HOW TO COMPLETE A SUCCESSFUL RESEARCH PROJECT

PEARSON

At Pearson, we believe in learning – all kinds of learning for all kinds of people. Whether it's at home, in the classroom or in the workplace, learning is the key to improving our life chances.

That's why we're working with leading authors to bring you the latest thinking and best practices, so you can get better at the things that are important to you. You can learn on the page or on the move, and with content that's always crafted to help you understand quickly and apply what you've learned.

If you want to upgrade your personal skills or accelerate your career, become a more effective leader or more powerful communicator, discover new opportunities or simply find more inspiration, we can help you make progress in your work and life.

Pearson is the world's leading learning company. Our portfolio includes the Financial Times and our education business, Pearson International.

Every day our work helps learning flourish, and wherever learning flourishes, so do people.

To learn more, please visit us at **www.pearson.com/uk**

**KATHLEEN McMILLAN &
JONATHAN WEYERS**

PEARSON

Harlow, England • London • New York • Boston • San Francisco • Toronto • Sydney
Auckland • Singapore • Hong Kong • Tokyo • Seoul • Taipei • New Delhi
Cape Town • São Paulo • Mexico City • Madrid • Amsterdam • Munich • Paris • Milan

Pearson Education Limited
Edinburgh Gate
Harlow CM20 2JE
United Kingdom
Tel: +44 (0)1279 623623
Web: www.pearson.com/uk

First published 2014 (print and electronic)

© Pearson Education Limited 2014 (print and electronic)

The rights of Kathleen McMillan and Jonathan Weyers to be identified as authors of this work have been asserted by them in accordance with the Copyright, Designs and Patents Act 1988.

The print publication is protected by copyright. Prior to any prohibited reproduction, storage in a retrieval system, distribution or transmission in any form or by any means, electronic, mechanical, recording or otherwise, permission should be obtained from the publisher or, where applicable, a licence permitting restricted copying in the United Kingdom should be obtained from the Copyright Licensing Agency Ltd, Saffron House, 6–10 Kirby Street, London EC1N 8TS.

The ePublication is protected by copyright and must not be copied, reproduced, transferred, distributed, leased, licensed or publicly performed or used in any way except as specifically permitted in writing by the publisher, as allowed under the terms and conditions under which it was purchased, or as strictly permitted by applicable copyright law. Any unauthorised distribution or use of this text may be a direct infringement of the authors' and the publisher's rights and those responsible may be liable in law accordingly.

All trademarks used herein are the property of their respective owners. The use of any trademark in this text does not vest in the authors or publisher any trademark ownership rights in such trademarks, nor does the use of such trademarks imply any affiliation with or endorsement of this book by such owners.

The screenshots in this book are reprinted by permission of Microsoft Corporation.

Pearson Education is not responsible for the content of third-party internet sites.

ISBN: 978-0-273-77392-4 (print)
         978-0-273-77409-9 (PDF)
         978-0-273-77408-2 (eText)

British Library Cataloguing-in-Publication Data
A catalogue record for the print edition is available from the British Library

Library of Congress Cataloging-in-Publication Data
A catalog record for the print edition is available from the Library of Congress

10 9 8 7 6 5 4 3 2 1
18 17 16 15 14

Print edition typeset in 9.5/13pt Helvetica Neue Pro Roman by 3
Print edition printed and bound in Great Britain by Ashford Colour Press Ltd, Gosport

NOTE THAT ANY PAGE CROSS REFERENCES REFER TO THE PRINT EDITION

SMARTER STUDY SKILLS

Instant answers to your most pressing university skills problems and queries

Are there any secrets to successful study?

The simple answer is 'yes' – there are some essential skills, tips and techniques that can help you to improve your performance and success in all areas of your university studies.

These handy, easy-to-use guides to the most common areas where most students need help, provide accessible, straightforward practical tips and instant solutions that provide you with the tools and techniques that will enable you to improve your performance and get better results – and better grades!

Each book in the series allows you to assess and address a particular set of skills and strategies, in crucial areas of your studies. Each book then delivers practical, no-nonsense tips, techniques and strategies that will enable you to significantly improve your abilities and performance in time to make a difference.

The books in the series are:

- *How to Write Essays & Assignments*
- *How to Write Dissertations & Project Reports*
- *How to Argue*
- *How to Improve your Maths Skills*
- *How to Use Statistics*
- *How to Succeed in Exams & Assessments*
- *How to Cite, Reference & Avoid Plagiarism at University*
- *How to Improve Your Critical Thinking & Reflective Skills*
- *How to Improve Your Memory for Study*
- *How to Write for University: Academic Writing for Success*
- *How to Research & Write a Successful PhD*

For a complete handbook covering all of these study skills and more:

- *The Study Skills Book*

Get smart, get a head start!

CONTENTS

About the authors — ix
Acknowledgements — xi
Preface — xiii
How to use this book — xv

INTRODUCTION

1 **Taking on a research investigation** – how to approach the challenges of project work — 3

PLANNING YOUR RESEARCH PROJECT

2 **Choosing a research topic** – how to decide on a theme for your investigation — 13

3 **Framing a research question** – how to set targets and formulate hypotheses to test — 21

4 **Writing a project proposal** – how to structure a formal research plan — 31

5 **Planning and managing time** – how to organise your investigation and submit on time — 38

6 **Working successfully with a supervisor** – how to make the most of your relationship — 50

RESEARCHING THE LITERATURE

7 **Finding relevant source material** – how to develop your information literacy skills — 61

8 **Assessing content in the literature** – how to evaluate published information in your field — 69

9 **Interpreting published data** – how to understand graphs, tables and basic statistics — 82

10 **Note-making from research sources** – how to record information for use in your investigation — 94

11 **Organising your research materials** – how to collect and file information and details of references — 108

RESEARCH APPROACHES

12 Using quantitative research methods – how to obtain and analyse numerical information — 119

13 Using qualitative research methods – how to obtain and analyse descriptive information — 127

14 Conducting experiments and field studies – how to design and perform lab and field investigations — 136

15 Designing and carrying out surveys and interviews – how to obtain relevant information from research participants — 151

16 Thinking in research contexts – how to apply method to produce valid, original ideas for your investigation — 166

17 Arriving at a position and supporting it – how to sift fact and opinion and express your conclusions — 182

18 Following guidelines on ethics and safety – how to observe good research practice in your investigation — 192

DATA ANALYSIS AND PRESENTATION

19 Analysing data – how to manipulate and interpret your results with simple, effective techniques — 203

20 Presenting data – how to display information, graphs and tables to academic standard — 213

THE WRITING PROCESS

21 Planning the writing phase – how to organise your work effectively to produce the best-quality product on time — 225

22 Writing up in the approved format – how to report on your research using standard structure and content — 235

23 Writing up in the appropriate style – how to use academic language and well-organised discourse to express your ideas and findings — 247

24 Citing, referencing and avoiding plagiarism – how to refer appropriately to the work and ideas of others — 264

25 Reviewing, editing and proofreading – how to enhance the quality of your write-up — 283

26 Acting on feedback – how to interpret and learn from what your supervisor writes on your drafts — 290

27 Presenting your project for assessment – how to submit your work appropriately — 296

List of references — 307

ABOUT THE AUTHORS

Dr Kathleen McMillan was formerly Academic Skills Advisor and Senior Lecturer at the University of Dundee.

Dr Jonathan Weyers was formerly Senior Lecturer in Biological Sciences, Director of the Learning Enhancement Unit and Director of Quality Assurance at the University of Dundee.

Both are now freelance authors and consultants specialising in books on skills development in higher education.

This book represents a synthesis based on over 60 years of combined administrative, teaching and advisory experience. We have supervised and supported numerous students, conducted induction events and led skills workshops covering such diverse topics as thesis writing and personal development planning. Our backgrounds in the arts and humanities and life sciences respectively mean that our support has covered a wide range of subjects – from biology to orthopaedic surgery; information and communication technology to law; as well as political science and English as a foreign language.

Above all, we have spoken to countless students, both individually and in focus groups, and have consulted with fellow academics about research skills that underpin a wide range of disciplines. As well as gaining relevant qualifications ourselves, we have also observed at close quarters our own children taking on project work at university.

Our former responsibilities involved drawing up regulations for academic study, responding to research student feedback and a wide range of university committee work related to learning and teaching. We have carried out a number of relevant tasks, most notably the writing and editing of an extensive website providing guidance for students studying at the University of Dundee. Our collaborative writing has produced ten books on diverse aspects of learning and writing at university level. Most of these have appeared in several editions and they have been translated into a total of seven other languages.

In short, we have read widely, thought deeply about relevant issues and tested many ideas related to the research experience. This book is a distillation of all the best tips and techniques we've come across or have developed ourselves.

ACKNOWLEDGEMENTS

As researchers ourselves, as well as supervisors, trainers and examiners of students, we have gained much from interactions with colleagues, students and external examiners. Our accumulated wisdom from many of these exchanges is expressed in this book. Some of the material was developed during the construction of the website *Advance@Dundee* (internal to the University of Dundee). We thank all of our colleagues and friends who helped us with that project, especially Margaret Adamson. We have also contributed to the training of research students at several different levels, especially in the area of writing up, and we thank both students and academic colleagues for the opportunity to develop our ideas and contribute in that area.

Many others have influenced us and contributed in one way or another to the production of this book, including: Rami Abboud, Richard A'Brook, Michael Allardice, Lorraine Anderson, John Berridge, Richard Campbell, Cathy Caudwell, Margaret Forrest, Martin Glover, John Hillman, Andy Jackson, Allan Jones, Rod Jones, Christine Milburn, Kirsty Millar, Dave Murie, Graham Nicholson, Fiona O'Donnell, Richard Parsons, Neil Paterson, Jane Prior, Mhairi Robb, Dorothy Smith, Eric Smith, Gordon Spark, David Walker and David Wishart. We are indebted to the support and interest of the Royal Literary Fund and particularly the RLF Writing Fellows in our university, distinguished authors in their own right, who have given wise words of counsel – Bill Kirton, Brian Callison, Jonathan Falla and Gordon Meade. Also, we acknowledge those at other universities who have helped frame our thoughts, especially our good friends Rob Reed, Nicki Hedge and Esther Daborn, as well as the membership of the Scottish Effective Learning Advisors who work so energetically to help students to develop the key skills that are addressed in this book.

We owe a special debt to the senior ex-colleagues who encouraged various projects that contributed to this book, and who allowed us the freedom to pursue various avenues of related scholarship, especially Robin Adamson, James Calderhead, Chris Carter, Alan Davidson, Ian Francis, Rod Herbert, Eric Monaghan and David Swinfen.

At Pearson Education, we have had excellent support and advice, especially from Steve Temblett, Simon Lake, Emma Devlin, Jen Halford and Lucy Carter.

Finally, we would like to say thanks to our long-suffering but nevertheless enthusiastic families: Derek, Keith, Nolwenn, Fiona, Tom and Eilidh; and Mary, Paul and James, all of whom helped in various capacities.

PUBLISHER'S ACKNOWLEDGEMENTS

We are grateful to the following for permission to reproduce copyright material:

Table 24.1 derived from *Concept of Citation Indexing* available at **www.garfield.library.upenn.edu/papers/vladivostok.html**, accessed 6 November 2013, reproduced courtesy of Dr Eugene Garfield; Proofreading symbols used in Tables 25.3 and 26.1 adapted from British Standards Institute, 'Marks for copy preparation and proof correction', BS 5261-2:2005. Permission to reproduce extracts from British Standards is granted by BSI Standards Limited (BSI). No other use of this material is permitted. British Standards can be obtained in PDF or hard copy formats from the BSI online shop: **www.bsigroup.com/Shop** or by contacting BSI Customer Services for hard copies only: Tel: +44 (0)20 8996 9001, Email: cservices@bsigroup.com.

In some instances we have been unable to trace the owners of copyright material, and we would appreciate any information that would enable us to do so.

PREFACE

We're delighted that you've chosen *How to Complete a Successful Research Project* and we'd like to think it's because this book promises insight into the research experience. Our aim has been to provide a highly practical guide to the planning, researching and writing up of a research project. The target audience is primarily advanced university and college students – for example, those taking on a penultimate or final-year dissertation, carrying out an honours project or conducting masters-level research. It should also suit those studying for baccalaureate or professional qualifications where research is required. The outcome of these exercises may be termed differently – for example, dissertation, report, paper or thesis. Readers should interpret our generic phrasing (for example, 'write-up') according to their situation.

At all levels of study, we feel that similar principles apply when conducting research, but at these advanced levels the stakes may be higher and the expectations of lecturers, tutors and examiners rather more demanding. Thus, there will be a need for greater accuracy in obtaining, summarising and presenting results; a requirement for deeper thinking in relation to ideas, positions and conclusions; and more exacting criteria in relation to referencing, editing and presentation. Guidance on these matters will often be valuable, if not essential, to ensure that the best possible grades are obtained.

We have tried to write material that will apply across subjects, although inevitably some of the content will be more relevant to certain subjects than others. This will also apply to its significance for students as individuals, who may have different experiences and training before arriving at this stage. For example, a student studying an arts subject might be quite familiar with the ways of arriving at and presenting a position on a topic (**Ch 17**), perhaps from practise during tutorial work, whereas a sciences student might gain hugely from reading about relevant approaches and methods. Similarly, a student of a maths-based science would probably find the content of the 'number crunching' chapter (**Ch 19**) rather simplistic as a result of their studies for past qualifications or modules, whereas an arts student may benefit greatly from a 'refresher' on this topic. The material is therefore presented so that each chapter is self-contained and the book can be dipped into as needs emerge.

Regarding the writing itself, we have adopted the tried-and-tested approach of our other books in the 'Smarter Study Skills' series. That is, we have aimed for a direct and no-nonsense presentation. We've tried to avoid jargon, have used devices such as bulleted lists and have kept the main text uncluttered by placing examples and tips in boxes, tables and figures. Our goal is to allow readers to assimilate the key points rapidly and be able to apply relevant guidance to their manuscript.

If we were asked to give one overarching piece of advice it would probably concern the need for compromise during your research project. Put bluntly, your project will never reach perfection – for a variety of reasons, including limitations of time, resources and even bad luck. Only effective planning and time management can allow you to get acceptably close to your ambition for the work, so full attention needs to be paid to these skills. Hence, it is essential that you tone down any perfectionist tendencies and accept certain flaws in your work if it is to be of even quality and presented on time. Do not feel guilty about this; it happens in every piece of research. Our hope is that by reading this book, you will be able to minimise flaws and optimise each aspect of the final report.

We wish you well in your research and would be pleased to hear your opinion of the book, any suggestions you have for additions and improvements and especially if you feel that it has made a positive difference to the way you have approached your studies.

Kathleen McMillan and Jonathan Weyers

HOW TO USE THIS BOOK

Each chapter in *How to Complete a Successful Research Project* has been organised and designed to be as clear and simple as possible. The chapters are self-contained and deal with particular aspects of the subject matter so that you can read the book through from beginning to end, or in sections, or dip into specific chapters as you need them.

At the start of each chapter you'll find a brief paragraph and a **Key topics** list that lets you know what is included. Within each chapter, the text is laid out to help you absorb the key concepts easily, using headings and bulleted lists to enable you to find what you need. Relevant examples are contained in figures, tables and boxes that complement the text. The inset boxes are of three types:

Smart tip boxes emphasise key advice that we think will be particularly useful to you.

Information boxes provide additional information that will broaden your understanding by giving examples and definitions.

Query boxes raise questions for you to consider about your personal approach to the topic.

Finally, the **Action points** section provides three suggestions for possible follow-up activities as you consider ideas further.

INTRODUCTION

1 TAKING ON A RESEARCH INVESTIGATION

How to approach the challenges of project work

Embarking on a research project can be exciting but also challenging. To succeed, you will need to understand fully what's required of you and set about your work with the right expectations and attitude. This chapter introduces the key phases of research, outlines the activities necessary at each stage and covers the skills you will need to develop.

KEY TOPICS
→ What's expected in a research project?
→ Approaching a research project

We are assuming in this book that you have started or are about to begin what might be termed a 'high stakes' undergraduate or master's research project. That is, one that accounts for a large proportion, if not all, of the grade or degree you hope to achieve, and, moreover, one that will involve an extended period of study and, as a result, a formal write-up. The aim of this book is to assist you in producing the best possible outcome from this period of study, by explaining the

Models of research study

Various models apply to project work. Your project may be carried out alongside lectures, practicals, tutorials (and associated assignments), or you may be allocated a dedicated period of time to carry out your research and write up your account of the project. The length of time allocated to the process may be weeks, months or even a full year. Regardless of the precise details, there are certain principles and approaches that apply in all situations.

processes, expectations and most effective approaches to project work, while also warning about difficulties you may encounter.

WHAT'S EXPECTED IN A RESEARCH PROJECT?

This is the first question you should ask yourself before starting your study. You may already feel you know part of the answer from information received during your previous studies and assignments, when the techniques used to establish received wisdom in your discipline may have been introduced. You may also have experienced 'tasters' in the form of brief projects or coursework carried out in earlier years of study. However, in all probability, none of this can prepare you for the authentic experience of advanced research. You will have to work at a new, higher level, paying meticulous attention to detail, technique and methods of analysis. Your work will need to be original and, ideally, will make a genuine contribution, however small, to knowledge in your field. You will also have to write up your work to the highest standard. For some, that particular aspect may seem harder even than conceiving new ideas or using advanced analytical techniques.

One way of finding out about the academic expectations for your project is to examine the learning outcomes (or objectives) associated with your programme of study. These can normally be found in the course handbook or within online resources. Typically they will cover general aspects such as:

- planning work and managing time
- making literature searches
- learning new research techniques
- applying theory and/or technology
- problem solving
- conducting research
- working ethically and safely
- adopting professional standards
- carrying out data interpretation and analysis
- evaluating your own and published work
- writing your findings up in a formal account.

Each of these terms means something different in any given field of study and not all will be relevant in your specific subject.

In addition to these academic outcomes, your department, supervisor and, more importantly, those who will assess your completed project will expect to see certain personal qualities, including:

- the dedication of time and energy to complete your project on time
- the application of intellectual integrity to your research task
- active participation in meetings to review the work in progress
- an approach involving a questioning and open mind
- the capability to demonstrate original thinking
- the stamina and application required to be productive in the conduct of your research and its write-up.

All this may sound like research is a demanding experience, and it will be. However, the hardship is balanced by rewards that are worth all the effort. You will, of course, have deepened your understanding of the topic and overall subject area. You will also have developed hugely as a person and, with luck, the work you have done will contribute to a grade or degree that will allow you to move forward towards your chosen career aspirations.

The endpoint of research project work

The most important tangible product of any project is the report that you will submit for assessment (in some cases, it may be called a paper, dissertation or thesis). This document will summarise your findings and it must normally be presented in the standardised format that applies to your discipline or department. In rare cases, your work may even be published in the academic literature (journals) of your field. However, there are other major outcomes that are less tangible. These are related to the development of your intellect, thinking, skills and ambition. In some cases project work can be life-changing – and it will certainly contribute to changing your personality and outlook.

APPROACHING A RESEARCH PROJECT

To be successful, and in particular to report on your investigation on time, you will need to be clear about your overall aims and the approaches required to achieve them. It will not be possible to map out all your work accurately and in detail (if this were the case, then perhaps the research would not be worth tackling). Nevertheless, you should try to anticipate what skills you need to develop. You should also be proactive in arranging the necessary meetings and visits in gaining access to research materials and facilities. Possibly most important of all, you will need to understand the need for 'closure' (most research is, after all, open-ended with no 'right answer') and be willing to accept the compromises required for completion in terms of the formal write-up. Most students experience highs and lows as they progress through what is necessarily uncharted territory. It will be important to remain upbeat during episodes when things may go less well than you hoped. Recognising this aspect of project work and remaining well-motivated is a vital key to successful research study.

Balancing your effort

No single part of your research effort should dominate over any of the others, or the overall quality of your work will suffer. Typical faults are:

- spending too much time on initial reading before getting down to work
- being obsessed with getting a 'perfect' set of results
- heading off down a blind alley that is not relevant to your main theme
- avoiding the writing-up phase.

To avoid these failings, create a work plan (**Ch 5**) and review your progress frequently.

Understanding how a project develops through time is vital if you are to organise yourself and submit high-quality work on the required submission date. Table 1.1 shows some of the key stages in a research project, with typical work activities and the skills required to perform them. With so many component parts, most of which could be open-ended, good time-management and planning are essential. **Chapter 5** provides tips on this aspect of research study.

How can I gain an understanding of the quality of work required?

Firstly, consult the marking criteria for the project and associated write-up (usually published in the course handbook). These may indicate for example, the emphasis placed on originality or on presentation. Submissions produced by students in previous years will help you gain a sense of style and standard – but don't feel intimidated by apparently sophisticated structure and style in these completed examples. Achieving this standard did not happen spontaneously. Your starting point may not be at this level, but the learning process will very likely result in a similarly high standard of document.

ACTION POINTS

1.1 Consider your personal strengths and weaknesses in relation to the challenges of research activity. This self-understanding may also help you to take anticipatory action – for example, by considering how you might need to develop skills such as calculating and interpreting statistics, data presentation, referencing or academic writing.

1.2 Review the timeline for research study shown in Table 1.1 and create a set of targets for yourself. Think about where you would like to be in your research at different times. Some research projects are completed in a hurry at the end of the study period, but you can avoid this by planning your work carefully and giving yourself the best possible chance of completing on time, avoiding a last-minute rush.

1.3 Get yourself organised. Regarding the points made in 1.2 above, one of the keys to meeting targets is being organised in your work, so ensure your filing (both computer and hard copy) is in good order right from the start – and periodically review its status, giving it an overhaul from time to time. Always remember to back up your files.

Table 1.1 Timeline for a typical research project. This is a generic model and so the nature of events and their order will differ according to individual contexts, disciplines and institutions. In particular, development in thinking and writing will depend on the individual.

Event and milestones	Focus of work activities	Development of thinking and skills
Selecting or identifying a research project	Scoping possible areas of research	Decision making and critical thinking (Ch 16)
Choosing and/or meeting supervisor	Researching past work	Thinking about personalities and interactions (Ch 6)
Writing a research proposal or plan	Writing proposal, possibly in defined format (Ch 4)	Basic review of research area, potential topics and approaches (Ch 7)
Carrying out a literature search or survey	Identifying relevant literature and initial assessment of literature	Information literacy (Ch 7); analytical and critical thinking (Ch 16)
Standardising information regarding sources	Deciding on a referencing system or following the recommended referencing system (Ch 24); organising materials and records (Ch 11)	Grouping resources thematically, thinking critically about content (Ch 16); learning how to use referencing software if appropriate
Planning research	Designing a research strategy including methodological approach (Chs 3, 12–15)	Clarification of research topic and related thinking (Chs 2–4, 12–15)
Seeking ethical approval	Using the formal application process as appropriate (Chs 4, 18)	Considering ethical aspects of the topic (Ch 18)
Undertaking experimental work or conducting a survey	Designing and testing (Chs 14–15)	Planning ahead; thinking about resources and activities (Chs 5, 14–15)
Searching literature and reading	Making a critical appraisal of existing work (Ch 8)	Deeper thinking about the research field, including generation of original ideas (Ch 16)

Continuing observational or experimental work (where relevant)	Carrying out work of high quality, suitable for final write-up	Collecting and analysing data (**Chs 19–20**)
Submitting interim reports on progress	Writing about research and associated ideas	Organising material and writing in appropriate format and style (**Chs 22–23**)
Having meetings with supervisor	Discussing progress, including review of agreed action points, assessment of results, presentation of data/ideas and assessment of their significance	Writing up drafts or conclusions (**Chs 21–23**)
Writing the main literature review	Summarising ideas in context for introduction or main thesis section (**Ch 23**)	Arriving at a position and supporting it (**Ch 17**); citation and referencing (**Ch 24**)
Completing the final observational or experimental work (where relevant)	Carrying out data collection and analysis (**Chs 19–20**)	Deciding on significance and writing provisional conclusions (**Ch 22**)
Writing the report, paper, dissertation or thesis	Attempting to write a near-final version from notes and early drafts	Planning both time for writing and formatting (**Chs 5, 21, 23**); academic writing skills (**Ch 22**)
Submitting drafts to supervisor	Preparing material to high standard	Learning from feedback (**Ch 26**)
Editing and proofreading the final draft	Preparing material to high standard; following guidelines to the letter (**Ch 27**)	Checking for consistency and completeness; creating final reference list (**Chs 23–25, 27**)
Submitting the completed work	Arranging for binding if required	Finding and correcting any remaining errors

PLANNING YOUR RESEARCH PROJECT

CHOOSING A RESEARCH TOPIC

How to decide on a theme for your investigation

The correct choice of project topic will improve the chances of a successful outcome. It is important to weigh up relevant issues as you select among the possibilities.

KEY TOPICS
→ Deciding on your personal research interests
→ Taking account of the options open to you
→ Making a final decision

The precise topic you choose to research has a great influence on how well you succeed in carrying out the investigation and in writing up your work. A crucial factor is whether you have a genuine interest in the subject, as this will motivate you to complete the task to the best possible standard. In addition, many practical matters need to be taken into account, such as the feasibility of the intended investigation, or the availability of relevant resources.

DECIDING ON YOUR PERSONAL RESEARCH INTERESTS

For any research project, it is essential that there is enough about the topic that is novel and challenging for you. If this is the case, then your levels of motivation will be high and may sustain you through any problems you encounter. If not, you will be liable to become bored or disillusioned, and this will hinder your ability to complete and write up your work.

By the time that you're considering a potential research topic, you will almost certainly have an above-average interest in the broader field of study. However, you may never have thought rigorously about your true underlying interests. Now, when you are forced into making a decision, these will need to be considered quite deeply. For some, stating a primary interest might be easy, but for many, it will be quite difficult to commit their efforts to one highly focused subject, or to settle on which option on a list interests them most. There may be a range of possibilities, each with a balance of attractions and negative aspects.

 Rewind your past experiences to focus your views

Reflect on those areas of your course where you found your curiosity and interest being fired. Remind yourself about appealing issues that arose in debate in the lectures, tutorials, seminars or practicals. This may help to give you some direction in selecting a topic.

TAKING ACCOUNT OF THE OPTIONS OPEN TO YOU

In many cases, you may find that the project topics are prescribed or restricted. The decision is not so much what you would like to research, but more which topic you will choose from a list of options provided by academic staff. A variation on this closed-option list is the semi-closed list, where academics provide a list of broad topics but leave the student to choose the detailed perspective that they wish to pursue.

Constraints such as these may feel limiting, especially at first when you do not know the details of the topics outlined. However, they are generally designed to provide you with a degree of freedom within parameters controlled by those who will need to supervise and assess the finished work, and who will have carefully considered the practicalities of each option and the chances of obtaining a successful outcome.

Where your choice is restricted, or from a fixed-menu of options, consider each option in turn. Do not reject any possibility out of hand until you know more about it. Obtain background information where necessary and if a reading list is offered, consult this. Rank the options according to how they appeal to you.

Make your decisions with speed but not haste

If a list of research options is presented, find out the details as quickly as possible, as there may be competition for specific topics or for particular supervisors. However, make sure you take all relevant factors into account in a deliberate decision-making process, rather than hastily choosing under pressure. You should give the matter high priority and allocate time and attention to activities that may help you make a decision, such as library or internet searches and discussions with potential supervisors.

A less restricted approach to the selection of research project topic may occur. In this case, no list is provided and you are asked to choose not only the topic but the specific research question to be addressed. In this open-choice case, you will be expected to make a selection largely on the basis of your personal interests within the discipline. These might have developed from your personal experience or from previous consideration of related topics arising from your course of study – for example, from reading carried out for coursework.

If you have this type of open choice, then one approach might be to brainstorm possible topics and sub-topics within your subject and then to rank these in order of your interest. You could do this in phases, moving sequentially from broader subject fields to more closely specified research areas, until you can narrow down the choices and a set of favourites emerges.

MAKING A FINAL DECISION

While you may have distinct preferences for specific areas of study, you should still consider the options at a finer level before making a final decision. Many factors will influence your ability to complete your studies to a high standard, and they should all be borne in mind as you weigh up different possibilities.

Potential research approaches

Is it possible for you to identify the approach that might be required? Is there a question to be answered, a problem to be solved or an issue to be debated? How will you restrict the potential areas to cover? How exactly will you set about researching the topic? You may alter this 'research angle' through time, but refining your thoughts at this stage might aid the decision-making process. If you have a distinct direction to your work from the start, this will increase your chances of success.

 Finding out more about a research option

If the answers to questions about the practicalities or relevance of a topic are not immediately evident, ask around. Sometimes it is useful to get more than one perspective on the issue, so try to find several people who can give you an opinion. If possible, discuss your options with a potential supervisor or other academic contact.

Time aspects

In selecting a topic, it is particularly important to guard against being over-ambitious. Ensure that you will have enough time to be able to demonstrate, through your written work, that you have addressed all the learning outcomes (**Ch 1**). You need to factor in not only the time that you will need to read, analyse or present the material, but also take account of potential delays in obtaining the material or data you need.

In some cases, approval for your work will be required from an ethics committee, and this may also take time (see **Ch 18**). Remember, too, that the writing phase for a project write-up requires a lot of time – more than many students recognise at the outset of the project. Where you can anticipate that simply identifying and obtaining the material, let alone reading and digesting it, is going to take an inordinate amount of time, then you may need to eliminate some of your first-choice possibilities.

Availability of resources or experimental material

Some research projects run into difficulties because it is not possible to obtain the material required to carry out the work.

1 Obtaining published material. You will need to evidence your work by reference to the literature (**Chs 7–8, 24**). In some cases, access to published material is critical to the research process. You need to review the materials relevant to each potential topic that:
   – are available locally in hard-copy book and journal format within your own institution's library
   – can be accessed electronically through your library's subscription to online journals

- can be obtained through inter-library loan (taking into account any cost implications)
- may require you to visit another library site for on-site access.

2 **Obtaining data.** You need to take into account the most realistic method of gathering data and recording and interpreting the findings within the time-frame that you have to complete the work. If you need to analyse quantitative data, then you should also consider what statistical analysis software packages you may need to access and learn. Where your data are qualitative in nature, then you should also consider with your supervisor the most appropriate methods for gathering and interpreting the information. For example, an action-research approach might require different techniques to a questionnaire-based approach (**Ch 12**).

How can I find out what resources are available to support a potential project?

Other than a potential supervisor, the best people to consult are the subject librarians in your library. They will know about:

- the resources already present in your library, including stored materials
- the main routes for obtaining information, including advanced online searches
- alternative approaches that you may not have thought about
- obscure resources and how to access these
- contacts at other institutions who can help
- professional organisations that may have exclusive databanks that you might be able to access through your department or library.

Research topics may focus on contemporary events and you may have to use recently published primary sources as the basis for your study. For example, you might consult material such as a recently produced Royal Commission Report, a new piece of legislation, or a newly published item of literature. Since the newness of the topic would make it unlikely that there would be very little, if any, critical appraisal of such things in the public domain, then your research task will include placing your own interpretation on this material. If you think you might encounter difficulty with this aspect, seek guidance from your supervisor.

Depth

Your research topic will need to offer sufficient depth to allow you to show off your skills. These may depend on your discipline, but might include the ability to think critically through analysis and evaluation, or the ability to design an experiment or survey and report it professionally. Avoid choosing a well-worked area, or even one that you feel is likely to provide easy results – especially if it will not allow you to demonstrate advanced research and intellectual skills.

Extent of support and supervision

At all levels of study, conducting research and writing this up are major tasks and you will not be expected to work on them alone. Incorporated into the process will be support provided by an assigned supervisor. However, you need to be clear at the outset about what you can expect in terms of this support (**Ch 6**). In some institutions, supervision is mapped onto the research/writing process with regular student–supervisor meetings, although under some regulations these may be of a limited number. In other situations, arrangements are agreed by the partners for meetings as required. Generally, the supervision will enable you to ask questions, seek guidance and debate some key issues. Be sure, however, that you reach an understanding with your supervisor about the extent to which you can expect them to review your research findings and provide feedback on your written work. This may not extend to reading the whole submission, nor to detailed proofreading of the text, as this is often regarded as being the responsibility of the student.

Choosing a supervisor

If you have a choice, try to ensure that this is a member of staff whom you feel comfortable talking to and whom you feel will offer support and guidance as well as inspiring you to work harder and complete on time. Ask recent students if you want the insider view on different tutors and the environment where you will be expected to work.

Impact on your CV and career options

Although this is rarely the primary aspect to consider, for some it is a factor to take into consideration when choosing a project. Perhaps your subject interests are already very closely aligned to your ideas for your future career. You may also wish to take into account specific skills you might gain that will be of interest to an employer. If you are an undergraduate interested in further studies, your choice of topic may be valuable in giving you experience to take to the next stage in your studies or research career.

> ### Weigh up the pros and cons and rank your options
>
> If you remain undecided after considering both your interest in potential topics and the practical aspects, try laying out your thoughts about the options in a set of simple tables with columns for advantages and disadvantages. This process may help you to order your thoughts and clarify the factors that are important to you. Consider each option in turn, and award it a mark out of 10. When you have completed a scan of all the options, look again at the ones that scored highly and reject the ones that scored weakly. You might also try to explain the reasons for your scores to someone else. This may force you to put into words how you feel, and thereby become more confident in your decision. The process may also help you to assess whether the topic holds sufficient challenge or whether it lacks the depth to provide you with an adequate project.

With luck, you will now have selected a potential topic. The next stages, in many cases, are to decide on a specific research question (**Ch 3**) and then construct a written research proposal (**Ch 4**). This may involve presenting a reasoned argument justifying the approach to be taken, and will be considered by the supervising academic or a panel of academics for consideration and approval.

ACTION POINTS

2.1 Set aside time to make your decision. As indicated throughout this chapter, you should consider your options very carefully and carry out the necessary research to ensure your decision is an informed one. This will take time, but you must act quickly or others may choose an option before you, or claim the supervisor(s) you favour. Therefore, as soon as information is available, lay aside the necessary time to focus your attention on this issue.

2.2 Go back to basics. If the choices are bewildering, it may pay to revisit your old lecture notes and general texts to gain an impression of potential research areas. It may also be valuable to look at introductory material that might be available online. These sources can provide an overview to a subject that might help you decide.

2.3 Speak to students who have already completed your type of study. Postgraduates in your department might be useful contacts to ask. Discuss with them any aspects in the process that they felt were important to them when they were researching and writing up their projects.

3 FRAMING A RESEARCH QUESTION

How to set targets and formulate hypotheses to test

Having a level-headed view of how you will approach your research is an essential starting point. This involves framing the research questions or hypotheses you will set out to answer. Setting provisional goals and milestones is an important way to get your studies off to a good start, even though your ideas and plans will be tested and refined as time goes on.

KEY TOPICS

→ Exploring the literature
→ Narrowing your options
→ Creating goals and framing research questions
→ Setting up hypotheses and explanations to test in science-related research

Depending on the type of research project you are carrying out (**Ch 2**), you will have different levels of decisions to make regarding the direction of your work. If the project area is relatively open, you will obviously have relative freedom to select a precise topic and targets. If the project area is well-defined, your choices will be narrower, but there will still be some need to select between options and decide upon an initial approach to the study. Both are reasons why some universities or departments ask students to complete a research proposal at an early stage, so that the scoping phase of the research process (Table 5.1, **Ch 5**) is well documented and can be checked by the relevant progress monitoring group. This requirement recognises the importance of having a strong starting point and clear aims right from the beginning, and also allows such matters as ethics approval (**Ch 18**) to be monitored. The structure and content of a formal proposal is explained in **Chapter 4**.

> ✓ **Importance of making the right choices for your research**
>
> Finding suitable research questions to ask and the best methods to answer them will clearly improve your ultimate chance of success. Ambitious students will probably wish to make an important advance in the subject area, but it is probably better to choose a topic with a high chance of obtaining results that you can analyse and discuss, than to attempt a difficult project with a low chance of success. Most topics are multifaceted and there is often the temptation to try to address too many issues. You may have to be selective in narrowing down the research topic to create achievable goals.

EXPLORING THE LITERATURE

Generating new ideas for research requires a certain amount of relevant knowledge – and even if your project is already quite well defined, you will probably need to learn some jargon and gain an understanding of the context of the work. You will therefore need to carry out some background reading. Your project supervisor may have provided a reading list that will be a good starting point. In addition, you may wish to carry out a literature search of your own, perhaps with the assistance of a subject librarian (**Ch 7**). **Chapter 8** provides tips for reading and analysing the research literature.

This phase of a project can consume valuable time. While surveying the literature you should maintain a balance between a focused consideration of options and the width and depth of your reading. Because of the appeal of the topic, you may find yourself easily distracted into areas of marginal value. Take a note of this interesting material, but move on swiftly at this stage to more relevant sources.

> ✓ **Getting to grips with jargon and difficult ideas**
>
> Having to comprehend the terminology and complex concepts of a new topic can result in a hazy understanding of the foundations of your work and, hence, difficulty in framing suitable questions. One way around this is to go back to basics, possibly by reading a general textbook of the area. You may also wish to create a personal glossary of terms to help you learn the meanings of the specialised terms involved.

Your initial literature trawl might involve:

- An analysis of up-to-date reviews of your subject area. The aim would be to explore the current state of knowledge and place your proposed research direction in context.
- A thorough read of key papers. These might have been suggested by your supervisor; otherwise, you may find them highlighted in subject reviews. You should read these sources for clues about evidence, methods and suggestions for your work – either written up in the paper, or that arise from your own thoughts while reading about the subject.
- Reading relevant publications published by your supervisor and his/her research colleagues. This will not only give you an appreciation of related topics and approaches, but may also provide you with useful sources for further reading.
- A study of the research methods used in your area. In the sciences this might be highly technical in nature, with much jargon and detail, while in the non-sciences it might involve broader, more philosophical approaches to the topic. You should be aware of the possibility of using methods from one subject or discipline in another, as these cross-disciplinary lines of enquiry can often be very productive. This is a reason for consulting a wide range of sources.

A quick read around a new subject – what should you be looking for?

When establishing your knowledge base around a new research area, you should attempt to find out:

- the past authorities in the area – that is, those who established the foundations of the topic
- the major schools of thought in the area
- the key research findings and relevant (international) publications
- the researchers and research groups currently active
- the areas currently being worked on and any trends in focus or findings
- the jargon of the subject, and what the terms mean
- the research methods in use, both in the past and currently
- sources of research materials and evidence
- pointers to productive new areas of work.

A brainstorm diagram (**Ch 16**) could be a good way of encapsulating the main themes on a single sheet of paper, allowing you to see connections and themes in the literature at a glance.

In the light of your early reading, and after thinking through the options, you should construct a short list of ideas about your project to discuss with your lecturer or potential supervisor.

NARROWING YOUR OPTIONS

One way of narrowing your research options is to try to answer the following questions:

- What really interests me? A topic that holds your attention and motivates you will keep you going through any tough patches.
- What am I equipped to do? This question refers both to your personal abilities and to the availability of equipment and other resources.
- What line of enquiry will ensure that I have some outcomes to discuss? It is vital that you can demonstrate your skills of analysis in your write-up – but this will be tricky if there is little to show from your researches.
- What barriers are there to studying a specific topic? These could prevent you making good progress. For example: you might need to obtain permissions (perhaps to study a site of special scientific interest); you may need to make a complex ethics committee submission (**Ch 18**); you may require training in a specific technique; or you may require a very expensive piece of equipment.

In some cases, and especially in the sciences, you will be interested in the minutiae of methods. Bear in mind that although published materials and methods are supposed to allow a competent worker to repeat research (**Ch 23**), this is not always the case in practice. The text may assume readers know about certain details that could make a difference to the success of the technique or subtly affect results. It might be a good idea to ask an experienced researcher about methods before you start any work. There may also be benefits from carrying out a pilot experiment or survey to familiarise yourself with the precise methods, to check that these work as you expect and to ensure your designs for your research are practical.

CREATING GOALS AND FRAMING RESEARCH QUESTIONS

After reading around your topic, the next phase is to draft a set of goals for your research. This involves framing a research question that you will be seeking to address and setting yourself realistic targets for what will be a short and intensive period of research. Note that the word 'address' is used deliberately here rather than 'answer', because a clear-cut answer or conclusion to any piece of research is rarely possible, and, in fact, you will gain credit by considering the evidence from all sides of an argument or case, arriving at a clearly stated viewpoint and giving reasons for adopting this position. A generalised approach that might be adopted is shown in Figure 3.1.

Your research goals should be:

- detailed – where possible, they should include specifics about outcomes, as opposed to vague wishes or a title encompassing a diffuse area of study
- measurable – they should have defined outcomes, so that you and others can decide that you have achieved the targets you have set
- realistic – they should be attainable given the resources at your disposal, including personal abilities, time, equipment, availability of research materials and relevant permissions.

These research goals will lead naturally to more specific research questions. A general approach to the framing of research questions might be to write down your goals as a series of statements that you would like your research to answer. An example could be, 'I would like to find out whether children from lower socio-economic backgrounds are more or less likely to fail if they come to university'. This might lead you to a series of narrower research avenues.

> **Time as an important resource** ✓
>
> Many students who have just completed a research project will tell you that time is the one thing they wish they'd had in greater abundance. It is easy to underestimate the time it takes to achieve your research goals. Things nearly always proceed at a slower pace than you imagine, either due to unexpected delays or problems along the way. Therefore, always take care not to be too ambitious in your plans and to leave plenty of time for dealing with contingencies.

For instance, in the above example, you would probably need to look into definitions of socio-economic backgrounds and set criteria for the notion of 'failure'. This thinking might even lead you to think of a tentative title for your project and possibly the potential titles for the different chapters within it. Even though you may change these at a later date, they will help to make the nature of your researches more concrete and outcome-led.

1. **Explore the wider topic area ('observation')**
   - Understand its key facts and concepts
   - Form an overview of the wider area
   - Decide on a specific topic of interest
   - Note the unknowns, controversies, or areas where knowledge might advance
   - Decide on a specific problem or issue
   - Survey current explanations and evidence

2. **Come up with your own ideas regarding the selected problem or issue ('theory')**
   - Create your own explanation(s) of, or solution(s)
   - Take a wide view of possible answers
   - Put these into words (an important part of the process)
   - Rule out the very unlikely
   - Arrive at a tentative explanation or explanations (hypothesis/es)

3. **Make a forecast from your explanation or hypothesis ('prediction')**
   - What sorts of evidence could support it?
   - If it is true, what follows?
   - What would be feasible tests of its viability?

4. **Test your explanation or hypothesis ('experiment')**
   - Does any existing evidence conflict with your explanation?
   - What experiments or evidence-gathering could you carry out to test it?
   - Does this support or disprove your explanation?

Figure 3.1 **The four-stage process of forming and testing a research question or hypothesis.** This is a commonly accepted description of the route for formulating or refining a research question or hypothesis and then testing it. The process can be cyclical, as indicated, with the results of tests being fed back to the start as new observations.

SETTING UP HYPOTHESES AND EXPLANATIONS TO TEST IN SCIENCE-RELATED RESEARCH

In the sciences, a research question can simply be the hypothesis you would like to test by seeking out relevant evidence and comparing with the theoretical expectation. This notion fits with the framework of understanding described in Table 3.1. However, many who study the philosophy of science feel that there may be more human intuition in 'real' research than is indicated by this analysis.

Each hypothesis normally is cast as a simple statement, such as 'the reason obesity reduces lifespan is because of the risk of diabetes and the consequent debilitating conditions'. The next stage is a statement along the lines of 'if that is the case, then we would predict that...' (for example, 'if so, we would expect mortality assigned to specific diabetes-related conditions to be correlated with the weight of the patient').

Nearly all science deals with the testing of small-scale hypotheses. This involves making a prediction and its testing via an experiment (Table 3.1). An experiment is a test under controlled conditions that reduces the number of changing variables (often called 'factors' or 'treatments'), ideally to a single factor of interest in the context of the hypothesis (Ch 14).

No hypothesis can be rejected with absolute certainty, especially when there is variability in the results of the experimental test (which there nearly always is). The field of statistics for a large part deals with assigning probabilities to the results of hypothesis-testing (Ch 19).

Someone who proposes a new theory in their research area will probably become quite famous and will be much quoted. These people may become the standing 'authorities' of the subject – but perhaps this is something to aspire to in your overall research career rather than in a short research project.

Table 3.1 A hierarchical view of the theory underpinning any particular research area. This model applies best for scientific areas of research.

Paradigm
At the top of the hierarchy is the paradigm, a theoretical framework of understanding that is so successful and well-confirmed that most research in the area is carried out within its context. By definition, such notions are rarely challenged by the results of research, and, even if they were, workers in the field would require reasonably extensive corroboration before they would shelve the framework. • An example of a paradigm might be: 'Physiological systems are capable of being controlled via the concentrations of chemical messengers called 'hormones'.'
Theory
Next in the hierarchy is the theory, a collection of hypotheses. This is more tentative in nature than a paradigm, and might be overturned if evidence justifies this; a theory is differentiated from a hypothesis by being applicable to a wider range of natural situations. • An example of a theory could be that the hormone ghrelin acts to increase hunger in mammals by acting on the hypothalamus. Related to a theory is the notion of a scientific law, a theoretical understanding that can be encapsulated in a mathematical equation. These are more prevalent in the physical sciences. • A familiar example of a law might be $e = mc^2$.
Hypothesis
The hypothesis is, in effect, the 'unit' of understanding. It is an explanation that can be tested by experiment and can essentially be found to be untrue if the evidence suggests so. This property of hypothesis is known as falsifiability. If confirmed, a hypothesis will be retained with greater confidence, but if falsified, it may be rejected outright or it might be modified and retested. • An example of a hypothesis could be that the hormone abscisic acid works by stimulating potassium efflux from stomatal guard cells.

? Where do the ideas for new hypotheses come from?

This may be a question that interests you if you are new to research. Generally speaking, they are said to arise from observations or the results of previous experiments. They normally require one or more of the following thought processes:

- analogy with other systems
- recognition of a pattern
- recognition of departure from a pattern
- invention of new methods for research
- development of a mathematical model
- intuition
- imagination.

Researchers who try to overturn a paradigm (Table 3.1) will meet a lot of resistance from the academic community (many of whom may have a vested interest in its continuance). Such new ideas are often met with incredulity and it may take time and the accumulation of new evidence to persuade others to change their views. These kinds of events are rare, and understandably those whose radical views are later accepted are fêted for their impact on a subject area. An example might be the concept of continental drift (later, plate tectonics), as originally championed by Alfred Wegener and others, which initially met great resistance from established geological scientists. As a student, attempting to overturn a paradigm may not be a constructive strategy to adopt. In short, try not to be overambitious.

> **The concept of repeatability**
>
> This is vital to the rationale of the scientific method. The essential result from an experiment should be reproducible, providing all aspects remain equal (not always easy). Acceptable non-consequential differences should be within the bounds of error predicted by statistical analysis. An accepted hypothesis should therefore be testable again and again, with the same result, except for the occasional 'blip' where, considering statistical variation, the error data suggest that there a finite but small (usually less than 1 in 20) chance of a different result (**Ch 19**). This predictability underpins the utility of most scientific disciplines.

Non-science research

In the non-sciences, investigative approaches in many areas are less rigid than within experimental methodologies. This means that the tactics that researchers adopt are diverse and rely very much on the contexts of individual studies as well as on the philosophical underpinning and the research objectives. Indeed, there may be considerable and vehement debate about the efficacy of different approaches that are used. In essence, there is no 'right way' to conduct research in many non-scientific areas. Hence, it may be that there is no clear hypothesis set as a preliminary to undertaking the research and that the research questions may arise from circumstances as they emerge – for example, from dialogue with subjects.

ACTION POINTS

3.1 Make contact with the relevant subject librarian in your university library. They may be able to assist with your initial research enquiries, either by showing you appropriate collections or by framing search queries for databases.

3.2 Identify the key paradigms, theories and hypotheses that underpin your preferred research area. In sciences, what hypotheses have been tested in recent research papers? Which might be important for your own project? In non-sciences, what philosophical approaches lie behind recent research publications?

3.3 Think of three goals for your research. Assess their quality using the three criteria given earlier in the chapter.

4 WRITING A PROJECT PROPOSAL

How to structure a formal research plan

A research or project proposal may be required by your department before you start studying in depth. Producing this plan may seem like a hurdle preventing you from starting the 'real' work. However, you should regard your proposal as much more than an administrative exercise; it can help you organise your preliminary thoughts, plan your approach and complete your work on time.

KEY TOPICS

→ Benefits of writing a proposal
→ What will be taken into account in assessing your proposal
→ Writing your proposal

A research proposal outlines the scope and methods of the research you intend to carry out and in some cases will indicate how you plan to organise your write-up. Your proposal may be used to allocate a supervisor for your project, if that is not already decided, and it may need to be referred to the appropriate ethics or safety committees within your institution (**Ch 18**). You will probably be offered feedback on your proposal and advice on your intended investigation. Once approval is given, you may be given permission to proceed with your studies under the guidance of your supervisor.

BENEFITS OF WRITING A PROPOSAL

The discipline of composing a proposal is a valuable exercise and you should approach this task positively. The benefits include:

- ensuring your research has aims and objectives that are achievable in the time allocated

- compelling you to identify, read and review some of the relevant background material to orientate your thoughts
- checking that you have a realistic notion of relevant research methods
- making sure that, at an early stage, you think about resources you may require and that these can be provided for you
- verifying that you have considered safety and ethical issues relating to your research

How to produce a successful proposal

- Carry out an appropriate amount of background reading beforehand, selecting the sources carefully: you don't need to read all of the papers at the start, as this will take up too much of your study time, but you do need to gain an up-to-date appreciation of key topics and trends in your chosen field. Choose recently published reviews of the area – especially those likely to prompt ideas about key aspects that need to be considered in more detail.
- Try to formulate a key hypothesis or idea to investigate (**Ch 3**). Your project needs a focus and this will come from trying to answer a specific question, investigate a key issue or highlight a specific topic. Use brainstorming techniques (**Ch 16**) as you read sources to help you develop your ideas and outline potential topics.
- Remember that your proposal is only a proposal. You do not need to write the complete work at this stage. You merely need to establish, for the benefit of the reviewing person or group, that you have chosen a reasonable topic and are likely to succeed in conducting a project that meets the regulations or fulfils the learning outcomes of your course.
- Discuss your proposal with staff beforehand. At an early stage, try to arrange an appointment with a relevant staff member for a brief discussion about possible directions. If you have been allocated a supervisor, then consult them; if not, think about who you would like to be a supervisor and ask them.
- Get feedback from your peers. Show an early draft to a friend or family member, or swap proposals with a fellow student. Ask for comments and respond to them. This kind of feedback is especially valuable to ensure that the logic of your proposal is transparent to readers.
- Ensure that you observe any word limits placed on proposal submissions.

- assisting you to create an outline structure for your write-up
- helping you to create a viable timetable for your work
- matching your topic, interests and needs to an appropriate supervisor.

WHAT WILL BE TAKEN INTO ACCOUNT IN ASSESSING YOUR PROPOSAL

The person or group reading your proposal will be considering it from several viewpoints. They will expect to be able to answer 'yes' to the questions in the checklist below:

- ❏ Do you have an up-to-date and accurate view of the research field?
- ❏ Have you outlined the focus of your studies in sufficient detail? (In some disciplines, this means the hypothesis you intend to test.)
- ❏ Is the scope of your proposed study realistic in the time allocated?
- ❏ Is your proposed research study sufficiently original?
- ❏ Is your proposed research sufficiently challenging?
- ❏ Will the research allow you to demonstrate your academic ability?
- ❏ Will the research give you the chance to develop and refine your skills?
- ❏ Are the proposed methods appropriate to your field and topic and are you aware of their limitations?
- ❏ Are you likely to gain access to all the resources you need?
- ❏ Are there any cost implications for your supervisor or the department?
- ❏ Are you planning to deal with ethical and safety issues appropriately?
- ❏ Is the proposed structure of the research evident?
- ❏ Will your proposed research and the underlying scholarship meet the requirements of the department or university regulations?
- ❏ Have you undertaken appropriate background reading?

Finally, and in summary:

- ❏ Will your intended project – and the resulting write-up – give you the chance to meet the required academic standard for your level of study?

Topics that will be looked on favourably are those that are novel, take an original perspective on a research area and are relevant within the research field as it stands at the time of writing. One possible mistake is to try to cover too 'large' a problem or too wide an area of discussion, rather than one capable of adequate analysis given the resources likely to be at hand. Set yourself realistic aims and objectives, bearing in mind the need for originality in your work. The people considering your proposal will be aware that a major reason for students having problems with project choices is that they were over-ambitious at the start. Remember that a key element that will be assessed is the research question, 'core hypothesis' or main idea underlying your project (Ch 3), so you should try to express this clearly.

> **? What is the difference between aims and objectives?**
>
> The distinction between these terms can be confusing because they are often used interchangeably. Widely accepted definitions generally indicate that aims are statements of intent or purpose that are broad in nature, and hence defined in general terms perhaps relating to an overall outcome, while objectives (goals) are outlined in more specific terms and tend to relate to individual, achievable outcomes that are required to achieve the ultimate aim. For example, the aim of a project might be to summarise viewpoints within a particular research field, while an objective might be to compare the various research methods in use to investigate a specific aspect.

WRITING YOUR PROPOSAL

In many cases, a form may be provided for your project proposal. This will normally include some or all of the components shown in Table 4.1, so that the person or committee evaluating your proposal can answer the questions noted in the previous section.

Present your proposal neatly. It should be word-processed and should stick very closely to any word limits. Regardless of any constraints, try to make your proposal succinct and to the point. There will be ample time to expand your thoughts when writing the real thing. Those evaluating your proposal will be trying to arrive at a quick decision and this will be made easier if your proposal is 'short and sweet'.

Table 4.1 **Typical components of a project proposal.** A selection of these categories will be used in individual cases. The choice of elements used in a proposal will depend on the discipline and level of study.

Component	Content and aspects to consider
Personal details	Required so that you can be identified and contacted
Details of your degree course or programme	There may be subtle differences according to your precise degree
Proposed title (it may alter as the work evolves)	This should be relatively short; a two-part title style can be useful
Description of the subject area/Summary/Background/Brief review/Statement of the problem or issue to be addressed	A brief outline that provides context such as: a synopsis of past work; a description of the 'gap' to be filled or new area to be explored; and a summary of current ideas and, where relevant, hypotheses
Aim of research	General description of the overall purpose; a statement of intent
Objectives	Listing of specific outcomes you expect to fulfil in order to achieve the aim
Literature sources to be examined	Examples of sources you intend to consult during your researches
Research methods or critical approach	How you propose to carry out your investigation
Preliminary reference list	Details (in appropriate format, Ch 24) of the key sources you have already consulted
(Special) resources required	Information sources, samples, instruments, people and other requirements for your investigation, especially where there could be an ethical, safety or financial consideration
Outline plan of the project write-up	For example, the likely section or chapter headings and subheadings
Indication of whether discussions have already been held with a nominated supervisor/indication of a potential supervisor	Valid only in cases where there is an element of choice of supervisor
Indication of whether discussions have already been held with the programme or course director	Valid only in cases where this is an administrative requirement
Names of possible supervisors	Your chance to influence this aspect
Timetable/plan	A realistic breakdown of the stages of your project, ideally with appropriate milestones
Statement or declaration that you understand and will comply with ethical and/or safety rules	The committee's guarantee that you have considered these; details may be required in certain cases (Ch 18)

> **✓ Choosing a project title**
>
> The point at which you write your proposal may be the first time you have deeply considered your project title. Consider adopting a two-part title – an attention-grabbing statement, followed by a colon or a dash, and a secondary title that defines the topic more closely. It is also worth noting that the title given at the proposal stage should be seen as provisional, for the nature of the study and the outcomes may dictate a change at the end of the process.

The language in your proposal should be clear to the non-specialist, but must include appropriate terminology to show that you understand key concepts and jargon (the language and specialised terms of the subject).

Try not to prepare your proposal in a rush – if possible, write out a near-final draft and leave it for a few days before coming back to it again with a critical mind. In this way you will be able to make considered modifications before your final submission.

> **ⓘ Example of refining a subject area for a project proposal**
>
> Let's say you are an arts student interested in bi-cameral systems of government. Clearly you cannot expect to write on this topic in its entirety. Suppose you had been enthused by a lecturer (a potential supervisor?) who talked about the checks and balances that arise from having two chambers of government. This stimulated an interest in contrasting the idea of an elected second chamber with one that is dependent on patronage and selection. Perhaps you wish to explore arguments for changes in the composition of the UK House of Lords as the non-elected second chamber in the UK. This might help you define a topic related to the implications of replacing the existing system with a method where the members of the House of Lords might be elected, rather than selected by birth or by patronage. You might then decide to examine the current composition of the Lords and research the levels of participation and contribution to the governmental process made by selected members in contrast to the activities of elected members of the Commons. This might be translated to a title such as: 'Representative Second Chambers: the House of Lords as a case study'.

ACTION POINTS

4.1 Imagine you are assessing your own proposal. Having completed a draft, answer all the questions in the checklist presented earlier in this chapter. If any answers seem problematic, go back to the proposal and try to improve on it. Alternatively, provide evidence to back up your case.

4.2 List potential project titles. Look at the titles of other projects completed recently to gain a feel for the modern style in your discipline. Write down a few options for your own work and ask your supervisor or fellow students what they think of them.

4.3 Use your proposal to focus your thoughts on a detailed timetable for your research and writing. Consult Chapter 5 for advice on managing time and remember to factor in some slippage time. Include suitable milestones – for example, 'finish first draft' (see Table 1.1).

5 PLANNING AND MANAGING TIME

How to organise your investigation and submit on time

Managing your time effectively is an important key to completing a research project successfully. This chapter provides ideas for organising your activities, with tips for maintaining focus on the main tasks in the research and writing processes.

KEY TOPICS
→ Creating an initial plan for your project
→ Starting off well
→ Making sure you work efficiently and effectively
→ Thinking ahead

As you carry out your research project, you will need to balance your time for your research, family duties, employment and social activities, as well as coursework, if this applies to your situation. You will also be expected to exercise considerable autonomy in conducting your research. While you will probably have more freedom over your schedule than many others, making the necessary decisions about how to use your time to your best advantage is still a challenge.

Time management is a skill that can be developed like any other. Coupled with a realistic approach to planning and work habits, adopting relatively simple routines and approaches can help you to improve your organisation, prioritisation and timekeeping. Weigh up the following ideas and use those most suited to your needs and personality. Some may be familiar, but there are always benefits from having a fresh look at your work patterns.

Advantages of being organised

Being well-organised is especially important for large or long-term tasks like a research project because it seems easier to put things off when deadlines seem distant. If you manage your time well, you will:

- keep on schedule and meet your submission deadline
- complete work with less pressure, avoid the build-up of stress and fulfil your potential
- build your confidence about your ability to cope
- avoid (or limit) overlapping commitments so that you don't have to juggle more than one piece of work at a time.

CREATING AN INITIAL PLAN FOR YOUR PROJECT

Laying out a plan for any academic research or writing helps you to clarify the likely structure behind your efforts. Writing out a fairly detailed plan is an aid to consolidating your thinking and also saves you time in the long run.

Each project is different, and among academic disciplines there are variations in approach. As a generalisation, however, it is possible to divide the work in a research investigation into six distinct phases (see Table 5.1).

Table 5.1 Six important phases of work when carrying out a research project and the associated writing.

Phase	Main work to be carried out
Scoping phase	Initial reading, framing a research question and preparing a research proposal (Chs 3 and 4)
Investigative phase	Carrying out the main research effort (Chs 7–18)
Planning phase	Planning, outlining and drafting your writing (Ch 21)
Writing phase	Composing the near-final version of your text, drawing on your drafts; putting the parts in the correct format and completing the final reference list (Chs 22 and 23)
Editing phase	Modifying your text following a detailed reading and taking on board any feedback your supervisor may have provided (Chs 25 and 26)
Submission phase	Focusing on presentational aspects and carrying out final checks (Ch 27)

At the outset, the date for final submission will seem to be some time away, but that time will pass very quickly. To keep yourself on target, create an initial plan for your work based on the six phases in Table 5.1:

1 work out the time in weeks between the submission date and your starting point (if you prefer, use days for your calculations here and below)
2 take away one week so that you aim to complete the work a week ahead of time (for rationale, see **Ch 21**)
3 subtract some further time to allow for contingencies, such as illness and problems with the research
4 deduct the number of weeks you are unlikely to do any significant work (for example, holidays)
5 divide the remaining number by 6 (the number of phases) – this will give the average length of time you can spend on each phase.
6 Now, using your judgement, swap weeks between phases so that you arrive at realistic times for each component. The total number of weeks should remain the same, but you will probably want more time for the investigative and writing phases than (say) for the editing phase.

Figure 5.1 shows an example of such a project time allocation (shown as percentages of a total period).

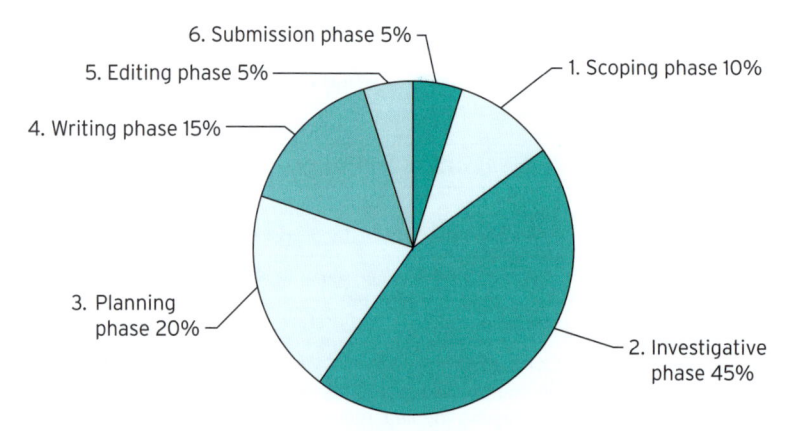

Figure 5.1 Representative time allocations for phases of a research project. This example could relate to the sciences, with an emphasis on scoping and investigation. The phases are presented as proportions of the total, for convenience, and in practice may overlap – as indicated in Figure 5.2. If the total time for the project work is 10 weeks, then the investigative phase, for example, would be planned to take 4.5 weeks (45% of 10 weeks).

It is important not to regard these phases as discrete units to be worked on sequentially. Rather, they are times when you should be focusing on a specific aspect of your project – but not to the exclusion of the others. This is because tackling each activity in a sequential manner is not usually an efficient approach: it is better practice to work in parallel on several aspects, while using the phase deadlines as an indication of when you should aim to complete each one. This is particularly true of draft writing, which can and should start from an early stage (see discussion in **Ch 21**). Those with the technical ability might prefer to draw up a Gantt chart (see e.g. ***www.smartdraw.com***), which allows for such overlapping activities in project work (Figure 5.2).

When you are happy with your timings, work out the end points for each phase and note these in your diary or on a wall planner. Keeping these completion points in mind should help to prevent you from 'drifting' – it is all too easy, for example, to spend a lot of time on unproductive scoping, without actually getting down to any real work.

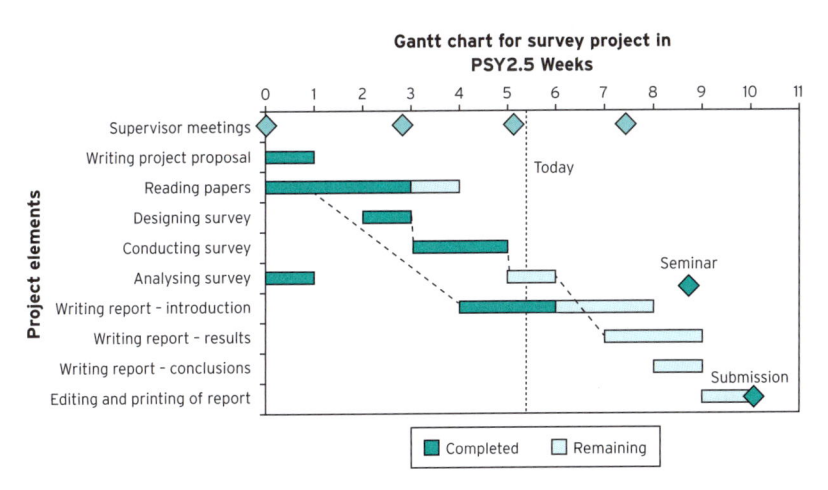

Gantt chart for survey project in PSY2.5 Weeks

Figure 5.2 Representative Gantt chart for project work. This chart was created using the 'stacked bar' type of chart in Excel, and illustrates progress at the start of the 6th week of a simple project based on a survey, culminating in a research report. Note how progress in each phase is shown by shading the horizontal bar for each element: this student is shown as 'behind schedule' with their reading of the literature and analysis of the survey results, but has started to write parts of the introduction to the report, so is 'ahead of schedule' on this aspect. Connections between elements are shown with a dotted line, such as the obvious need to complete the design of the survey before conducting it. Key milestones (lozenges) shown include meetings with the student's supervisor, a seminar to be presented in week 8 and the final report to be submitted in week 10.

5 Planning and managing time

You may wish to 'nest' your plans – creating, for example, a separate sub-schedule during the main writing phase that gives timings for completion of the different sections of your submission. Always view your plan as flexible and, if necessary, revisit it from time to time, reconstructing it with new endpoints.

> ✓ **Assisting serendipity**
>
> In research work – whatever your discipline – make sure that you leave some time for serendipity (chance discoveries) to take over. The germs of some of the most famous ideas, discoveries and inventions arose unexpectedly during moments when the person was thinking about or doing something else (**Ch 16**). So, for example, leave some space in your schedules to browse among the library shelves – not looking for anything in particular, but just opening books because their titles look interesting or intriguing. You never know what you may find or what thought process will be sparked by what you have read.

STARTING OFF WELL

It is vital to start your project and its write-up as you mean to go on, and to establish good working habits from the outset.

- Make sure you fully understand what you are being asked to produce, and how. You can do this by reading the supporting material in the course handbook or regulations (particularly the learning objectives or outcomes), or by speaking to your supervisor.
- Try to connect with your research or source material. Sometimes the topic will appear bewildering in its breadth, obscure in its jargon or genuinely difficult to master. The only way to overcome this is to immerse yourself in the topic, read background material and ask questions. The sooner you take this step, the better.
- Identify the basic concepts at an early stage. You might do this by reviewing a chapter from an introductory text or by revisiting relevant course notes.
- Try not to luxuriate in the comfort of having a deadline many months away. Every part of the process will take longer than you estimate. The time will quickly evaporate, and the earlier you start each phase of the task, the more likely you will be to avoid stress near to the end.

- Try to do something active at all times. Appropriate actions will depend on your subject, but will probably include taking notes of your background reading, or creating a plan of action or timetable. In some research projects it will involve making initial observations or setting up a pilot experiment; in others, getting your hands on the right textbooks, references or primary source material, or realia.
- Be prepared to work hard, fast and focused right from the first moment.
- Starting off well also means understanding what constitutes good working practice and avoiding common errors. There follows a quick summary of these aspects, as they apply to the research and writing phases of your project.

MAKING SURE YOU WORK EFFICIENTLY AND EFFECTIVELY

Efficient working means using your time well. If you can do this, it will mean you have more time available for thinking and relaxing – creating a virtuous cycle that will result in a better end-product. Some key pointers for working efficiently are:

- thinking and planning ahead for each day or part of a day
- understanding what you are trying to achieve during each day or part of a day
- getting down to work as quickly as possible
- scheduling important work for when you generally feel most intellectually active
- prioritising tasks appropriately
- avoiding distractions
- keeping your papers and workplace well organised
- taking breaks when you need to rest.

Effective working is effort that results in meaningful results. It involves having a continual focus on the final outcome and making sure that for each subsidiary task undertaken you keep this in mind. Some key pointers for working effectively are:

- getting started quickly
- focusing on the end-product
- minimising unproductive work

- breaking larger tasks down into smaller parts
- identifying things that are barriers to progress
- finding ways to overcome obstacles to progress
- making sure you complete every component of the task, even if this means some loss of quality.

To avoid common difficulties, watch out for the following and take avoiding action where necessary.

- You may underestimate the time it takes to carry out the research – try to relate to the time you spent on coursework. You should consider how this might be similar, less or more than what you will be required to do for the research project. You will know best how you work and this should enable you to achieve a more realistic assessment of the time you will need.
- Your initial reading may be aimless – seek the advice of your supervisor to ensure that your reading material is appropriate and that you select resources that expand your understanding rather than repeat information or ideas that you have read elsewhere.
- You will need to organise large amounts of information – ensure that you have a system for organising your material in a logical way, such as thematically or sequentially.
- You will need to keep records of research sources so you can cite them properly – systematically record the publication details (**Ch 24**) for everything that you read so that you already have this information when you are ready to create your reference list.
- You will need to be aware of copyright infringement and plagiarism – ensure that you understand how to quote directly from printed resources (**Ch 24**) and, if paraphrasing or summarising, that you remain faithful to the meaning of the original.
- You may need to carry out advanced forms of data analysis (**Ch 19**) – take early steps to understand relevant theory and learn how to use appropriate software.
- You may need to adopt a professional approach to data presentation (**Ch 20**) – study publications in your field to grasp the standards required and learn how to produce similar results, perhaps via specific software.
- You may underestimate the time it takes to write, suffer from writer's block, or your writing skills may be rusty; adopt a strategy of 'speed

writing' – that is, writing a paragraph or two about an aspect of your research at the start of each day. Reread it at the end of the day and amend or develop it so that it flows well. These mini-writing exercises may be useful later on when you are completing the final write-up and will build your confidence in your ability to write quickly and well.

- You may need to allow time for your supervisor to provide feedback (**Ch 26**) – if possible, agree a time schedule with your supervisor where you give a date when you aim to submit drafts and ask for an indication of how long might be required to give you feedback. This will help both you and your supervisor to work to complementary time goals.

- You may need to allow time to take your supervisor's feedback into account – sometimes supervisor's remarks on a draft may require a rethink of text or an aspect of the content. Take time to work through their comments and take advantage of the guidance they offer.

- For longer pieces of work, you will need to allow time for typing your submission, or, if you need this service, for graphics to be produced or printed, and for binding, if this is required (**Ch 27**). Establish at an early stage where, when and by whom any printing, graphics or binding work will be done. If everyone has the same submission date, then some services may be particularly busy, so planning ahead on this aspect may be advisable.

THINKING AHEAD

Anticipating events that need to be included in your time planning is important. For example, if you need to book a particular piece of equipment, this must clearly be done in advance. Failure to place the booking can upset your planning and waste valuable time – not only your own, but that of others whose work schedules may have been adversely affected because of your last-minute requirements. Similarly, if you need to monitor the subjects of your research, perhaps in a clinic or classroom, then you will need to schedule a visit that coincides with the availability of those you need to observe. If you fail to do this, then you may have missed the opportunity and damage your research objectives and timetable.

> ### ✓ Organising your activities
>
> A well-maintained diary or calendar, whether maintained in hard copy, computer or on a mobile device, is the obvious way to keep track of your day-to-day schedule (for example, meetings, seminars and other activities) and to note any deadlines you have. Wall-planners are another way of charting out your activities, with the advantage that you can see all your commitments and deadlines at a glance. Similarly, if available, a white-board can be valuable to mark up and amend a flexible plan.

Listing and prioritising

At times you may run into problems because you have a number of different tasks that need to be done. It is much better to write these tasks down as a list each day, rather than risk forgetting them. You will then have a good picture of what needs to be done and will be able to prioritise the tasks more readily.

Once you've created a list, rank the tasks by numbering them 1, 2, 3 and so on, in order from 'important and urgent' to 'neither important nor urgent' (see Figure 5.3). Your 'important' criteria will depend on many factors – for example, your own goals and submission dates.

Each day, you should try to complete as many of the listed tasks as you can, starting with number one. If you keep each day's list achievable, the process of striking out each task as it is completed

	High ← Urgency → Low	
Importance → High	1	2
Low ←	3	4

Figure 5.3 The 'urgent–important' approach to prioritising. Place each activity somewhere on the axes in relation to its importance and urgency. Do all the activities in sector 1 first, then 2 or 3, and last 4.

provides a feeling of progress being made, which turns into one of satisfaction if the list has virtually disappeared by the evening. Also, you will become less stressed once high-priority tasks are tackled.

Carry over any uncompleted tasks to the next day, add new ones to your list and start again – but try to complete yesterday's unfinished jobs before starting new ones of similar priority, or they will end up being delayed for too long.

This technique works well for practical aspects of researching. Once you get to the writing-up phase, it becomes less easy to apply list-making on the writing task itself. However, keeping lists of non-writing things you need to do could help you to deal with each item separately and keep your mind free to focus on the writing in progress.

How can I decide on my priorities?

This involves distinguishing between important and urgent activities.

- **Importance** implies some assessment of the benefits of completing a task against the loss if the task is not finished.
- **Urgency** relates to the length of time before the task must be completed.

For example, in normal circumstances, visiting the barber or hairdresser will be neither terribly important nor particularly urgent, but if you have to attend a work interview, then the 'shaggy dog' look you have been cultivating may require some attention, meaning that making a hairdressing appointment moves further up your 'to do' list. Hence, priorities are not static and need to be reassessed frequently.

Routines and good work habits

Many people find that carrying out specific tasks at special periods of the day or times of the week helps them to get things done on time. You may already adopt this approach with routine tasks, such as doing your shopping every Tuesday morning or visiting a relative on Sunday afternoons. You may find it helps to add work-related activities to your list of routines – for example, by making Monday evening a time for literature-searching in the library.

Good working habits can help with time management:

- Do important work when you are at your most productive. Most of us can state when we work best (perhaps morning, afternoon or evening). When you have worked this out for yourself, timetable your activities to suit: academic work when you are 'most awake' and routine activities when you are less alert.
- Make the most of small scraps of time. Use otherwise unproductive time, such as when commuting or before going to sleep, to jot down ideas, edit work or make plans. Keep a paper or electronic notebook with you to record your thoughts.
- Keep your documents organised. If your papers are well filed, then you won't waste time looking for something required for the next step.
- Extend your working day. If you can deal with early rising, you may find that setting your alarm earlier than normal provides a few extra hours to help you achieve a short-term goal.
- Allocate a specific period each week for 'housekeeping' your research. Taking the time to audit your achievements and progress over the previous week and anticipate your next steps will stimulate your planning for the following week. This can also be an opportunity to catch up on routine tasks such as administration or managing your work space, materials and equipment. Using this strategy means that you start your next research period with a clear desk and a plan of action for the following week.

Examples of work patterns that *don't* work well for lengthy projects

1. Working long hours for an extended period – and not having the energy to complete the task.
2. Last-minute completion – sacrificing quality due to a last-minute rush.
3. Being naïve or over-confident – not allocating enough time to tasks.
4. Being a perfectionist – trying for the best possible result on one aspect and compromising quality elsewhere.
5. Not being focused – wasting time on diffuse activities.
6. Doing too much outside work – not allocating enough time to the task and potentially losing energy.
7. Procrastinating – finding other less important things to do rather than your project work.

ACTION POINTS

5.1 Create an initial plan for your project – and act on it. Follow the guidance in this chapter, deciding on lengths of time for each phase as fits both the project and its methods. If some of the times for phases seem rather short, then let this be a wake-up call. You will need to work hard and in a focused way to complete your project, and there is no better time to start than the present.

5.2 Analyse your time-management personality. Can you recognise any character traits that might prevent you from organising your time effectively? Might any tips in this chapter help you become better at time management? How could you adapt them to your own situation?

5.3 Experiment with listing and prioritising. If you haven't used this strategy before, test it out for a week or so. Make a list of all your current and future tasks, academic commitments, appointments and social events. Rearrange the list in order of priority. Take special care to take account of events that depend on other jobs being completed. Now try to complete the different components, ticking them off the list as you go. After your trial period, decide how effective the method was in organising your activities and helping you to ensure that tasks were done on time. You might find it helpful to use a free App such as 'Remember the Milk' (*www.rememberthemilk.com/services/*) or 'Wunderlist' (*www.wunderlist.com*) to help you with the process of managing your time. Note that there may be charges that apply to such applications.

6
WORKING SUCCESSFULLY WITH A SUPERVISOR

How to make the most of your relationship

Your supervisor is vital to the success of your research activity. You want to produce a project worthy of an excellent grade and your supervisor will try to assist you in making this possible. It is essential that both parties work together to ensure that your project is successful.

KEY TOPICS

→ The self-directed nature of a research project
→ The duties and responsibilities of a supervisor
→ The pressures on your supervisor's time
→ Supervisor and student personalities
→ Your supervisor's role in your project write-up

Other than yourself, your supervisor will probably be the most important person in relation to your research. He or she will be in a position to help you in many ways. Arriving at a good working relationship with your supervisor is therefore a vital component of successful research. In many cases, this association develops easily through the various phases of the project and may last well beyond into later degrees and employment. In others, there may be a mismatch between the personalities or expectations of either party, and problems may ensue. This chapter aims to clarify the ground rules for supervised research and to provide suggestions for remedying any difficulties that arise.

> **Having multiple supervisors**
>
> There are a number of scenarios where you might have more than one supervisor. They might have complementary expertise relevant to your project, or one may be performing a mentoring role for another who is at the start of their career. Throughout this book we will use the term 'supervisor', while acknowledging that, on occasion, this might properly be 'supervisors'.

THE SELF-DIRECTED NATURE OF A RESEARCH PROJECT

Research-based study is not intended to be an exercise in the student awaiting direction from a supervisor who dispenses instructions. The student has to learn to exercise a degree of autonomy in a number of ways. This need for independent thought and action involves recognising a number of important responsibilities.

Firstly, you will need to take a certain amount of responsibility for your own research by planning your time and pacing your work so that you achieve objectives on time (**Ch 5**). However, carrying out autonomous work in itself is not your only responsibility – you must support it with independent thought. You are expected to be able to produce fresh ideas that you can develop and defend (**Chs 16 and 17**). Although you will probably start by 'working to guidance', increasingly it should be you, rather than your supervisor, who drives the research.

Your period of research study will therefore involve the development of a number of personal transferable skills – for example, advanced data presentation techniques. It is your responsibility to explore the means of developing such skills. For instance, this might involve using appropriate software tools to help you present your work competently. You may be expected to seek out help by yourself if this is required.

Writing skills are vital to your progress and ultimate success (**Chs 21–27**). Many graduates will readily admit that their early research experiences led to major improvements in their abilities in this area and that their supervisor's advice was an important influence on their progress. You should take a proactive role by reacting positively to his or her feedback (**Ch 26**), adapting your writing to the style adopted in your subject area and gaining and transferring skills from relevant experience, writing manuals and reference works.

> **Key expectations of supervisors**
>
> These are the main qualities that a supervisor will expect you to display:
>
> - honesty
> - autonomy (once trained)
> - hard work
> - the desire to learn how to write effectively
> - openness about problems.

THE DUTIES AND RESPONSIBILITIES OF A SUPERVISOR

Before you even started your project, your supervisor's role may have included proposing the project and (in certain cases) obtaining specific funding to support your studies. They may well have created or assembled the components of your working environment. In the sciences, for example, your supervisor may have obtained vital equipment through research grants. In other areas, they may have accumulated vital resources or access to evidence that will underpin your work, such as old books, manuscripts and papers. They may have had to negotiate desk and/or lab space for you and the raw materials you will need for your research study.

Your supervisor may provide or bring the ideas that will form the basis of your work. In some cases, these may be defined in great detail (for example, putting forward hypotheses and laying out clear milestones). In others, they may simply be a general area of study and associated intellectual framework, encapsulated perhaps in a project title and single descriptive paragraph, that you yourself will be expected to develop independently in a detailed proposal or plan (**Ch 4**).

When you begin as a researcher, your supervisor's role will probably include some of the following:

- helping you to settle down when you first start – for example, by providing advice on finding your way around your department and important research facilities
- supporting you in developing appropriate skills to pursue your work – these may include, for example, guidance on how to use software,

or a particular set of analytical techniques, or tips on assembling a reference collection (**Chs 7, 8 and 24**)
- assisting you to develop the research project from the initial ideas, perhaps helping you to refine hypotheses or ideas on the basis of your early results or findings (**Ch 16**)
- putting you in touch with those locally or at a distance who can help with your studies or can contribute to your work.

Once your work is under way, your supervisor's role may include some of the following:

- ensuring that you work safely at all times
- being available for discussions and meetings
- providing adequate resources and facilities for your work, including training in necessary skills
- providing pastoral care, if required, or putting you in touch with those who can help you
- enthusing you about the work in hand and helping you get through the inevitable low points when everything seems to be going wrong
- making sure your work does not end up in a dead end and that you do have something to write up when you finish
- keeping you informed about any milestones or deadlines within your study periods (such as those for writing interim reports on progress)
- helping you to interpret the rules and regulations and codes of practice that govern your studies
- helping you to analyse your findings
- giving you feedback on your research and the related written work you produce
- helping you as you write up your findings and, where applicable, suggesting opportunities to disseminate them via posters, seminars or other forms of presentation
- providing guidance about the *viva voce* exam and other assessments, as applicable
- supporting your onward progress when your studies are finished.

> ✓ **Always go well prepared to meetings with your supervisor**
>
> Have all your materials well organised and neatly written up. Create a list of discussion points beforehand and if you have questions, be prepared to show you have made some attempt to answer these independently.

When you have completed the research project, your supervisor may be able to give you guidance on possible careers, help you find a job after your work is finished and write references for you when you apply for jobs – but you should always inform your supervisor about jobs you are applying for and provide them with an up-to-date CV.

THE PRESSURES ON YOUR SUPERVISOR'S TIME

All the above duties and responsibilities of a supervisor take time, and it is important to realise that your supervisor undertakes these duties while carrying out a wide range of other tasks. Typically, these could include:

- carrying out his or her own research
- writing up his or her research
- refereeing others' work
- applying for research funding
- going to seminars and conferences
- working with other students, postgraduates, post-docs and technical staff
- teaching
- marking exam papers or conducting oral exams
- carrying out departmental administration
- attending university committees and working groups
- (if they are lucky) having some sort of private life.

This means you should make sure your notion of the amount of time your supervisor can spend with you is realistic. After all, research study is primarily about learning to work and think on your own. That does not mean that your supervisor can ignore you. It might mean, however, that you will have to be patient in waiting for feedback on drafts of your work. Normally, you will have a good idea of the context in which your supervisor is working and can adjust your expectations accordingly. Just before a lecture might not be a good time to ask for a considered opinion on your work; in the run-up to an important conference, all of your supervisor's attention might be on putting together his/her contribution; and in vacation periods, he/she may be away from the lab or office for several weeks on research work.

Time your approaches to your supervisor

Be sensitive to their working patterns and to any one-off tasks they are doing. If possible, suggest diary dates for meetings in advance.

SUPERVISOR AND STUDENT PERSONALITIES

Although there may be times when you will doubt it, supervisors are human beings and hence are fallible. They may be near-geniuses and have heroic research achievements to their name, but at the same time they may have difficulty empathising with students or seem rather abrupt. In the majority of cases, this simply requires adjustment on the part of the student.

While you will inevitably focus on your supervisor's traits, he or she will also have a view on your personality. The emphasis may be on qualities supervisors are pleased to see, such as being:

- hard-working
- well-organised
- punctual

What should I do if I do not feel my supervisor is giving me enough of their time?

1. Compare notes with others in your department to see whether you are relatively disadvantaged in this way
2. Try to be more proactive in setting up meetings, perhaps by helping to set up diary dates or a regular meeting slot
3. Raise the matter informally when your paths cross
4. As a last resort, you might wish to consult the course leader or head of department.

6 Working successfully with a supervisor

- focused
- technically adept
- intellectually bright.

A supervisor will probably not want to deal with personal matters extraneous to the research itself. Examples might include: lack of motivation; being homesick; financial problems; or issues with relationships. Nevertheless, because these issues may have a direct effect on your progress, you should explain your feelings frankly – just don't expect much more than sympathy in return. Supervisors are not social workers and their attention will nearly always be directed to the outcomes of students' work. If you need further help, consult the relevant student services unit directly.

> **What should I do if I have more than one supervisor and they give me conflicting advice?**
>
> The situation where conflicting advice is given is a difficult one to resolve. It can only really be dealt with through a discussion with all parties present. You should confront an issue of this kind as soon as possible as it could lead to huge problems nearer to the submission date. If it seems that matters will not be resolved easily, it might be a good idea to have a confidential chat with the course leader or head of department.

YOUR SUPERVISOR'S ROLE IN YOUR PROJECT WRITE-UP

The end point of your research period will be the submission of a report, paper, dissertation or thesis summarising your findings (**Ch 21**). Communicating your work in this way is a vital part of any research programme and in most cases it will be a major determinant of your grades or degree award.

While you may be asked to sign a statement to the effect that your submission is 'all your own work' (**Ch 22**), there is necessarily an element of collaboration between student and supervisor. If there is a *viva voce* exam, this will be designed to ensure that the research and the write-up reflect your own work, and that you fully understand what has been done. Despite the need for autonomy, you should have a legitimate expectation of guidance and constructive criticism concerning your efforts. However, your supervisor may insist on including material you do not agree with or insist on removing material you think is important. Before getting too annoyed with this, do bear in mind your supervisor's experience and wisdom. He or she may well have good reasons for adopting a particular stance – perhaps sensitivity to the 'political' aspects of your research, or the wider picture in your research area.

> ### How much will my supervisor help me in writing up?
>
> Misunderstandings on this issue can act as a major source of dissatisfaction. International students in particular, who may be paying large fees for the experience, might expect that this payment is in part for help with writing up. It isn't, normally. Moreover, most supervisors will be unable to have the time to help with putting your ideas into scholarly English. You may need to consult a specialist writing centre in your university where special courses may be available.

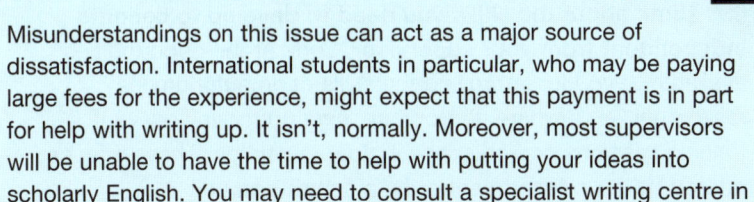

Your supervisor may feel that aspects of your work are not ready for writing up. He or she may insist that you repeat your procedures several times; or that you analyse something in greater depth. Again, you should respect their wisdom in such matters. If your results are important or go against other work it might be extremely important to have a high level of confidence before 'going public'. Your supervisor will be well aware of the rigour with which external examiners will look at your work and the sorts of comments they are likely to make and may wish to forestall most of these.

Expect some differences to emerge in your writing styles. Your supervisor will probably have had a different type of schooling/training from you and therefore may write in a different way – perhaps one that you feel is overly formal and pedantic. Almost certainly, however, your supervisor will have the same or a better qualification than the one you aspire to and a greater experience of writing in academic style. Listen and learn. Writing up is likely to be a valuable experience as far as learning about academic English is concerned. There is much to be gained from sensible discussions about the issues that arise. It is not uncommon, for example, for there to be lengthy supervisor–student discussions on the use of commas, or sentence or paragraph construction. You should be prepared to defend some aspects of your writing style (as long as it meets the standards) as this is unique to you, but should always consider the advice of your supervisor carefully.

ACTION POINTS

6.1 Analyse how your personality will interact with that of your supervisor. Reflect on how you might forestall or respond to the challenges you feel might emerge in your continuing relationship. What kind of research student are you? What traits do you display that your supervisor may like or dislike?

6.2 Think about the skills you need to develop to become independent from your supervisor. Look at the opportunities available to you for improving the skills of an autonomous researcher, and, where appropriate, sign up for any relevant training sessions or workshops in your institution. These may be offered by your department or by a centralised unit.

6.3 Find out more about your supervisor's research. Seek out some of his or her recent research publications and explore what topics appear to be of interest. How have his or her findings been presented and explained to the wider academic community through journal articles or conference papers? What style has been adopted when writing up the work? This may be highly relevant for your own report (Ch 22).

RESEARCHING THE LITERATURE

7

FINDING RELEVANT SOURCE MATERIAL

How to develop your information literacy skills

In researching literature for your project, you will generally be expected to source material for yourself. Your supervisor may suggest some resources to get you started, but after that it will be very much up to you to explore further, according to your specific project aims. Therefore, learning more about your university library from the viewpoint of a researcher is a priority.

KEY TOPICS

→ Understanding information literacy
→ First steps for new researchers
→ Basic types of source material
→ How to access your university library's e-resources
→ Obtaining difficult-to-find resources

Although you might already be familiar with how university library resources are organised through your experience of researching and reading for undergraduate coursework, your research project studies will probably mean that you need to delve into areas and facilities that you may not have explored or used before. For example, you may need to find out about and read journal articles in obscure or highly specialised or advanced journals, or access archived resources. Indeed, familiarising yourself with a new range of sourcing methods for this purpose may present a challenge.

UNDERSTANDING INFORMATION LITERACY

The library is a key resource in any research project. Modern university libraries are not just repositories of books, journals and archived material. They are information centres that coordinate an electronic gateway to a massive amount of online information. Accessing these resources requires a set of seven skills known collectively as 'information literacy' (SCONUL, 2011). This term, coined by library experts, has been defined as: 'knowing when and why you need information, where to find it, and how to evaluate, use and communicate it in an ethical manner' (CILIP, 2012).

> **The seven key information skills associated with information literacy (SCONUL, 2011)**
>
> 1 The ability to identify a personal need for information ('identify' information)
> 2 The ability to assess current knowledge and identify gaps ('scope' information)
> 3 The ability to construct strategies for locating information and data ('plan' information)
> 4 The ability to locate and access the information and data needed ('gather' information)
> 5 The ability to review the research process and compare and evaluate information and data ('evaluate' information)
> 6 The ability to organise information professionally and ethically ('manage' information)
> 7 The ability to apply the knowledge gained: presenting the results of the research, synthesising new and old information and data to create new knowledge and disseminating it in a variety of ways ('present' information).
>
> These skills are discussed at various points in this book – most notably in this chapter and Chapters 8 and 9, but also in Chapters 11, 16–18 and 24.

Spending time at the start of your research period considering the different aspects of information literacy will bring later rewards. It will provide valuable clues about the expectations for your work at this new level, and you should assess how well you can carry out each of the seven skills. Essentially, you will be expected to be able to carry out most or all of them at a high level of competence. Consult library staff if you feel you need assistance with any specific skill.

FIRST STEPS FOR NEW RESEARCHERS

For project work, it will be assumed that you will have a working knowledge of how a university library functions, such as:

- how to use an electronic catalogue for your own and other libraries
- how hard-copy resources are shelved, probably using one of the two commonly used methods – the Dewey decimal system (numerical coding) or the Library of Congress system (alphanumeric system)
- how to find a periodical or journal in hard copy or online
- the borrowing rules, including the borrowing periods and fines.

If you are unfamiliar with any of these aspects of library-use in your institution, you should ask for assistance from a librarian.

Library information systems are constantly changing as your library enters into agreements with new or different suppliers of online information through subscriptions to electronic media, especially e-journals, which are of particular importance in researching. Although you will probably find that your library provides an online information portal, part of which may be dedicated to your subject area, you may find it easier at the outset to contact the librarians with responsibility for connecting you with discipline-specific resources. You will benefit from the expertise and guidance they can provide and this will help to get your research on track.

How can I learn more about what my library has to offer?

Apart from contacting the librarian with responsibility for your discipline, you may find that library staff offer training sessions on how to use referencing packages or on the use of new or subject-specific databases. Your library's website may also carry useful tips and online access routes to databases and e-journals. Many libraries have hard-copy leaflets providing tips and guidance for using a range of facilities and resources.

7 Finding relevant source material   **63**

BASIC TYPES OF SOURCE MATERIAL

You will be expected to research your topic extensively using a variety of resources. These include:

- Textbooks – good for gaining an overview of a new field.
- Monographs – books on a single, often narrow, subject.
- Reference works – useful for obtaining facts and definitions, and a concise overview of a subject. These include general and subject-specific encyclopaedias, yearbooks and dictionaries, and can be found in the area of the library reserved for reference material. These items usually cannot be borrowed. While some may be available online, others might only exist in hardcopy because it would be too expensive to create online versions for a limited audience. Hence, you should familiarise yourself with them at an early stage in your studies.
- Research papers – very detailed 'articles' published in journals, covering specific subject areas. Proceedings of conferences where cutting-edge research has been presented would also fall into this category. These may also be available online.
- Reviews – analyses of a defined research area, often detailed and more up-to-date than books. These are important for orientation in a specific research field, sometimes looking at the subject from a particular academic stance.

Some of these resources may be stored elsewhere, so don't assume that the only books in the library are those on display – consult the catalogue(s) using appropriate search words.

> ✓ **The value of using more than one source**
>
> Consulting a number of sources on any given issue is fundamental to the research process. While some sources may corroborate each other, others may take different views or support different interpretations. Interrogating these different 'schools of thought' is sometimes referred to as 'reading around' a subject. Your interpretation of this reading involves the analytical processes of critical thinking (**Ch 16**) which are essential for effective research.

HOW TO ACCESS YOUR UNIVERSITY LIBRARY'S E-RESOURCES

This is normally done via the library's website. Some resources are open-access, but others will require a special password. This may depend on the system used in your library – for example, Athens or Shibboleth. Note that different institutions will operate slightly different systems, but if in doubt, ask a member of the library staff. Many current items are now available online in each of the categories listed above. For example, libraries take out subscriptions to e-book repositories, e-journals, e-newspapers and online dictionaries and encyclopaedias. Your institution will have its own method of giving access to these resources, probably via the library's online portal or a virtual learning environment (VLE). The main advantage of this method of accessing information is that it is available 24 hours a day from any computer connected to the internet. Some e-book facilities, such as ebrary, offer features such as searching, note-making and linked online dictionaries.

Shibboleth and (Open)Athens

These are systems that provide a gateway to a number of different databases used by academic researchers. In many cases access is automatic when you are recognised as a logged-in member of your university, but in other instances you may gain access solely via a 'library' computer. Where these automatic systems do not function, you may have to obtain a password through your institutional library. This will identify you as an authorised user for as long as you are a student.

Web-based material may be published by official bodies and should therefore be reliable in content; however, other websites without such provenance are not wholly reliable as sources, although they may be useful for comparing viewpoints and sourcing other information. One important point to note is that copying/printing out from online sources is governed by copyright restrictions just as much as paper-based material (**Ch 11**).

Key online research techniques

For project work, your research skills will need to become more thorough than in your early years of study, because your investigation and write-up need to be based on reliable evidence that is both up-to-date and comprehensive. For example, it will not be sufficient to base your work on a few isolated references, augmented by searches of the internet or Wikipedia. You will need to identify and access new sources. To find sources new to you, there are, essentially, three key approaches.

1 Subject searches. These find sources based on key words related to your research topic, including, where relevant, author names. The output is usually a listing of reference details plus abstract/summary material from a wide range of sources. From this list, you can select references that might be of particular relevance, although it may only be possible to judge how significant they really are when you read the full paper.

2 Searches based on references cited in a given source. With this kind of search, you start with a source and its reference list. From this list, you backtrack through selected references, making judgements about their relevance and value and, potentially, looking at items cited in their reference lists. This enables you to gain a perspective on the literature of your subject area, working backwards from the starting point of your most recent source, but it does not enable you to identify more recent research.

3 Searches based on citations of a given source. These searches rely on the availability of databases that give details of publications that have cited a given reference. In other words, they allow you to work forward in time towards more current research. This can be very useful if your original sources are slightly dated.

A number of online databases are available to assist with these searches – for example, British Humanities Index, Google Scholar, Scopus or Web of Science. Some of these may require a subscription, and your library's website or staff will indicate which ones are available and recommended for your purpose. Their interfaces are usually self-explanatory, but online tutorials are available via a simple web search.

✓ **Record information about all sources that you find**

Sometimes, keyword searches and even seemingly relevant titles and abstracts can lead you to papers that are not of immediate value. If this is the case, don't discard these sources but keep the reference information and brief notes about the content in a filing system, electronically or in hard copy. It is very frustrating to forget, mislay or be unable to relocate details of sources that later transpire to be highly relevant.

OBTAINING DIFFICULT-TO-FIND RESOURCES

Access to the sources identified by any of the above methods is not guaranteed. They may be published in journals to which your library does not subscribe. However, most materials are obtainable via a system of inter-library loans that can be arranged through your own library site, often by a specialist librarian. There may be cost implications in this process – usually, the cost is borne by the borrower, especially if the material is in hard copy.

Most libraries share resources with those of neighbouring institutions and all are linked to the British Library (**www.bl.uk**) – the national library of the UK. This receives a copy of every publication produced in the UK and Ireland, and its massive collection of over 150 million items increases by 3 million items each year. Some university libraries are designated as European Documentation Centres, holding key documents of the European Union (**http://ec.europa.eu/europedirect/visit_us/edc/index_en.htm**).

Accessing 'raw' data

Electronic databases make it easier to access information from public bodies, and much of that kind of information is also more readily available online. For example, in the UK statistical population details are available through the National Statistics website (**www.statistics.gov.uk**), while papers and publications produced by the Houses of Parliament can also be accessed electronically (**www.parliament.uk**). Clearly, the types of data in this category that you may wish to access will depend on your research topic.

Accessing archive material

The use of primary sources is fundamental to research in many disciplines, but especially in the arts and humanities. Many universities hold archive material of original documents, collections, artefacts and other source material that can be of particular relevance to some research studies. Your university web page will give you further information about how to access such resources, usually through an in-house archives service. There it may be possible to speak directly with an archivist to explain your research topic and find out what locally-situated resources might be of possible interest and relevance to your project.

Internet searches

'Browsing' your topic using one of the major search engines will probably produce a wealth of links, some of which may not turn up on library databases. On the one hand, this approach can produce good material that has been provided for open access. On the other, you will need to be sure that the sites you consult are authoritative sources and do not contain unsubstantiated and possibly erroneous information. As a ground rule, if the material appears to be useful, then try to triangulate it with references from within recognised academic publications, whether online or in hard copy.

The nature of the internet means that it is a constantly changing environment where material is made accessible very quickly – and can, of course, be altered or even removed with similar speed. Thus, it is important to keep a detailed record of all references you have found online, and provide the relevant 'Accessed' date (**Ch 24**).

ACTION POINTS

7.1 Take time to explore the shelves covering your subject area. Identify this area from the library catalogue and the information in the shelving aisles. Browsing the books on the library shelves may reveal interesting resources you might not find by other searching methods. Note that relevant research journals may be stored in a different area of your library.

7.2 Spend some time becoming thoroughly acquainted with the electronic library resources available to you. Look, in particular, at any subject-specific resources that are provided on the catalogue system or via the library website.

7.3 Find out about alternative library facilities. In some cases, there may be additional libraries on different campuses or in different buildings. Some of these may be departmental libraries, containing specialist resources. These can contain duplicate holdings of books in the main library. Importantly, you may find they represent convenient or preferable study areas. Even if they do not cover your subject area, you may find their atmosphere more suited to your mood, learning style or personality.

8

ASSESSING CONTENT IN THE LITERATURE

How to evaluate published information in your field

A search for information sources related to your research topic will identify a variety of sources to consider: some relevant, some less so; some reliable, some less so. To evaluate these, you will need to develop the skills of considering the origin, reading for meaning, assessing content and, consequently, the value of information.

KEY TOPICS

→ The initial survey of a new source
→ Examining the structure of the writing
→ Text-reading techniques
→ Checking the reliability of source material
→ Identifying bias and error in text

Whatever the subject of your research project, the ability to evaluate the information and ideas in source material is essential. This is a key aspect of 'information literacy', involving multifaceted skills (**Ch 7**). Your analysis may centre on the accuracy or truth of the information itself, the reliability or potential bias of the source of the information, or the value of information in relation to some argument or case. You may also come across contradictory sources of evidence or conflicting arguments based on the same information. You will need to assess their relative merits. To do any or all of these tasks, you will need to read the text effectively and appraise the origin and nature of the information you find.

You will need to be discerning about your reading choice, and in this chapter it is assumed that you have found a new publication (**Ch 7**) and wish to evaluate it in order to establish its value to your appraisal of the literature. The focus here will be on the most common sources of information – research papers or reviews, books and websites – but similar principles apply to other types of source.

> ✓ **Reader as author**
>
> The points in this chapter about the organisation of printed material and the structure of text are important for you as a reader, or 'decoder', of text. This awareness should also come into play when you act as an academic author yourself and have to write about your own ideas.

THE INITIAL SURVEY OF A NEW SOURCE

You should first carry out a quick survey to familiarise yourself with what any new source contains. For books and longer reviews you might find contents or section listings near the front, and some websites have site maps, links or tabs that will help. For journal articles, the content may be clear from the title, abstract (sometimes called a summary) and/or section headings, but these can mislead, so a more in-depth look may be necessary. Use elements of the structure to answer key questions about the content, as indicated in Table 8.1. The answers to these questions will help you to decide whether to investigate further, whether you need to look at the whole source, or just selected parts, or whether the source is of limited value at the present time.

EXAMINING THE STRUCTURE OF THE WRITING

Learning how to access the content of academic publications quickly will significantly save you time. In order to grasp the main thrust of a resource you plan to read in full, you need to understand the structure of academic text. Well-structured academic writing usually follows a standard pattern, with an introduction, main body and conclusion in each element (**Ch 23**). Sometimes the introduction may comprise several paragraphs; sometimes it may be only one paragraph. Similarly, the conclusion may be several paragraphs or only one. Figure 8.1 illustrates a model layout for a piece of text with five paragraphs, comprising an introduction and conclusion with three intervening paragraphs of varying length.

Table 8.1 Questions to ask when reading a new source. The individual questions will have greater or lesser relevance depending on the nature of the source (i.e. book, paper/review or website) and your specific area of research.

Who wrote it and why?
Details of authorship are usually given alongside the title or on the preliminary pages. The status of the author(s) might be useful (academic qualifications imply some authority and reliability, for example). You might find their affiliation there too (perhaps a university or company). The authors may be well-known authorities in the subject area – or previously unknown to you. Whatever is the case, you should carry out the same rigorous analysis of the content. It can be difficult to find out who wrote a website, and indeed parts may have been written and edited by a range of contributors. This is especially the case with 'Wikis'. The preliminary information may also give reasons for publication (for example, scholarship, publicity, sponsorship) that might influence your analysis.
Who published it?
Well-known publishers have a vested interest in ensuring content is reliable and valid. Consequently, they often put in place rigorous refereeing/reviewing/editing procedures to ensure this is the case. Websites may be sponsored or part of a bigger web presence, and have the same controls.
When was it written?
This is usually pretty obvious from the title pages – usually on a left-hand page beside the copyright symbol. The date of publication will help you to put the source in its context and decide, for example, whether its assumptions, methods or conclusions remain valid. Old material can remain valid for a surprising amount of time in some disciplines, but be outdated very quickly in others. Web-based material can be difficult to date as it may be modified frequently after its first appearance (**Ch 24**).
Can I rely on the information within?
You will get clues from the author's affiliation (see above) and publisher, but you will need to focus on the content too. Your judgement should be influenced by: standard of presentation; the methods used; analysis with statistics; and the support given to the position within by the literature that is cited (**Ch 24**).
What does it say?
The title (and abstract for a paper or review) should be informative, but it may mislead because key aspects may have been omitted for space, or because the authors wish to make a headline-grabbing statement. For books, the contents listing or index may be helpful to find relevant material. There is quite frequently a mismatch between what the author(s) think(s) or say(s) they've done and what you may feel after reading the main body of the paper or book.
How does it fit with my current interests?
This clearly depends on your research question (**Ch 3**) and the relevant section of your project and its write-up. If you have used a pictorial or tabular structure to lay out your key thoughts on relevant issues, then you can add the citation alongside or in a parallel structure. Those who like to use reference cards (**Ch 11**) may like to lay these out over a desk or table to find groupings or trends.

Introduction	Topic paragraph	First paragraph
Main body	Topic sentence / Topic development	Second paragraph
	Topic sentence / Topic development	Third paragraph
	Topic sentence / Topic development	Fourth paragraph
Conclusion	Terminator paragraph	Final paragraph

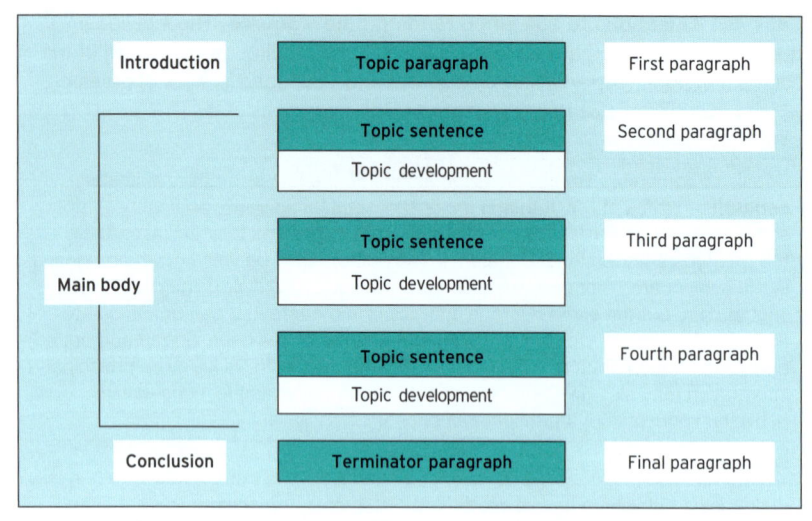

Figure 8.1 **Sample textual layout.** Most samples of academic text will be similarly organised, although the numbers of paragraphs of different types may vary.

Within the structure of well-written academic text, each paragraph will be introduced by a topic sentence stating the content of the paragraph. Each paragraph, in turn, performs a specific function. For example, while some may describe, others may provide examples, or examine points in favour of a particular viewpoint, or points against that viewpoint. The function of these paragraphs, and the sentences within them, is usually signalled by use of 'signpost words' that guide the reader through the logical structure of the text. For example, the word 'however' indicates that some contrast is about to be made with a point immediately before; 'therefore' or 'thus' signals that a result or effect is about to be explained. Examples of signpost words are shown in Table 8.2. You can use this knowledge of the structure of writing to establish quickly the substance of a piece of text.

TEXT-READING TECHNIQUES

With good technique (Ch 7), your searches will provide plenty of information to assess. There will be much to read, and you will need to develop the skills of doing this quickly, while simultaneously abstracting meaning and assessing relevance. There are several strategies to help you to do this.

Table 8.2 Examples of signpost words and phrases used to indicate and manage the flow of writing. These are sometimes called 'discourse markers' or 'cohesive devices' because they contribute to the construction of the discussion within a text (Ch 23).

Type of link intended	Examples of signpost words
Addition	additionally; furthermore; in addition; moreover
Cause/reason	as a result of; because (mid-sentence)
Comparison	compared with; in the same way; in comparison with; likewise
Condition	if; on condition that; providing that; unless
Contrast	although, by contrast; conversely; despite; however; nevertheless; yet
Effect/result	as a result; hence; therefore; thus
Exemplification	for example; for instance; particularly; such as; thus
Reformulation	in other words; rather; to paraphrase
Summary	finally; hence; in all; in conclusion; in short; in summary
Time sequence	after; at first; at last; before; eventually; subsequently
Transition	as far as … is concerned; as for; to turn to

- Filleting the text for content. This is where you read the topic and terminator paragraphs, or even just their topic sentences, to gain a quick overview of a specific part. Follow this by reading the topic sentences for the intervening paragraphs to provide an overview of the entire section or chapter you are evaluating. This will aid your understanding before you study-read the whole text in detail. At this point, you may be able to make a judgement about whether this text is appropriate and whether you rate it as relevant to your investigation.
- Skimming. This is where you pick out a specific piece of information by quickly letting the eye run down a list or over a page looking for a key word or phrase, as when seeking a particular topic in an index.
- Scanning. Here, you let your eye run quickly over a section before you commit yourself to study-read it. Sometimes headings and sub-headings may be used, which will give some indication of the sequence being followed in delivering information. This will help you to gain an overview of the content before you start.

- Identifying the signpost words. As noted in Table 8.2, these help guide you, as the reader, through the logical process that the author has mapped out for you.
- Recognising clusters of grammatically allied words as well as subject word 'strings'. Subliminally, good readers will group words in clusters according to their natural alliances. This helps the reader to make fewer fixations (see below). Research-level texts often contain specialised word 'strings' that form a single meaningful concept (**Ch 23**); looking for such word strings will help you to assimilate content and hence evaluate its merit more quickly.
- Taking cues from punctuation. As you read, you will gain some understanding by interpreting the text using the cues of full-stops and commas, for example, to help you gain understanding of what you are reading.

Fast readers tend to operate by using their peripheral vision (what you see, while staring ahead, at the furthest extreme to the right and the left). This means that they absorb clusters of words in one 'flash' or 'fixation' on the text. A reader who does this is reading more efficiently than the reader who reads word-by-word. Research has indicated that people who read slowly word-by-word are actually less likely to absorb information quickly enough for the brain to process.

Note that problems can occur when reading online text. For example, it is very easy to jump from link to link and stray from the main focus of the reading. Furthermore, unless a 'breadcrumb' trail is available allowing you to retrace your searches, it is all too easy to stray from the original text and not be able to find a way back to it. Some people therefore prefer the traditional paper-based approach, in which case they print out a hard copy of the document. For those who prefer to read material onscreen, then peripheral vision still plays an important part, since the ability to scan and skim first of all, using the scroll bar, can help readers to obtain an overview of the whole piece. Then, a more intensive reading 'sweep' of topic sentences, again using the scroll function, can achieve the overall survey of the text. The use of colour, highlighting and other features popularly used in online text, but less so in paper-based text, can help the reader to be more selective in the extent of the text that they read intensively.

> **Text-reading onscreen** ✓
>
> There are two approaches to mounting text for online reading.
>
> 1 Where 'normal' text that was produced in paper format is uploaded. This allows the traditional speed-reading approaches to be applied, as described in this chapter.
> 2 Where the text has been created particularly for the computer screen. This may include interactive images and hypertext links. The language may be truncated or simplified to conform to web-writing conventions.
>
> In both cases, if the text is in Portable Document Format (pdf), then there may be limited options for manipulating the document. However, in both approaches it is usually possible to search more efficiently than in a textbook for key words or phrases, link to related material or jump to an electronic dictionary for words that you may not understand.

To be effective, reading quickly must be matched by a good level of comprehension, whatever the source. Clearly, you need to incorporate tests of your understanding to check that you have understood the main points of the text. One method of reading that incorporates this is called the SQ3R Method – Survey, Question, Read, Recall and Review (see Table 8.3).

CHECKING THE RELIABILITY OF SOURCE MATERIAL

Essentially, the content of source material contains facts and ideas originating from someone's research or scholarship. These can be descriptions, concepts, interpretations or numerical data. At some point, information or ideas must be communicated or published, otherwise no one would know about them. Generally, the literature in any subject can be categorised as a 'primary' or 'secondary' source. Information and ideas usually appear first in the primary literature and may be modified later in the secondary literature (see Table 8.4). Understanding this process is important not only when analysing and evaluating information, but also when deciding on the evidence or references to cite (Ch 24). Logically, the closer you can get to the primary source, the more consistent the information is likely to be with the original.

Table 8.3 Reading for remembering: the SQ3R Method. The point of this method is that the reader has to engage in processing the material in the text and does not simply read on 'autopilot' where very little is being retained. In the context of reading for research purposes, this method helps to avoid the risk of plagiarising source material because readers are required to reconstitute the information using their own words.

Survey stage
• Read the first paragraph (topic paragraph) and last paragraph (terminator paragraph) of the relevant section of text • Read the intervening paragraph topic sentences • Focus on the headings and sub-headings, if present • Study the graphs and diagrams for key features
Question stage
• What do you know already about this topic? • What is the author likely to tell you? • What specifically do you need to find out?
Read stage
• Read the entire section quickly to get the gist of the piece of writing • Go back to the question stage and revisit your initial answers • Look especially for keywords, key statements and signpost words • Do not stop to look up unknown words – go for completion
Recall stage
• Turn the text over (or look away from the screen) and try to recall as much as possible • Make relevant notes • Turn the source over again or look back at the screen • Check over for accuracy of recall; suggested recall periods – every 20 minutes
Review stage
• After a break, try to recall the main points

✓ **Assessing sources of facts**

Some sources and facts can be considered very reliable. In the sciences, one interpretation of reliability is that the observation or experiment can be repeated by a competent peer – well-established 'textbook' knowledge usually falls into this category. In other areas, reliability may be bound up with the academic record and authority of the person making the assertion, or in the nature of the evidence that is cited to support a case.

Table 8.4 **Characteristics and examples of primary and secondary sources of information.**

Type of resource	Comments
Primary sources – those in which ideas and data are first communicated	• The primary literature in your subject may be published in the form of papers (articles) in journals. Such literature is usually refereed by experts in the authors' academic peer group. Referees check the accuracy and originality of the work and report their opinions back to the journal editors. This system helps to maintain reliability, but it is not perfect. • Books (and, more rarely, articles in magazines and newspapers) can also be primary sources but this depends on the nature of the information published rather than the medium. These sources are not formally refereed, although they may be read by editors and lawyers to check for errors and the legal implications of content. • Original materials that have been published to provide information to a wide and not necessarily expert audience. For example, Parliamentary White Papers, financial statements, public enquiry reports and epidemiological reports are all primary sources that differ from other categories in this list in that they provide the 'raw' information without interpretation by others. This kind of material allows you, as a researcher, to come to independent and perhaps original conclusions. Such documentation is particularly important in the arts and social sciences, where incisive interpretation can be an indicator of critical thinking (Ch 16), and hence the quality of the research.
Secondary sources – those that quote, adapt, interpret, translate, develop or otherwise use information drawn from primary sources	• It is the act of recycling that makes the source secondary, rather than the medium. Reviews are examples of secondary sources in the academic world, and textbooks and magazine articles are often of this type. • As people adopt, modify, translate and develop information and ideas, alterations are likely to occur – whether intentional or unintentional. Most authors of secondary sources do not deliberately set out to change the meaning of the primary source, but they may do so unwittingly. Others, consciously or unconsciously, may exert bias in their reporting by quoting evidence primarily on one side of a debate. • Modifications while creating a secondary source could involve adding valuable new ideas and content or correcting errors.

One important method of establishing reliability is to see whether the original source has been 'peer-reviewed' (see Table 8.4). This is where the material is reviewed by one or more academics ('referees') working in the same field, prior to being accepted for publication. This helps to ensure that:

- the material is original
- significant past work is cited
- conflicting theories and opinions are mentioned
- any data and calculations are checked
- interpretations of information and data are valid.

Such reviews cannot guarantee reliability, and it can be argued that they may act to entrench 'established' viewpoints: radical new ideas often encounter extreme resistance when they are first put forward. It is the journal editor's task to ensure that a balance between freedom of expression and satisfactory reasoning is maintained, while acknowledging that there can be healthy controversy concerning different viewpoints and approaches.

Other sources can be a lot less reliable. They may not cite evidence, or this may not be available for examination by others. In the worst cases, evidence may be fabricated or impossible to assess or test. What you read could be misquoted, misrepresented, erroneous or based on a faulty premise. The data presented may carry no indication of error levels. These risks are particularly important when looking at internet-based information, as this is less likely to be refereed or edited.

> **? How can I check whether a source is peer-reviewed?**
>
> For academic journals, the answer may lie in or close to the 'information for authors' section, which appears every three months or so in current volumes, or on specific web pages, and may provide valuable insights and background information about the submission, refereeing and editing process. Some journals also indicate who edited or refereed specific articles. In books, the acknowledgements section may indicate whether a peer has assisted by reading a draft.

An obvious way to assess reliability is to make cross-referencing checks. 'Triangulating' in this way involves looking at more than one source and comparing what is said in each. The sources should be as independent as possible (for example, do not compare an original source with a secondary one that is based directly on it). If you find the sources agree, you may become more certain of your position. If two sources differ, you may need to decide which is more reliable – and this may become a focus for your discussion.

The quality of academic work may be indicated by the extent and quality of citations provided by the author. This applies particularly to articles in academic journals, where positions are usually supported by citations of others' work. These citations may demonstrate that a certain amount of research has been carried out beforehand, and that the ideas or results are based on genuine scholarship. If you doubt the quality of the work, these references might be worth looking at. How up-to-date are they? Do they cite independent work, or is the author exclusively quoting him- or herself, or the work of one particular researcher? Is there reference to works published in other countries or languages?

This leads to another form of cross-referencing, which is to look at who else has cited the author's work, and how. You can use databases such as the Web of Science, available at **www.wokinfo.com**, to find out how often an article or author has been cited and by whom (**Ch 7**). You may then be able to consult these sources to see how others have viewed the original findings. Reviews of a subject area published after your source may also provide useful comments.

IDENTIFYING BIAS AND ERROR IN TEXT

In many subjects it is important to differentiate fact from opinion. To do this when reading material that is unfamiliar, you may need to answer the following questions:

- To what extent has the author supported a particular viewpoint?
- Has relevant supporting information been referred to, via literature citations or the author's own researches?
- Are numerical data used to substantiate the points given?
- Are these data reliable and can you verify the information – for example, by looking at a source that was cited?
- Might the author have a hidden reason for putting forward biased evidence to support a personal opinion?

At some point, you should concentrate on analysing the method being used to put the points over, rather than the facts themselves. This will help you detect fallacious arguments and logical flaws (**Ch 16**).

> ✓ **Analyse the language used in order to assess a source**
>
> Words and their use can be very revealing. Have subjective or objective sentence structures been employed? The former might indicate a personal opinion rather than an objective conclusion. Are there any tell-tale signs of misinformation? Bias might be indicated by absolute terms, such as 'All the evidence suggests...' or 'We can be sure that...', or by a seemingly unbalanced consideration of the evidence. How carefully has the author considered the topic? A less studious approach might be indicated by lack of citation, exaggeration, ambiguity, or the use of journalese and slang. Always remember, however, that the underlying content and ideas should be judged above the presentation.

In 'scientific' subjects, in particular, you will often need to interpret and check the reliability of data. This is essential for setting up and testing meaningful hypotheses and, therefore, is at the core of the scientific approach (**Ch 3**). If numerical information is used, do not rely on the author's interpretation or even their calculations. Do your own cross-checks to ensure the data are consistent – this will also give you a better understanding of the theory and methods being used. Look closely at any data and graphs that are presented and the way they have been analysed (**Chs 9 and 20**).

In 'non-scientific' subjects, ideas and concepts tend to be important, and you may need to carry out an objective analysis of information and arguments in order to construct your own position, backed up with evidence (**Chs 16 and17**).

ACTION POINTS

8.1 Try to gain a feel for the primary literature in your subject area. This may be shelved in the library building or you may be expected to access it online (or both). Read one or two articles to gain a flavour of the format, style of writing, language and sources used. Initially, expect to find some of the subject matter relatively impenetrable; as you progress, you will master most of the concepts and jargon used.

8.2 Use the questions in Table 8.1 to assess a source about which you are uncertain. If you are unable to establish its reliability, you should research further around the topic.

8.3 Practise analysing excerpts of text for their underlying structure. Can you identify the types of paragraphs and sentences being used? Can you identify how and where signpost words are being used to direct or redirect your thoughts as a reader? Understanding how these methods are used in practice is a valuable route to developing your own proficiency in writing in your specialist area.

9 INTERPRETING PUBLISHED DATA

How to understand graphs, tables and basic statistics

Research work often calls for detailed examination of published results. Data can be presented and interpreted in different ways. To glean their full meaning, you will need to understand how they are presented in graphs and tables and have an awareness of statistical methods.

KEY TOPICS

→ How to 'read' a graph
→ How graphs can mislead
→ Abstracting information from tables
→ Important descriptive statistics
→ Concepts of hypothesis-testing statistics

There are many ways of presenting data sets, and the methods chosen can affect your analysis or favour certain interpretations. A healthily critical approach is therefore essential when you are examining graphs, tables and statistics. Equally, when creating these items to condense and display your own information, your primary aim should always be to do this in a manner that is simple to understand and is unbiased (**Ch 20**). It is beyond the scope of this book to discuss all the possible modes of presentation and analysis. Instead, this chapter provides a quick refresher on data interpretation based on basic principles.

Graph types

Some common forms are illustrated throughout this chapter, but a quick way of finding out about different types is to explore the forms available in a spreadsheet program, such as Microsoft Excel. Look at the 'Insert>Chart>Standard Types' menu, which illustrates many sub-types and provides brief descriptions. This is also a good way of exploring ways of presenting your own data (**Ch 20**). Note that 'Chart' may be the term used in Excel and other programs to refer to graphs.

HOW TO 'READ' A GRAPH

A graph is a pictorial representation showing the relationship between sets of numerical data. In academic text, graphs may be referred to as 'figures'. The following elements are present in most graphs. Use them to work out what a specific graph means, referring to the example shown in Figure 9.1.

- The figure title and its caption. These should appear below the graph. Read these first to determine the overall context and gain information about what the graph shows. If the caption is detailed, you may

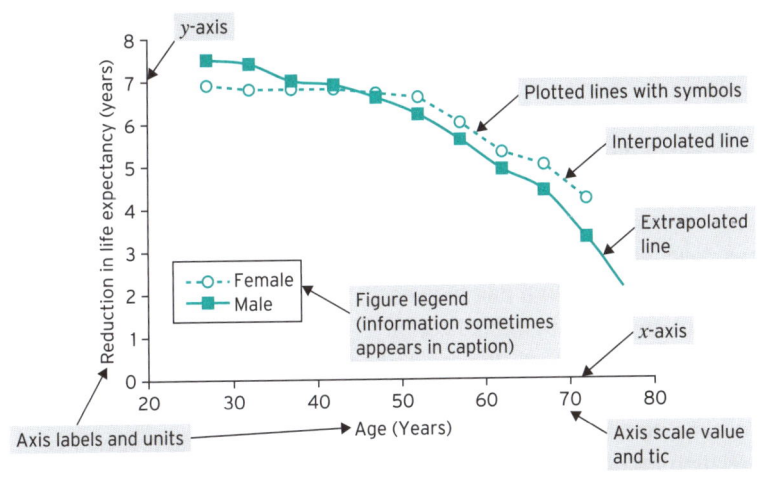

Figure 89 **A standard plotted curve.** This figure type uses *x-y* axes and points and lines to illustrate the relationship between two variables. *Source*: Data modified from Rogers, R.G. and Powell-Griner E., 1991. Life expectancies of cigarette smokers and non-smokers in the United States. *Soc. Sci. Med.*, 32, 1151-9.

Figure 9.1 **The basic components of a graph.**

need to revisit it later to aid your interpretation.

- The type of figure. With experience, you will come to recognise the basic chart types (Figure 9.2) and others common in your discipline. This will help you to interpret the data displayed. For example, a pie chart is usually used to show proportions of a total amount.

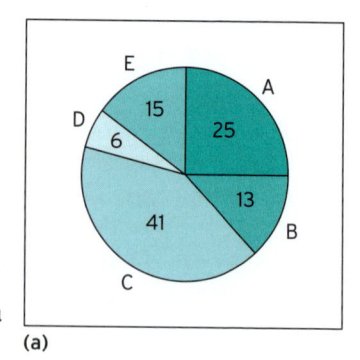

> **Checklist for interpreting a graph**
>
> ❏ Consider the context by reading the title, legend and main text
> ❏ Recognise the type of graph
> ❏ Examine what the axes show
> ❏ Inspect the scale of the axes
> ❏ Study the symbols and plotted curves
> ❏ Evaluate what any error bars or statistics mean.

- The axes. Many forms of graph represent the relationship between two variables, called *x* and *y* for convenience (conventionally presented as italic letters). These are often presented between a pair of axes at right angles, with the horizontal *x*-axis often relating to the 'controlled' variable (for example, concentration or time) and the vertical *y*-axis often relating to the 'measured' variable (for example, income, weight (mass), or response). More than one measured variable may be plotted on the same graph, either using the same *x*-axis or a second one (Figure 9.3(b)). Some

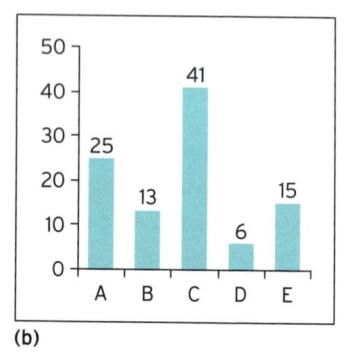

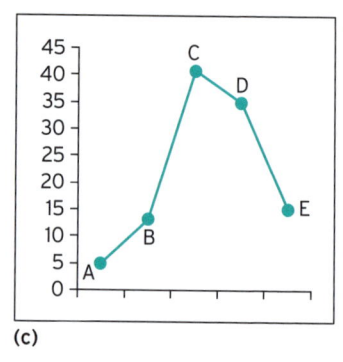

Figure 9.2 **Common forms of graph.** These are in addition to the standard plotted curve shown in Figure 9.1. (a) Pie chart, showing proportions of a total – here expressed as percentages. (b) Histogram, showing amounts in different categories. (c) Frequency polygon, showing distribution of counted data across a continuous range.

84 Researching the literature

types of graph don't follow this pattern, and if you are unfamiliar with the form being used you may need to investigate further.

> **Plural terms**
>
> The following plurals are often misused or misunderstood:
>
> **Axis** = singular; **Axes** = plural
>
> **Datum** = singular; **Data** = plural (hence, the correct way to refer to data is 'the data are presented in Figure 14', rather than 'the data is presented in Figure 14').

- The axis scale and units. An axis label should state what the axis means and the units being used. Each axis should show clearly the range of values it covers through a series of cross-marks (tic, or tick, marks), with associated numbers to indicate the scale. To interpret these, you'll also need to know the units. Some axes do not start from zero, or incorporate a break in the scale; others may be non-linear (for example, a logarithmic axis is sometimes used to cover particularly wide ranges of numbers). Pay attention in these cases, because this could mean that the graph exaggerates or emphasises differences between values (see Figure 9.3(a) and (b)).

- The symbols and plotted curves. These help you to identify the different data sets being shown and the relationship between the points in each set. A detailed legend or key may be included to make this clearer. Symbols may also include information about variability in the data collected (for example, error bars), which provides useful clues about the reliability of data and assumed trends. Your interpretation is likely to focus on differences in the relationships and, inevitably, on the plotted curves (also known as 'trend lines'). In so doing, you should remember that curves are usually hypothetical interpolations between measured values, and in some cases may be extrapolations beyond them.

> **Definitions: trend lines**
>
> **Interpolation** – an assumed trend or relationship between available data points.
>
> **Extrapolation** – an assumed trend or relationship before or after (below or above) available data points. Extrapolation is risky because the assumption may be made that a trend will continue when there may be little evidence that this will happen.

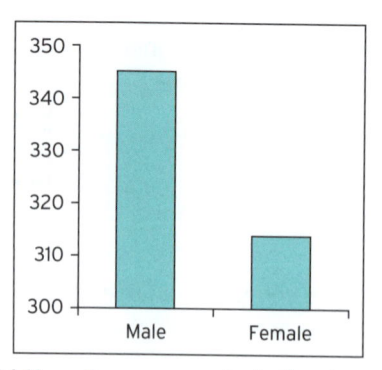

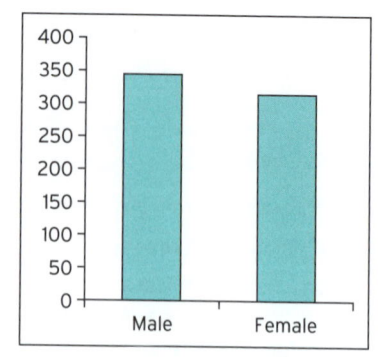

(a) Use of non-zero axis. In the chart on the left, it looks as if the differences between males and females are large; however, when the y-axis is zeroed, as on the right, the differences are much less noticeable.

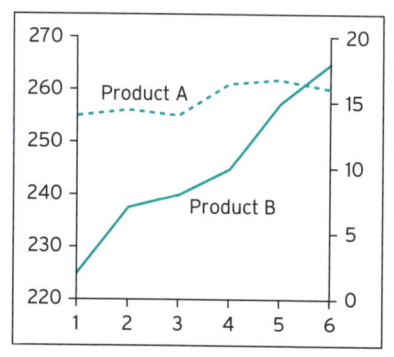

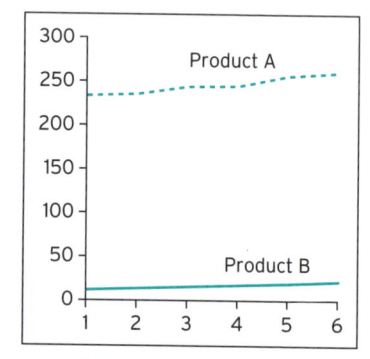

(b) Use of different y-axes for different curves. In the chart on the left it looks as if sales of product A (left-hand axis) are being caught up by those of product B (right-hand axis); however, when the same axis is used for both curves, then it can be seen that product A vastly outsells product B.

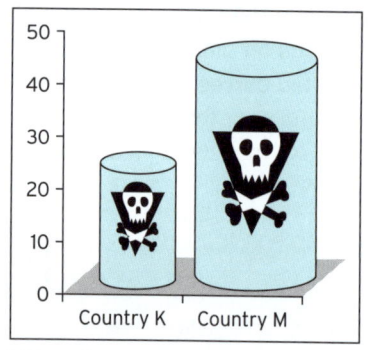

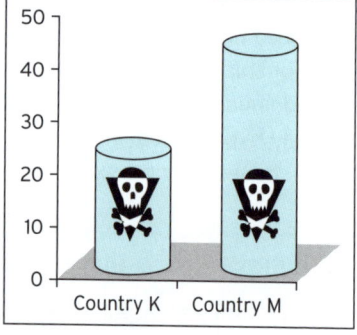

(c) Use of a two- or three-dimensional object to represent a linear scale. In the chart on the left, the barrel retains its shape in relation to the y-axis scale, so it makes it look as if country M produces much more toxic waste than country K. On the right, a truly linear representation is shown.

Figure 9.3 Three common examples of misleading graphs.

HOW GRAPHS CAN MISLEAD

You can learn a lot about data interpretation by reviewing misleading graphs and understanding why they give an erroneous impression of results. A selection of examples is shown in Figure 9.3. Particular things to take into account include:

- use of a non-zero axis, which can act to over-emphasise differences between observations or treatments (Figure 9.3(a))
- use of different axes for different observations or treatments, which may exaggerate differences (Figure 9.3(b))
- use of three-dimensional representations, which can give the wrong impression if not constructed carefully (Figure 9.3(c))
- lack of error bars on data (Table 9.1), which may indicate that the differences between points or plotted curves are real, whereas they may be within the scope of natural variability
- interpolation or extrapolation of fitted curves, which may involve unwarranted assumptions about trends in the data.

ABSTRACTING INFORMATION FROM TABLES

Tables are used to summarise numerical data, and particularly where precise values are of interest. They can also be used to present qualitative data – perhaps most often where comparisons are valuable. Tables are laid out in 2-D grid form, with sets of horizontal rows and vertical columns. Complex tables can be difficult to interpret, especially where they consist of many rows and columns of numerical data. However, the following elements are present in most tables; use the descriptions to work out what the data in a specific table means, referring to the example shown in Figure 9.4.

- The title and caption. These provide a guide to the content, just like a figure or graph caption. Read these first to orientate yourself, before looking at the detail of the table. You may need to refer back to the caption from time to time, as it may contain information vital for interpretation of the values that are presented.
- Columns and their headings. Each vertical column normally displays a particular type of data, and the descriptive headings reflect these contents, giving the units where data are quantitative.

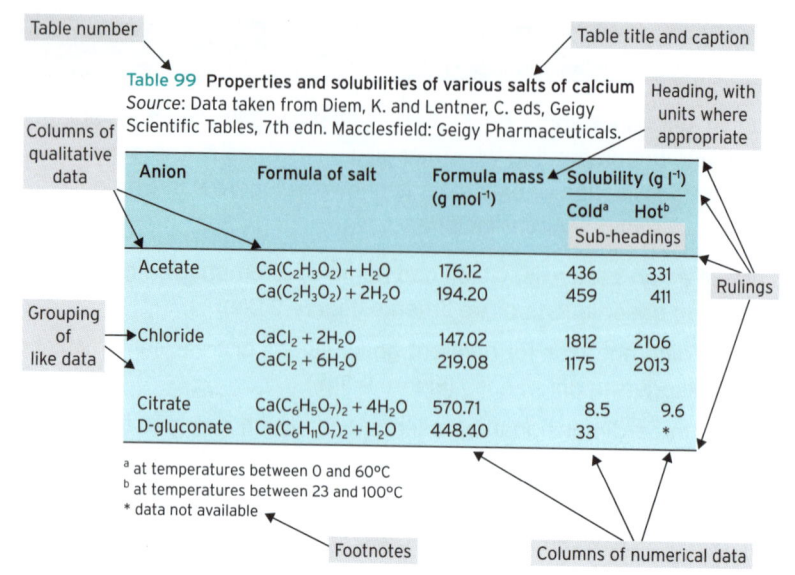

Table 99 Properties and solubilities of various salts of calcium
Source: Data taken from Diem, K. and Lentner, C. eds, Geigy Scientific Tables, 7th edn. Macclesfield: Geigy Pharmaceuticals.

Anion	Formula of salt	Formula mass (g mol^{-1})	Solubility (g l^{-1}) Cold[a]	Hot[b]
Acetate	Ca(C$_2$H$_3$O$_2$) + H$_2$O Ca(C$_2$H$_3$O$_2$) + 2H$_2$O	176.12 194.20	436 459	331 411
Chloride	CaCl$_2$ + 2H$_2$O CaCl$_2$ + 6H$_2$O	147.02 219.08	1812 1175	2106 2013
Citrate D-gluconate	Ca(C$_6$H$_5$O$_7$)$_2$ + 4H$_2$O Ca(C$_6$H$_{11}$O$_7$)$_2$ + H$_2$O	570.71 448.40	8.5 33	9.6 *

[a] at temperatures between 0 and 60°C
[b] at temperatures between 23 and 100°C
* data not available

Figure 9.4 The basic components of a table. Note that shading is included here to emphasise the heading and data sections, and would not usually be present.

- Rows and their headings. Each horizontal row might show different instances of the types of data given in the columns, including sometimes the units used; therefore, when making comparisons, you will probably be looking across a given row.
- Data values. These should be presented to an appropriate number of significant figures. Look carefully for an indication of errors, which may be given in parentheses after data values. The column's heading or caption should make it clear what statistic is being quoted.
- Footnotes. These are used to explain abbreviations or give details of specific cases. You will normally be pointed towards these via superscript letters or numbers. Read them carefully, because they may detail exceptions or other points that might affect your interpretation.

IMPORTANT DESCRIPTIVE STATISTICS

If you are looking at numerical (quantitative) data, there are a number of questions that need to be addressed.

- How have the data been arrived at? For example, are they averages of several observations, or just based on a single observation?
- Have the errors of any data been taken into consideration and, where appropriate, quantified? If so, does this help you arrive at a conclusion about how genuine the differences are between important values?
- Have the appropriate statistical methods been used to analyse the data? Are the underlying hypotheses the right ones? Have the results of any tests been interpreted correctly in arriving at the conclusion?

Definitions: data

Quantitative data – data that can be expressed in numbers, such as length, height or price.

Qualitative data – data that are descriptive and non-numerical, such as colour, place of manufacture, or name.

Descriptive statistics are used to simplify a complex data set, to summarise the distribution of data within the data set and to provide estimates of values of the population frequency distribution. Two aspects that are often quoted are:

- a measure of location – this is an estimate of the 'centre' of the frequency distribution;
- a measure of dispersion – this is an estimate of the spread of data within the frequency distribution.

Basic measures of location and dispersion are outlined in Table 9.1. More complex descriptive statistics such as standard error (describing the precision of a mean), or quantifying the shape of frequency distributions, are outside the scope of this book and a specialist text should be consulted.

The following are reasons why the values and hence the descriptive statistics of samples of data from a given population may vary:

- sampling error, due to the selection of a small number of individuals from a larger, variable population
- measurement error, due to the method of measurement of the variable
- rounding error, due to an attempt to use an appropriate number of significant figures, but often compounded in calculations

Table 9.1 Descriptive statistics and their uses

Measure	Statistic	How to calculate*	Uses, advantages and disadvantages
Location	Mean	The sum of all the data values divided by the number of values, n.	The most commonly used measure. It takes account of all the values in the data set, but can be influenced by the presence of outliers and is not representative of the whole body of data if this is asymmetric. Units are the same as the data.
Location	Median	The mid-point of the data values when they are ranked in numerical order. For odd-sized data sets, it is the value of the middle datum, while for even-sized data sets, it is the mean of the two central values.	May represent the location of the majority of the data better than the mean if the data set is asymmetric or there are outliers. Units are the same as the data.
Location	Mode	The most common value in the data set.	Easily found and unaffected by outliers; however, especially when the data set is small, it may be susceptible to 'random' variation in the distribution of values. Units are the same as the data.
Dispersion	Range	The difference between the largest and the smallest values in the data set.	Easy to determine, but its value is greatly affected by outliers and the size of the data set. Units are the same as the data.
Dispersion	Semi-interquartile range	The difference between the first and third quartiles, which are the median values for the data ranked below and above the median value of the whole data set.	Less easy to calculate than the range, but less affected by outliers and the size of the data set. Suitable to match with the median as a measure of location. Units are the same as the data.
Dispersion	Variance	The sum of the squares of the difference between each data value and the mean, divided by $n - 1$.	Measures the average difference from the mean for all the data values. Good for data sets that are symmetrical about the mean. Units are the square of those of the data.
Dispersion	Standard deviation	The positive square root of the variance.	A measure of the average difference from the mean for all the data values. Good for data sets symmetrical about the mean. Units are the same as the data, so preferable to the variance.
Dispersion	Coefficient of variation	The standard deviation multiplied by 100 and divided by the mean.	A dimensionless (%) measure of variability relative to location. Allows the relative dispersion of data sets to be compared.

- human error, due to inaccurate writing or copying of data, mixing up of samples and so on
- error from unknown sources, or unappreciated effects of sampling.

CONCEPTS OF HYPOTHESIS-TESTING STATISTICS

Hypothesis testing in a statistical context is used to compare the properties of a data set with other samples, or to compare the data set with some theory about it. Error and variability exist in all data sets, which means that it is impossible to be 100 per cent certain about differences between sets. Are the differences 'genuine' and due to a true dissimilarity between the samples, perhaps because of a treatment you have administered to one of them, or are the differences you observe just the result of random errors? Hypothesis testing works by trying to put a probability on these alternatives.

Definitions: population, sample and frequency distribution

These terms have special meanings in quantitative research and statistics.

Population – the whole group of items that might be part of a study: for example, all men in the UK; all individuals of a species of bivalve mollusc on a particular beach; all Birmingham householders who use gas as a heating fuel.

Sample – a sub-set of individuals from a specific population: for example, the 28 men whose blood sugar level was measured and compared with that of 34 who had taken drug X for five weeks beforehand; the 50 bivalves collected from beach A, measured and compared with a similar sample from beach B; the 45 householders selected for telephone interview about their satisfaction with the service provided by their energy supplier.

Frequency distribution – a description of the occurrence of values of a variable. You may be interested in the actual distribution in the sample you have taken over its range of values, and you might use a frequency polygon (Figure 9.2(c)) to represent this. You might also be interested in the underlying population frequency distribution. This is often theoretical in nature, and a smooth curve representing a model function might be used to represent it. **Chapter 12** provides definitions of sample and population.

The norm is to set up a 'Null Hypothesis' (NH) that says that the samples are the same or that they conform to some theoretical description. By making certain assumptions about the data, calculating a hypothesis-testing statistic and looking up tables of probability (or calculating), you can find the probability (P) of the NH being true. The lower P, the less likely you are to accept it in favour of the hypothesis that the differences were 'real' and due to your treatment or a genuine difference between the samples. Conventionally, if $P<0.05$ (i.e. 5%), then the NH is rejected.

Hypothesis-testing statistics differ in their assumptions about the data and what they set out to test. Some common ones and their uses are:

- Student's t-test – for comparing two means
- Chi-squared (χ^2) test – for comparing observed against expected values
- Analysis of variance (ANOVA) – for comparing several means.

Chapter 19 includes information about how to conduct these tests using Excel spreadsheets. Precise details can be found in specialist texts.

> **? What are parametric and non-parametric statistical tests?**
>
> The former make the assumption that the data are distributed according to a particular mathematical function, often the so-called 'Normal' function; the latter make no assumptions of this kind, but are less powerful in distinguishing between samples that differ marginally.

Statistical analysis, properly used, can be used to support an argument, opinion or conclusion. However, don't be blinded by statistics. Leaving aside the issue that statistical methods don't actually deal with proof, only probability (**Ch 19**), it is generally possible to analyse and present data in such a way that they support one chosen argument or hypothesis rather than another (as in the adage 'you can prove anything with statistics'). You should look critically at the assumptions of a test, whether it is appropriate for the data that are being analysed and whether the conclusions have been expressed correctly. For example, has the chance of the Null Hypothesis being correct or incorrect been fully taken into account?

ACTION POINTS

9.1 Explore the chart options within Microsoft Excel. Finding your way around this program or a similar spreadsheet tool will be time well-spent. You should try to find out which data presentation options might be applicable to your research and how to modify relevant aspects of chart presentation.

9.2 Find out how tables are normally presented in your discipline. This may vary, for example in the use of cell borders and lines, so an understanding of the style usually adopted will help you to interpret the content more easily. Moreover, you will probably be expected to adopt the style evident in text and journal articles in your own work. However, note that these aspects are not always consistent even with the discipline. It is best to be guided by your supervisor if this is the case.

9.3 Research further on relevant statistics for your discipline. Where a particular descriptive statistic or hypothesis-testing method is frequently used, it will repay you to have full understanding of its mathematical basis and the assumptions that may underpin its use.

10 NOTE-MAKING FROM RESEARCH SOURCES

How to record information for use in your investigation

Keeping a record of what you read in the literature or hear in spoken presentations is an essential preliminary to the use of that information for your project. There are many options for keeping a condensed record of what you read and hear so that this remains meaningful to you when thinking about and writing your own material.

KEY TOPICS

→ Why notes are important as an input to your thinking and writing
→ Note-taking and note-making with purpose
→ How should you lay out your notes?

Early in your academic career, you will have developed note-taking strategies for recording information from lectures. However, there is a

Note-taking in lectures and seminars versus note-making from written sources

In a lecture (or seminar, tutorial or lab) you are in listening mode, you are *taking* notes spontaneously, based on the interpretation offered by the speaker and organised in ways that fit their logic and sequenced within the time constraints of the listening episode. You will be taking these notes under a certain amount of time pressure. By contrast, in a reading mode you are the person in control – hence, you are *making* notes reflectively, based on your interpretation of the text and framed in a format that suits your logic, your purpose in recording information and within your own time constraints.

range of methods you can adopt to record key points of content from the literature and spoken presentations, such as seminars, tutorials, labs and meetings. You may wish to modify the methods you use in order to meet the needs of researching, as both the purpose and context are different.

WHY NOTES ARE IMPORTANT AS AN INPUT TO YOUR THINKING AND WRITING

When examining potential sources of information for your project (Ch 8), you will receive information through a variety of media. Note-making is a form of writing that ensures that your reading has a purpose. The act of writing is part of the thinking process, so creating a condensed version of what you have read, or what you think about what you have read, can help you to clarify and record your thoughts.

A key task is to gather and organise this information in ways that are meaningful, logical and retrievable. If your notes are rough and disorganised, then you will be unlikely to comprehend their full meaning or achieve good writing when later referring to them.

Good notes can only be achieved if you are clear as to why you are creating them. In a research context, possible reasons include:

- constructing a framework or overview for the subject via general textbook resources
- examining specialist texts for detail, e.g. sequences or processes, analysis of issues, controversies or problems
- extracting the logic of an argument, perhaps comparing and contrasting different perspectives or authorities
- allowing you to isolate relevant quotes for later use
- facilitating addition of your own commentary on the topic, perhaps by linking key points with notes or points from other sources.

The reason(s) for creating notes will influence the style, detail and depth adopted. However, it is always important to make sure that your notes, if in handwritten form, are legible and memorable.

Several aspects of note-making will pay dividends when it comes to drafting your own writing. Good notes should:

- contain accurate information about source material
- save time in relocating source material

- allow comparison and contrast between literature sources
- aid understanding of complex issues
- include your own additional thoughts and ideas in response to the information you have heard or researched.

Try to develop a personal style – but adopting the following guidance to ensure that your note-making will provide you with a summary that will be meaningful in six days, six weeks or six months.

1 Attend to general record-keeping:
   - include the date each note was taken/made and how/where the resource was accessed
   - number each page of your notes
   - file your notes carefully and in a logical (easily retrievable) sequence.

2 Record full details about the source, including:
   - author details
   - title of paper or chapter
   - name of journal/book
   - date of publication
   - publisher and place of publication.

   You will need these details to enable you to cite the source of information (**Ch 24**).

3 Develop your own note-making 'codes'. For example:
   - underline or highlight key points you wish to emphasise
   - add asterisks (*) for points or new words to look up later
   - use block capitals for sub-headings or keywords to break up the text
   - use or create special abbreviations relevant to your subject
   - use a symbol (such as #) that indicates that a note is your own response to a point
   - add colour coding for themes
   - use bulleted and numbered lists for aspects or sequences
   - use 'call out' boxes to highlight important points.

4 Consider whether writing on one side of the paper leaves scope for later additions or annotations about content on the facing page.

Alternatively, if you decide to write on both sides of the paper, then don't cram too much information onto each sheet so that there is still enough white space around lists or other important items of information for adding further detail and thoughts later

5 Add diagrams, sketches and doodles – by using the 'visual' part of your brain, you will aid creativity and recall.

NOTE-TAKING AND NOTE-MAKING WITH PURPOSE

From written sources

The techniques described in **Chapter 8** will help you to identify the most relevant parts of the text quickly and then select the basic source material for your notes. Avoid making purposeless notes that are merely a rewrite or rehash of the original text. This is time-consuming and pointless. By consciously deciding on the reason for the note-making and adopting a style that is suited to that situation, you will be more likely to be reading with purpose (Table 8.3). You will also save time in the long run by producing a resource that will contribute usefully to your thinking and writing. This process involves:

1 identifying your purpose in relation to your research project aims and anticipating the most appropriate layout or approach in this instance

2 scanning the section to be read to establish the writer's purpose – for example, a narrative of events or a process, a statement of fact, or an explanation of reasoning or presentation of a logical argument

3 working out the author's view on the subject, and how this relates to your purpose

4 ensuring you paraphrase using your own words rather than transcribe; if you do transcribe, use quotation marks ('...') and note reference details including page number (**Ch 24**)

5 following stages 1–3 of the SQ3R method (Table 8.3) to allow you to:
   – judge whether the printed sources you have obtained will require intensive reading
   – obtain a clear idea of what is covered in the content before making notes in an appropriate style.

> **❓ When is it better to annotate a photocopy rather than take notes?**
>
> Sometimes you may find that the extent of notes you require is minimal, or that a particular book or other resource is in high demand and has been placed on short-loan in the library. It may be more convenient to photocopy the relevant pages, which can then be highlighted and annotated. However, remember that there are strict photocopying restrictions imposed on readers due to copyright law (**Ch 11**) – details will be displayed prominently in your library.

From spoken presentations

During conferences, seminars, lectures, tutorials or meetings your note-taking needs to be quick and you may need to compromise neatness and structure for content. In these situations:

- identify and list the aims (declared purpose) of the event, and try to identify and note the detail of these aspects as they come up in the presentation
- be selective in what you write down – trying to write every word (*verbatim* notes) is impossible – you'll miss out on understanding ideas, explanations and examples
- listen for sense – people often do not speak in full sentences and so repetition and pauses have to be taken into account when filtering out what you note
- listen for and note the key ideas
- listen for transition cues – these might be signpost expressions, such as 'firstly, secondly…', 'however', 'to summarise'; these will possibly signify a new element or direction for your notes
- identify any references to written sources – these may be given only as the author surname and the year of the publication; highlight relevant references for follow-up action on your part.

Creating electronic notes during spoken presentations

Logic suggests that using modern technological aids such as electronic notebooks, tablets and similar devices makes sense – especially for those whose handwriting is slow or illegible. Should you opt to take notes in this way, and your typing skills allow, then you will need to evolve strategies that will allow you to type up what you want to record in real time. One problem with this approach is that the relative rigidity of the screen limits layout possibilities. To optimise your ability to record key points using a keyword approach, a useful strategy might be to create a template ahead of time – like the one shown below (Figure 10.1). This will enable you to use the tab key to shift quickly from keyword to note content without having to format text.

Keep all your notes ✔

Never discard notes, even if your project topic changes or you feel the source is out of date or irrelevant. What you discounted in early planning and drafting of your writing may transpire to be relevant later in the writing process, and if you have thrown away your notes then you will waste precious time trying to relocate, reread and reinterpret the source material.

HOW SHOULD YOU LAY OUT YOUR NOTES?

The method you use to create notes should reflect the time that you can allocate to the task and what is best suited to the material and the subject area you are considering. In an ideal world, it should also reflect your learning style (consult **www.vark-learn.com** if in doubt on this). There are several strategies that you might consider using. Table 10.1 provides an analysis of the relative advantages and disadvantages of seven of these approaches, while representative examples of each type are given in Figures 10.2–10.8 which follow.

Title:		Presenter:	Date:
Keyword	Notes relating to keyword		

Figure 10.1 **Format of generic table for note-taking using a keywords approach.**

Table 10.1 **A comparison of the different methods of note creation.** The different types are illustrated in Figures 10.2–10.8.

Note type	Example	Advantage	Disadvantage
Keyword notes	Figure 10.2	Good as a layout for easy access to information; clearly demarcated aspects	Dependent on systematic structure in lecture/text
Linear notes	Figure 10.3	Good for classifying ideas and for analysis, especially from texts	Restrictive format; difficult to back-track to insert new information in lectures
Timeline notes	Figure 10.4	Sequences events or stages in a process; assists in narrative writing	Limited information possible; less useful for analytical writing
Flow chart notes	Figure 10.5	Allows clear path through complex options; favours sequential narrative in writing	Takes up space; may be unwieldy without special software; unsuited to electronic note-making
Concept maps/ Mind maps/ Explosion charts	Figure 10.6	Good for recording information on a single page; allows overview and aids analysis for planning writing	Can become messy; can be difficult to follow; not suited to all learning styles; needs to be synthesised for planning writing
Matrix notes/ Grid notes	Figure 10.7	Good layout for recording different viewpoints, approaches, applications, obtaining an overview; good for producing analysis and evaluation in writing	Space limitations on content or amount of information
Herring-bone maps	Figure 10.8	Good for laying opposing sides of an argument; good for visual learners when planning writing	Space limitations on content or amount of information

Topic: DEPOPULATION OF THE COUNTRYSIDE	Source: Ormiston, J., 2002. Rural Idylls. Glasgow: Country Press.
Problem:	Population falling in rural areas Traditional communities disintegrate Incomer settlement – dormitory villages
Reasons:	Mechanisation of farming Creation of farming combines Bigger farms, fewer employed Decline of traditional farming & related activities
Effects:	Families dispersed – fewer children Closure of shops, post offices, schools, surgeries Transport links less viable
Solutions:	Housing subsidies to encourage families to remain Diversify economic activity, e.g. tourism/action holidays Stimulate rural economy – farm shops, farmers' markets Diversify from traditional crops – seek new markets

Figure 10.2 **Example of keyword notes.** This style allows for easy identification and thus analysis of the key aspects of an issue.

Topic: OBESITY IN CHILDREN   Source: Skinner, J., 2001. Diet and Obesity. Edinburgh: Castle Publishing.

1. Lifestyle
    1.1 Television, computer-games generation
    1.2 Unsupervised leisure time – sedentary
2. Diet
    2.1 Constant 'grazing' – junk food
    2.2 Additives/processed foods
    2.3 Lack of adequate fresh food, including fruit + vegetables
3. Exercise
    3.1 Sport by spectating rather than participating
    3.2 Decline in team sports in schools
    3.3 Children over-protected from 'free play' outdoors
4. Family
    4.1 Parents overeat; children likewise
    4.2 Instant food
    4.3 Food as incentive + reward
5. Schools
    5.1 School meals spurned in favour of snack bar/chip shop
    5.2 Healthy-eating programmes as part of curriculum
6. Health service
    6.1 Less emphasis on prevention
    6.2 Limited health education of parents and children

(a)   *Continued overleaf*

Figure 10.3 **Examples of linear notes.** These are samples drawn from three diverse disciplines (a, b and c), where topics lend themselves to hierarchical approaches.

Topic:
GENERAL FEATURES OF ORGANIC MATERIALS

Source: Barker, J., 2001. Chemistry for University. Manchester: Midland Publishing

1. Solid state – molec. crystal – powder, poly. Thin films
2. Unique physical properties – exploit for high-tech applications
3. Advantages
   3.1 Versatile properties – reg. by organic chemistry
   3.2 Readily accessible – via organic synthesis
   3.3 Low cost – cheap raw materials
   3.4 Tractable – fusable, soluble: easy to fab.
4. Disadvantage
   4.1 Relatively fragile
5. Important types
   5.1 Conducting CT salts
   5.2 Conducting poly

(b)

Topic: **OPERATIONAL AMPLIFIERS**

Source: Scott, D.I., 1977. Operational Amplifiers. Coventry: Circuit Publishers.

1. Usually an integrated circuit; can be discrete
2. Uses all technologies: bipolar; FET; MOS; BI-FET
3. Effectively a highly stable differential amplifier
4. Advantages
   4.1 High voltage gain – typ. 100,000
   4.2 High input impedance – typ. 1MΩ – can be much higher, FET, MOS
   4.3 Low output impedance – typ. 600Ω
   4.4 Low drift, BI-FET best
   4.5 Wide supply voltage range
5. Disadvantages
   5.1 Relatively narrow bandwidth – GBP typ. 1MHz (but operates to DC)
   5.2 Very unstable in discrete versions – requires matched transistors
6. Common types
   6.1 741 – most common
   6.2 LM 380 – common AF AMP
   6.3 TDA 2030 – common power amp. – 20W into 4Ω

(c)

Figure 10.3 Continued

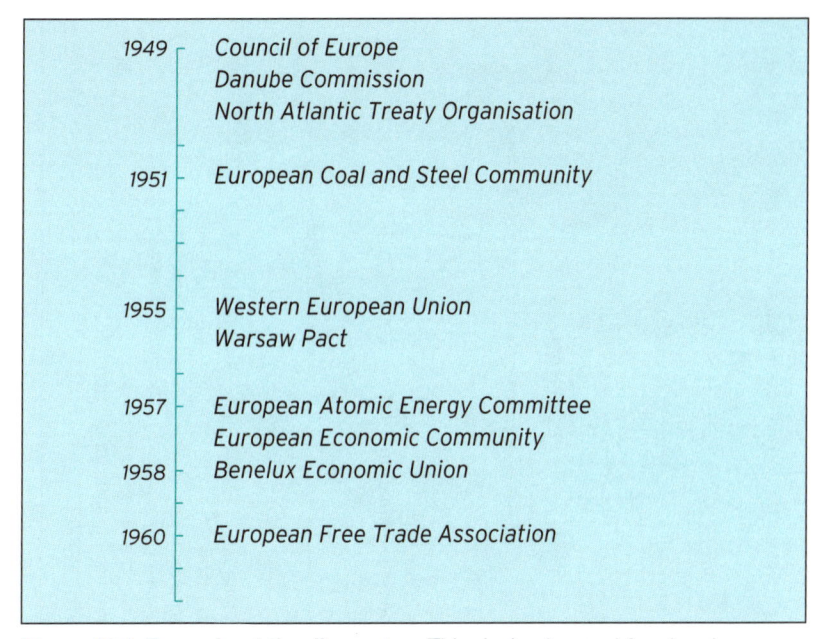

```
1949 ─ Council of Europe
       Danube Commission
       North Atlantic Treaty Organisation

1951 ─ European Coal and Steel Community




1955 ─ Western European Union
       Warsaw Pact

1957 ─ European Atomic Energy Committee
       European Economic Community
1958 ─ Benelux Economic Union

1960 ─ European Free Trade Association
```

Figure 10.4 Example of timeline notes. This design is good for showing a sequence of events – in this case, the development of European organisations.

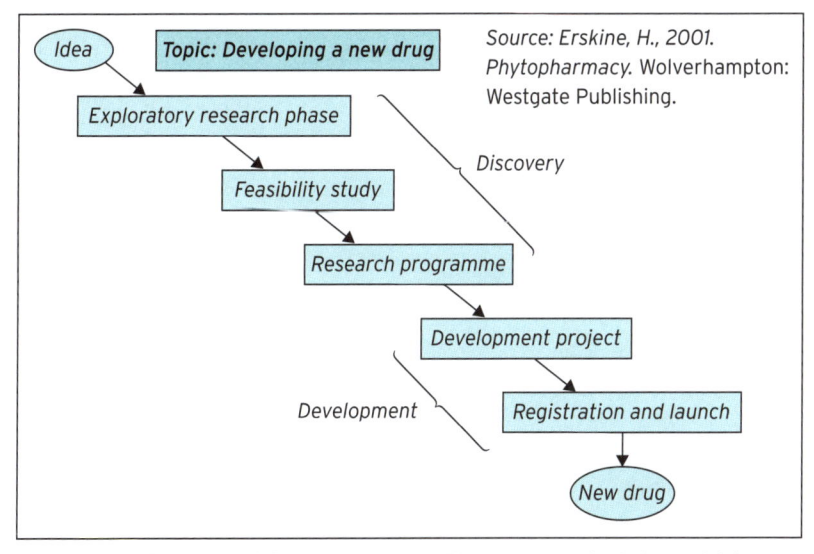

```
(Idea) → Topic: Developing a new drug      Source: Erskine, H., 2001.
           ↓                                Phytopharmacy. Wolverhampton:
        Exploratory research phase          Westgate Publishing.
           ↓                    ╲
        Feasibility study        Discovery
           ↓                    ╱
        Research programme
           ↓            ╲
        Development project
           ↓            ╲ Development
        Registration and launch
           ↓
        (New drug)
```

Figure 10.5 Example of flow chart notes. These are particularly useful for describing complex processes in visual form.

10 Note-making from research sources 103

Topic: INTERNET/DISSEMINATION OF INFORMATION

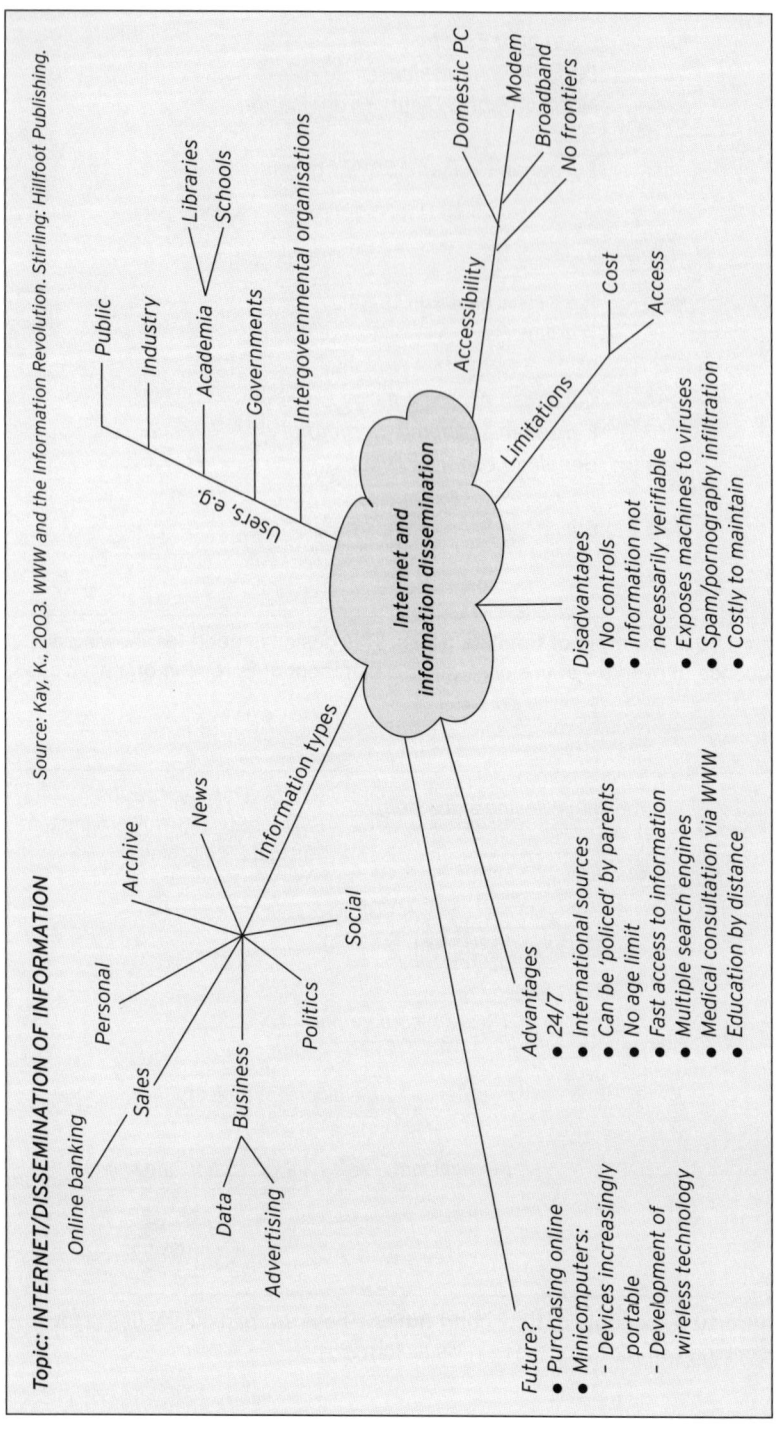

Source: Kay, K., 2003. WWW and the Information Revolution. Stirling: Hillfoot Publishing.

Internet and information dissemination

Users, e.g.
- Public
- Industry
- Academia
  - Libraries
  - Schools
- Governments
- Intergovernmental organisations

Accessibility
- Domestic PC
- Modem
- Broadband
- No frontiers

Limitations
- Cost
- Access

Disadvantages
- No controls
- Information not necessarily verifiable
- Exposes machines to viruses
- Spam/pornography infiltration
- Costly to maintain

Advantages
- 24/7
- International sources
- Can be 'policed' by parents
- No age limit
- Fast access to information
- Multiple search engines
- Medical consultation via WWW
- Education by distance

Future?
- Purchasing online
- Minicomputers:
  - Devices increasingly portable
  - Development of wireless technology

Information types
- Social
- Politics
- Business
  - Advertising
  - Data
- Sales
  - Online banking
- Personal
- Archive
- News

Figure 10.6 **Example of a concept map.** This may also be called a mind map and suits visual–spatial/visual learners.

104 Researching the literature

Topic: TRAFFIC CONGESTION

Source: Walker, I.M.A., 2005. Urban Myths and Motorists. London: Green Press.

Solutions	Council view	Police view	Local business view	Local community view
Pedestrianisation	+ Low maintenance − Initial outlay	+ Easier to police + Less car crime + CCTV surveillance easier	+ Safer shopping and business activity − Discourages motorist customers	+ Safer shopping + Less polluted town/city environment
Park and ride schemes	+ Implements transport policy − Capital investment to initiate − Car park maintenance	+ Reduce inner-city/town traffic jams + Reduce motor accidents − Potential car park crime	− Loss of custom − Lack of convenience − Sends customers elsewhere	+ Less polluted town/city environment − Costly
Increase parking charges	+ Revenue from fines − Costly to set up	− Hostility to enforcers	− Loss of custom − Delivery unloading problematic	− Residents penalised by paying for on-street parking
Restrict car journeys, e.g. odd/even registrations on alternate days	+ Easy to administer	+ Easy to police	− Seek exemption for business vehicles	+ Encourage car-sharing for daily journeys − Inconvenience
Levy congestion charge for urban journeys	+ Revenue raised − Cost of implementing tracking system	− Traffic jams on alternative routes	− Cost of loss of custom	− Inhibit work/leisure activities − Cost

Figure 10.7 **Example of matrix notes.** This particular analysis lays out positive (+) and negative (−) viewpoints on an issue from a range of different perspectives.

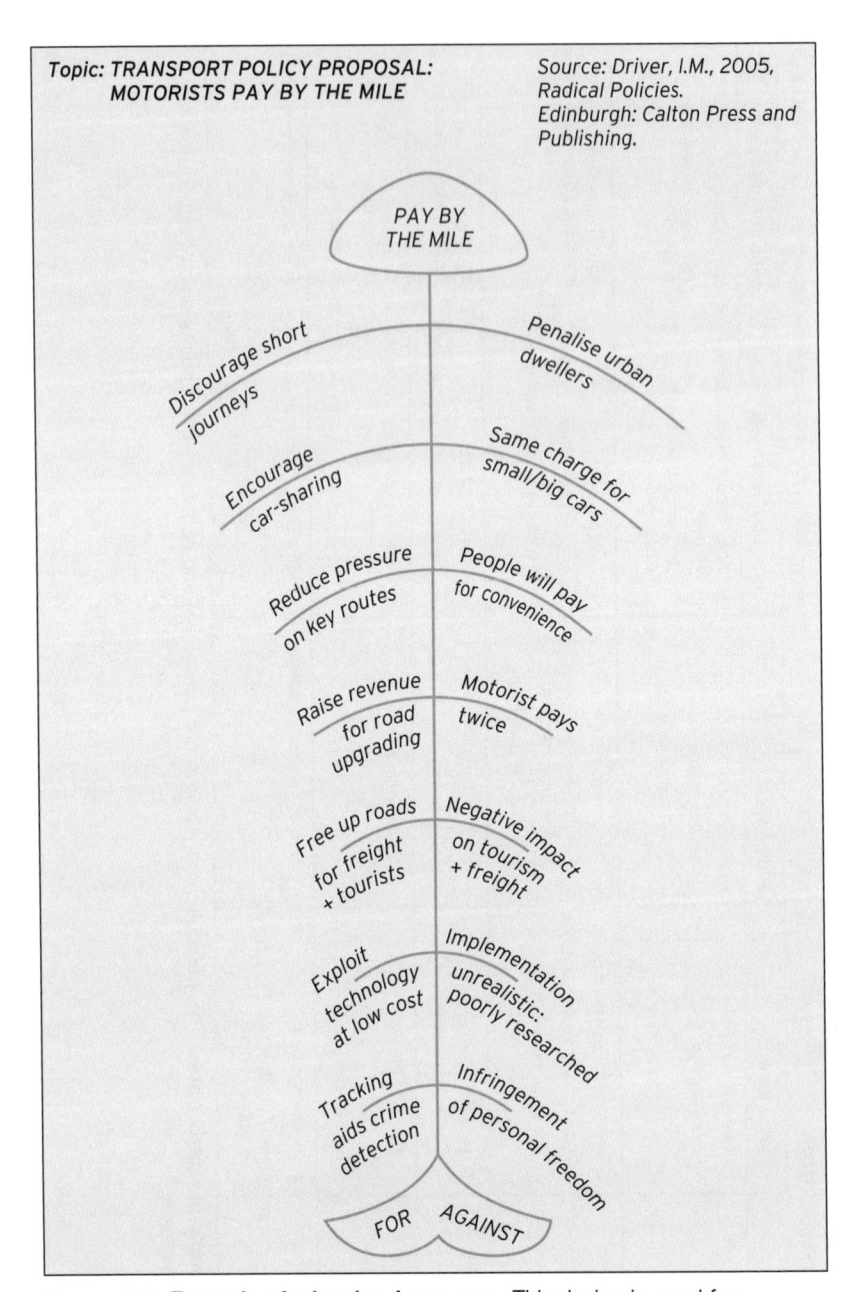

Topic: TRANSPORT POLICY PROPOSAL: MOTORISTS PAY BY THE MILE

Source: Driver, I.M., 2005, Radical Policies. Edinburgh: Calton Press and Publishing.

PAY BY THE MILE

FOR:
- Discourage short journeys
- Encourage car-sharing
- Reduce pressure on key routes
- Raise revenue for road upgrading
- Free up roads for freight + tourists
- Exploit technology at low cost
- Tracking aids crime detection

AGAINST:
- Penalise urban dwellers
- Same charge for small/big cars
- People will pay for convenience
- Motorist pays twice
- Negative impact on tourism + freight
- Implementation unrealistic: poorly researched
- Infringement of personal freedom

Figure 10.8 **Example of a herring-bone map.** This design is good for showing, as in this case, two sides to an argument. It may be particularly appealing to visual learners.

ACTION POINTS

10.1 Experiment with different styles of notes. Recognise that information is presented in different ways according to resource type, author and presenter. The style of notes you elect to create should be a response to these different methods of information delivery. For example, keeping track of a seminar that has many digressions may mean that you adopt a mind map rather than a linear note format; similarly, a complex text may be easier to understand and record in a grid format rather than as a keyword note. Only by considering the different techniques shown in Figures 10.1–10.8 will you be able to identify methods that suit you and the material best.

10.2 Keep a list of relevant abbreviations. This is an obvious way of saving time when recording specialist words and phrases, but can also apply to more general terms that are repeated a lot. A good general dictionary will normally provide a comprehensive list of useful abbreviations from which to draw, while a specialist (subject) dictionary will give a list of approved specialist abbreviations.

10.3 Compare your notes with those of a friend. There is often more than one possible interpretation of a text or presentation. If you and a friend exchange your notes relating to the same material, you may be surprised to find that your perceptions, and hence notes, differ concerning an approach or issue. This can lead to fruitful discussion about the content and the effectiveness of the style of note-creation.

11 ORGANISING YOUR RESEARCH MATERIALS

How to collect and file information and details of references

You will come across a large amount of potential source material in your researches. If you wish to copy any of this, you will need to take account of copyright law as it applies to copying for 'educational purposes'. You will also need to file the hard copies, reference details and any notes you have made in such a way that relevant information can easily be retrieved during the planning and writing phases of your project.

KEY TOPICS
- → Copying or printing out source material
- → Indexing and organising your resources and research notes
- → Creating a mini-database of themed research notes

Research activity always generates a great deal of paperwork and related information. This needs to be organised so that you can recover it easily when necessary. In addition, comprehensive reference details will be required for those sources you quote in your write-up. Formats for citation and reference lists are discussed in **Chapter 24**; this chapter deals with ways in which you can store or record the detailed information required for creating reference lists.

COPYING OR PRINTING OUT SOURCE MATERIAL

Having a paper copy of your source material can be extremely convenient. You can view this when needed, annotate it and store it for later reference. It can take the form of an original printed version, a photocopy, a scan or a printout. Increasingly, digital media are used for these purposes, but although computerised filing and annotation systems offer convenience, they are unlikely to supplant paper copies entirely.

When you copy or download any resource, you must take account of copyright law. This 'gives the creators of a wide range of material, such as literature, art, music and recording, film and broadcasts, economic rights' (UK Intellectual Property Office, ***www.ipo.gov.uk***). Copyright infringement is regarded as equivalent to stealing, and legal rights are sometimes jealously guarded by companies with the resources to prosecute.

In the UK, authors have literary copyright over their material for their life, and their estate has copyright for a further 70 years. Publishers have typographical copyright for 25 years. This is why the copyright symbol, ©, is usually accompanied by a date and the owner's name. For example, you'll find this information on the publication details page at the start of a book (as in this one).

Use of the copyright symbol

The © symbol indicates that someone is drawing your attention to the fact that something is in copyright. However, even if © does not appear, the material may still be under copyright.

You will be at risk of breaking the law if you copy (for example, photocopy, digitally scan or print out) material to which someone else owns the copyright, unless you have their express permission or unless the amount you copy falls within the limits accepted for 'fair dealing'. 'Educational copying', for non-commercial private study or research, is sometimes allowed by publishers (they will state this on the material, and may allow multiple copies to be made). Otherwise, for single copies for private study or research, you should only copy what would fall under the 'fair dealing' provision, for which there is no precise definition in law.

What is 'private study or research' in copyright terms?

'Private' means exactly what it says: the limits discussed here apply to that use and not to commercial or other uses, such as photocopying an amusing article for your friends.

Established practice suggests that you should photocopy no more than five per cent of the work involved, or:

- one chapter of a book
- one article per volume of an academic journal
- 20 per cent (to a maximum of 20 pages) of a short book
- one poem or short story (to a maximum of ten pages) from an anthology
- one separate illustration or map up to A4 size (note: illustrations that are parts of articles and chapters may be included in the allowances noted above)
- short excerpts of musical works – not whole works or movements (note: copying of any kind of public performance is not allowed without permission).

These limits apply to single copies – you can't take multiple copies of any of the above items, or pass on a single copy for multiple copying to someone else, who may be in ignorance of the source or of specific or general copyright issues. In legal terms, it doesn't matter whether you paid for the source or not: copyright is infringed when the whole or a substantial part is copied without permission – and 'substantial' here can mean a qualitatively significant section, even if this is a small part of the whole.

Approved copyright exceptions

Some copying for academic purposes may be licensed by the Copyright Licensing Agency (CLA) on behalf of authors. Other electronically distributed material may be licensed through the HERON (Higher Education Resources On-Demand) scheme. In these cases, you may be able to copy or print out more than the amounts detailed in the main text here, including multiple copies. Your university may also 'buy in' to licensing schemes, such as those offered by the NLA (Newspaper Licensing Agency) and the Performing Rights Society. As these can refer to very specific sources, consult your library's website or staff if in doubt.

The same rules apply to printing or copying material on the internet, unless the author gives explicit written clearance. This applies to copying images as well as text from the internet, although a number of sites do offer copyright-free images. A statement on the author's position on copying may appear on the home page or a page linked directly from it. If none appears, then you should assume the material is copyright protected. Where material is copyright free, this will be clearly stated on the document or in the book.

> **Complexity of copyright law**
>
> The material in this chapter is a summary, and much may depend on individual circumstances. Note also that copyright legislation is the subject of international cooperation and is supported by a network of international agreements.

INDEXING AND ORGANISING YOUR RESOURCES AND RESEARCH NOTES

Having a considerable quantity of source material, either in original hard copy or as printouts and photocopies, presents three related problems:

1 how to file and organise the hard copies you have obtained (usually by photocopying, but sometimes directly from an author)
2 how to create a database or other method that allows you to produce a reference list for all the references you wish to cite
3 how to store and cross-reference your notes on the material, so you refer to the right references in the right places.

The solution is to adopt a system of indexing your references. These systems can range from the simple to the complex, as outlined below. Select the most appropriate for your needs.

Hard-copy approaches

One simple, 'low-tech' method for storing hard copy and related reference information involves creating an index card for each item. Each hard copy document is given an 'accession' number in sequence (1, 2, 3...) indicating the order of archiving and is stored sequentially in boxes or files so that frequent reorganisation is not required as your collection expands. Each document is matched by an index card of the same number. On the card you write essential bibliographical information and any comments you want to note in particular – for example, details of the research methods used. You then store the cards in alphabetical order by author. Thus, if you recall that an article written by E. Burke (2003) is relevant, you can find the card, identify the accession number and immediately retrieve the relevant document from your filing system.

This method will help you become more familiar with your material and its content. The accession numbers or the record cards themselves can be used as a way of identifying and grouping references in different topic areas, and the relevant cards can easily be reordered alphabetically when writing up your reference list. This system is labour-intensive and has the disadvantage that the final list will probably have to be typed up as a single exercise; nevertheless, it might suit some learning styles better than the computer-based models described below.

> ✓ **Use reference index cards as an informal database**
>
> If you prefer to use handwritten index cards, these can also be physically grouped in themes and/or by date of publication to facilitate the writing process. Remember to note both the date that you created the notes and especially the date when you accessed online material, since this can change frequently and/or, without warning, may be withdrawn and thus be impossible to recover. The date you access online material is also important when listing online references.

Personalised computer-based approaches

Following the 'accession number' approach of the hard-copy model, an alternative, computer-based system involves creating a file folder in which you store copies of completed templates, similar to those discussed below. These should be filed in order of 'accession number', corresponding to the filing system for any hard copies. When creating a reference list, the reference information can then be cut and pasted into a word processor file and sorted alphabetically or numerically, eliminating any duplication. This method has the advantage of allowing onscreen manipulation of bibliographical data and interpretations.

Both the hard-copy and computer-based methods have the disadvantage of requiring extensive cross-checking and proofreading of the final list to ensure that all the conventions of the referencing method are applied consistently.

Using commercial bibliographic software

These systems offer great potential for organising citations within your text and for preparing your reference list. Appropriate bibliographic data must first be entered into fields within a database (you can also search online databases and import reference data from these). The database can then be searched and customised in the style of your choice to create a consistent reference list for your report or paper. Research notes, as described above, can also be added. One advantage is that the database system will avoid punctuation inaccuracies in the final version. In addition, most packages offer the functions of inserting citations according to different referencing methods and output can be altered to suit different requirements for different publication contexts. However, on the negative side, you have to consider whether the effort taken to learn how to use whichever package is available to you (for example, EndNote, ProCite, Reference Manager or Zotero) is worthwhile for a research project that may have relatively few references. If you decide to use this type of software, consider attending a training course if one is offered by university staff, or seeking guidance online. Ensure that servicing your database doesn't become an end in itself.

CREATING A MINI-DATABASE OF THEMED RESEARCH NOTES

During your investigation you may accumulate many notes from your sources, with the attendant risk that these become disorganised. The following suggestion will help you to avoid the frustration of 'losing' a particular note or idea and can help during the writing process. The method involves creating a word-processed file for each specific aspect of your research consisting of a series of templates in the form of the small table illustrated in Figure 11.1(a). Each time you read a new source, details of the reference are completed – as shown in Figure 11.1(b).

Alongside the reference details, you can record notes of your thoughts about the content and findings in relation to your own study. Within the same folder, you might also wish to keep any detailed quotes that you have taken directly from source material, any downloaded materials on that theme and any pieces of ongoing written work.

As this mini-database develops, you will have a composite record of related material that you will be able to use when you reach that particular aspect in your writing. You could choose to handwrite such notes, but the time spent typing them up will add value – enabling

(a)

Theme	
Publication details	
Direct quotation or paraphrase	
Importance/relevance/ Anticipated location in thesis	
Personal appraisal	

(b)
Source 1

Theme	Disadvantages of eco systems in house building
Publication details	Green, A. 2012. The EcoHouse. London: Earth Press.
Direct quotation or paraphrase [with page reference]	"Eco measures will only work if the home owner understands the underlying principles of the materials and services incorporated in the building." Page 59.
Importance/relevance/ Anticipated location in thesis	Need for eco education for home owners. Could be included in disadvantages. Either in intro. or critique chapter.
Personal appraisal	Useful as recognition that as eco homes become more the norm, their efficacy has to be matched with owner's knowledge.

Source 2

Theme	Disadvantages of eco systems in house building
Publication details	Brown, B. 2010. Building green. Ely: Fens Press.
Direct quotation or paraphrase [with page reference]	"The builder has to engage with the eco concept for successful project completion." Page 25.
Importance/relevance/ Anticipated location in thesis	Need for eco education of trades involved in construction. Could be included in disadvantages. Either in intro or critique chapter.
Personal appraisal	Supports idea of need for commitment from all stakeholders in the project.

Source 3

Theme	Disadvantages of eco systems in house building
Publication details	Black, H. 2009. Financing green-ness. Dublin: Green Press.
Direct quotation or paraphrase [with page reference]	"Financial houses need to be included in 'green education' so that mortgage applications for eco homes can be sympathetically appraised." Page 95.
Importance/relevance/ Anticipated location in thesis	Need for eco education for business. Could be included in disadvantages. Either in intro or critique chapter.
Personal appraisal	Useful as recognition that as eco homes become more the norm, their efficacy has to be matched with owner's knowledge.

Figure 11.1 Example of a word-processed template for recording details of references in an easily accessed format: (a) template; (b) examples of a completed template.

the details to be searched, copied and pasted using word-processor commands. Either printed out as hard copy or viewed on the screen, the completed template entries can be shuffled around to help group and visualise connections between sources. The key advantage is that you have all the related material in an easily readable format in one place.

Chapter 24 covers some key aspects of documenting sources, including ways of recording and citing quotations and ideas taken from them.

ACTION POINTS

11.1 Next time you are in the library, read the documentation about photocopying that should be on prominent display, often beside the photocopiers. This will provide detailed information about current legislation and any local exceptions. The library website may also be a useful source of information – for example, about HERON-licensed material.

11.2 Review how you currently store information. If this is in note form, consider storing like with like – for example, in folders by theme or topic. If you have print-out material, consider whether you need to create box-file storage that groups materials, again by topic and theme. Although this may not seem important at early stages of the research process, at later stages these decisions could have time- and labour-saving implications.

11.3 Decide on your referencing system at an early stage. Consult Chapter 24, and also any regulations about the recommended reference system given by your department, before you start taking notes or setting up a database for storing reference details. This will allow you to note details in the correct order and format and avoid the need for time-consuming reformatting when you finalise your document.

RESEARCH APPROACHES

12 USING QUANTITATIVE RESEARCH METHODS

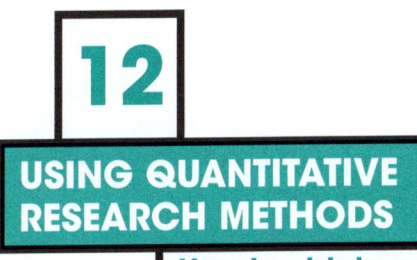

How to obtain and analyse numerical information

Quantitative research methods are commonplace in the sciences, but are also relevant to some non-science subjects. If carrying out this type of research, you will need to understand the rationale for obtaining numerical data and be proficient in the main techniques used to obtain, analyse and present them.

KEY TOPICS

→ Key features of quantitative research
→ Typical quantitative research methods
→ Correlation and causality
→ Analysing and presenting your results

Quantitative research methods are defined as investigative approaches resulting in numerical data, in contrast to those methods resulting in qualitative textual information (**Ch 13**). This type of research is especially valuable when:

- obtaining measurements (for example, in biochemistry and physiology)
- estimating error (for example, in physics and engineering)
- comparing information and opinions (for example, sociology and psychology)
- testing hypotheses (for example, in most investigative science disciplines).

The ideal in this type of research is for the investigator to be detached and impartial to the results of the study. Quantitative and qualitative research methods are not mutually exclusive and they may be used in the same investigation. For example, a full textual description of a sampling environment (qualitative information) may be vital to make sense of the numerical (quantitative) data obtained within it. Similarly, surveys and interviews (Ch 15) can yield outcomes that are quantitative ('over 45 per cent of respondents agreed with this statement') or qualitative ('respondent X stated that, in her opinion, the standard of service had declined in recent years').

KEY FEATURES OF QUANTITATIVE RESEARCH

Quantitative research is generally 'conclusive' in nature. It is especially important in the sciences, where its aim may be to provide a reliable value for a measurement or to test a hypothesis. Typical outcomes might be:

- for a set of measurements: 'The average insect wing length was 3.40 mm with a standard error of 0.14 mm, $n = 24$'
- for an experiment: 'Treatment A resulted in a statistically significant increase in weight gain compared with the control group'.

In quantitative research, your aim would normally be to base results on large, unbiased samples. Large sample size is important to ensure that measurements based on the sample are representative of the population as a whole, and to improve your chances of arriving at a statistically significant conclusion (Ch 9). However, time or resource limitations on your research may limit the sample size you can use in practice – your supervisor will probably provide guidance on this aspect.

Bias in quantitative research

Obtaining numbers to describe your results reduces subjectivity and allows comparisons between data sets. The inherent objectivity of quantitative research relies, however, on an unbiased approach to data collection. Some commentators on the quantitative approach claim that experiments, surveys and the like are rarely entirely free of observer bias, even if this is unintentional.

> **Definitions: objectivity and subjectivity**
>
> **Objectivity** – the ability to arrive at a detached, unprejudiced viewpoint, based on the evidence and without the influence of feelings or emotion (the object = the thing observed).
>
> **Subjectivity** – the ability to arrive at a viewpoint that takes account of personal impressions, feelings and interpretations (the subject = the observer or researcher).

Bias can be defined as a partial or one-sided view or description of events. Although the aim in most research is usually to reduce bias as far as possible, it can arise because of subconscious decisions by the investigator, which can mean that individuals selected for observation or experiment do not represent the population, or that values or measurements associated with them are skewed in a particular way.

Numerical results can be analysed with statistical techniques. These allow you to compare sets of observations or treatments, to test hypotheses and to allocate levels of probability (chance) of your conclusions being right or wrong. These are powerful tools and lie at the heart of much scientific scholarship.

However, just because you can measure something, or can compare data sets, this does not mean your conclusions are certain or relevant. For example, many researchers accept the conclusions of their studies on the basis that there could be a 5 per cent chance of their being wrong, so, on average, this will be the case 1 in 20 times (**Ch 9**). Even when a hypothesis is accepted as correct, the results may apply only to the very artificial experimental or observational environment. Moreover, statistical significance of this type should not be confused with significance in the sense of 'importance' or 'value'.

> **Take care with the concept of proof**
>
> The word 'proof' should be used cautiously when applied to quantitative research – the term implies 100 per cent certainty, whereas this is very rarely justified owing to the ambiguity inherent in statistical analysis and experimental design. Hence, when writing up your project, 'hedging' language (**Ch 22**), such as 'this indicates that...' or 'this appears to show that...', is preferable to 'absolute' or categorical phrases such as 'it is always the case that...' or 'this proves that...'.

TYPICAL QUANTITATIVE RESEARCH METHODS

This section describes methods used in the most common types of investigation. If your discipline favours a different or modified method, then consult relevant texts as suggested by your supervisor.

Measurements and error determination

A measurement is an estimate of some dimension of an object or event as a ratio of a standard unit. It therefore consists of both a number and the symbol for the unit – for example: 0.5 metres; 1.6 litres; 39 kilograms. The units chosen for most scientific studies are those of the *Système International d'Unités* (or SI) – a metre–kilogram–second scheme with defined symbols for units and prefixes for small and large numbers that differ by multiples of 1,000 (10^3). These units are discussed further in **Chapter 19**.

All measurements contain error, which can be of two types: accuracy or precision. In practice, measurements are often assumed to be accurate and the more important thing to estimate is the precision.

There are two main ways of estimating precision.

- By providing a range that relates to the observer's or instrument's ability to discriminate between readings. For example, if measuring length with a ruler, you might write 104 ± 0.5 mm because you were using the scale divisions on the ruler to estimate to the nearest mm; that is, the dividing points between adjacent values below and above 104 are at 103.5 and 104.5 mm.

- By providing an estimated error that is based on repeated measurements of the same quantity. For quantifying measurement error alone, this would be obtained from several independent attempts at measurement – for example, five independent values obtained from the same weighing machine of someone's weight (mass). In many scientific studies, this error is taken to be included in the overall sampling error obtained from replicates.

When reporting measurement data, you should use appropriate measures of location and dispersion to describe them. These are outlined in Table 9.1.

> ### Definitions: accuracy and precision
>
> **Accuracy** – the closeness of a measured or estimated value to its true value. Example: a balance would be said to be inaccurate if, instead of giving you a value for a standard 1 kg weight as 1 kg, it consistently gave a value of 1.02 kg. All measurements of similar weights from the instrument would thus be approximately +2 per cent wrong.
>
> **Precision** – the closeness of repeated measurements to each other. For example, if you weighed a specimen several times on the same balance and got very different results each time, then the instrument would be said to be imprecise. A mean of 1.000 kg might be considered to be accurate, but if the standard deviation of the measurements was 0.25 kg, this would be considered rather imprecise.

Experiments

An experiment is a contrived or designed situation where a researcher attempts to isolate the effects of changing one variable in the system or process, and then compares the results with the condition where no change has occurred. The aim behind many experiments is to help to establish causality – that is, to establish that a change in factor A causes a change in variable B. Experiments can also help elucidate in more detail how A causes B (see later section on correlation and causality).

Experiments are at the core of the 'scientific method', in which an experiment is set up that will allow a hypothesis to be accepted or rejected (Ch 3). Much of the progress in the modern world has been made through scientific advances based on experiments. Nevertheless, it is useful to recognise some limitations and difficulties.

- The situations required to allow manipulation of relevant variables are potentially artificial. Indeed, they may be so contrived as to be unnatural – making any conclusions of dubious value.
- It may be impossible to change one variable only in any treatment. Inevitably, other aspects change simultaneously. These are known as confounding variables. For example, if you attempt to change atmospheric temperature, you will probably also change humidity. Adding 'control' treatments are the way in which experimenters attempt to rule out the effects of confounding variables (Ch 14).
- There will be uncertainty in conclusions. Sampling and other errors can be taken into account in statistical analysis, but the results must always be expressed with a degree of uncertainty (Ch 9).

- There may be an unwitting element of subjectivity or bias in the choice of treatments, the choice of conditions (sometimes selected to accentuate effects of a particular treatment) and, in some cases, in the recording of results.

The conduct of experiments is discussed further in **Chapter 14**.

CORRELATION AND CAUSALITY

Correlation is a way of describing the relationship between two measured variables – for example, the number of cigarettes smoked per day and life expectancy. A variable is well-correlated with another if their values alter together, either in a positive fashion or in a negative fashion. This is illustrated in Figure 12.1.

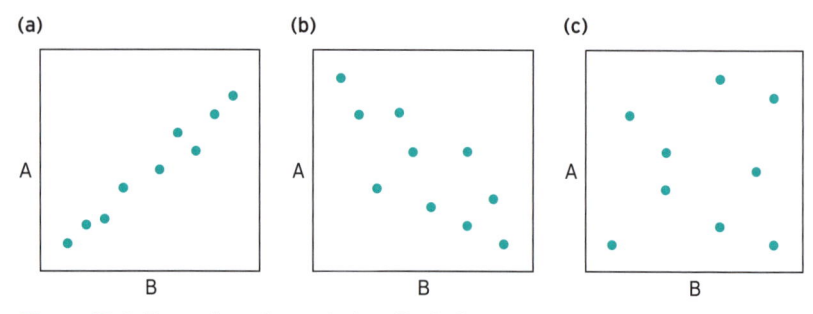

Figure 12.1 Examples of correlation. Each dot represents an experimental subject measured for variables A and B: (a) the two variables have a strong positive correlation – that is, if one variable increases, so does the other; (b) the two variables are negatively correlated – that is, if one variable increases, the other decreases – but in the case illustrated, the points are more widely scattered, so the correlation is less strong than in the first example; and (c) the two variables have no strong correlation – that is, they show no discernible relationship.

How can I measure the strength and significance of a correlation?

A statistic called the correlation coefficient can be used to express the strength or degree of linear correlation between two variables. This takes values between −1 and 1; the closer its value is to these extremes, the higher the degree of correlation, and the closer to zero, the lower. The sign indicates whether the correlation is positive or negative. The coefficient can be used in a statistical test to find out whether the correlation is significantly different from zero.

Vital to an understanding of quantitative research is an awareness that correlation does not always imply causality. If A is well correlated with B, this alone is not enough evidence to state that A causes B. It could be something related to A, or even, due to coincidence, something unrelated to A. So, if people with high blood pressure are more likely to have heart attacks, this alone does not show that high blood pressure is a cause of heart attacks, although if there were no relationship between the two you might be inclined to rule out this possibility. The only way to become more certain is to gather more evidence supporting a link – for example, by providing evidence of a possible mechanism of connection between the two variables.

ANALYSING AND PRESENTING YOUR RESULTS

Results of observations or experiments are rarely reported without subsequent analysis. Indeed, your ability to analyse and present your results will be judged as part of your assessment.

- Adequate description of your methods is vital. One goal of quantitative research is to produce repeatable results from which general conclusions can be drawn. This normally means that a 'Materials and Methods' section of a paper or report contains enough information to allow a competent peer to repeat your work (Ch 22).
- Descriptions should use clear, unambiguous language, and qualitative terms used should be defined if possible. For example, rather than describing the colour of a specimen as 'red', it might be described with reference to a standard colour chart.
- Repetition is vital. Simple measurements should be repeated if possible, so that a figure indicating their accuracy (dispersion, Ch 9) can be provided.
- Figures and tables should be used appropriately. When describing results, appropriate use should be made of figures and tables and these should be constructed according to the usual discipline conventions (Ch 20).
- The results of experiments should be analysed using statistical tests (Ch 9).

ACTION POINTS

12.1 List potential forms of bias in your research. Being aware of these will help you to avoid or manage them. Discuss your list with your supervisor to establish whether you have missed anything, and to explore methods of avoiding the most important sources of bias in your work.

12.2 Plan out a pilot experiment, or the procedures necessary for a measurement. Aim to identify the different steps in the process and, in particular, resource constraints. In the case of an experiment, this might include the availability of test subjects or equipment; and for measurements, the number of replicate readings it is possible to carry out in a given time.

12.3 Find out about the statistical tests that can be carried out using the specific software available to you. Will you be able to accomplish your aims using tests within a spreadsheet program such as Excel, or will you need more sophisticated software? What 'learning curve' is required to understand and master these tests? To help overcome potential difficulties, try out the software functions using dummy values, before using them with real data.

13 USING QUALITATIVE RESEARCH METHODS

How to obtain and analyse descriptive information

Qualitative research methods are commonplace in a wide range of arts, social sciences and scientific research work. When carrying out this type of research, you should understand the rationale for obtaining descriptive data, and be familiar with the main techniques used to obtain and present them.

KEY TOPICS
→ Theoretical perspectives
→ Key features of qualitative research
→ Typical qualitative research methods
→ Coding and analysing qualitative data

Qualitative research methods are those investigative approaches whose outcomes are summarised as textual information, in contrast with quantitative methods where results are usually summarised numerically (**Ch 12**). Qualitative approaches have wide application and are especially useful when examining complex information that needs to be disentangled in order to make sense of it. Typically, this might entail scrutinising:

- opinions, feelings and values (for example, in philosophy, political science, social policy)
- participant interpretations and responses (for example, in psychology, sociology)
- behavioural patterns (for example, in anthropology, ethnography, geography)
- processes and patterns (for example, in biology, economics, education)

- case studies including critical incidents (for example, in education, nursing, social work).

A range of methods have been developed in each of these areas, and if conducting this type of research yourself it will be useful to have a thorough understanding of the theoretical base from which qualitative study methods have grown.

THEORETICAL PERSPECTIVES

In qualitative research, there is recognition that collection and interpretation of data are influenced by a set of values belonging to the researcher. A range of theoretical perspectives apply to evaluating information of this type. A good starting point when scoping your study would be examination of four commonly used observational approaches:

1 **Field research**. This approach to qualitative research involves the collection, analysis and description of observations from natural environments beyond the laboratory. The method requires methodical and detailed note-making that is then coded before it can be analysed and the phenomena described. Fieldwork research is used in many disciplines and can be part of the process of some of the approaches listed below. The nature of collecting, coding, analysing and describing will differ according to discipline and context.

2 **Ethnography**. This approach aims to describe and understand cultural phenomena. It is based on participant observation and is a form of field research. In this approach, groups or organisations are observed in their natural contexts over a relatively short period. Members of such groupings share common experiences, whether by virtue of social context, location or practices, and it is their behaviours in the context of this mutual experience that researchers aim to investigate.

3 **Grounded theory**. This approach aims to understand social phenomena through 'real life' or 'grounded' observations in group contexts. Through an iterative coding process, a better understanding is reached regarding both events or problems and then explanations or solutions for them. The process does not begin with a hypothesis (**Ch 3**), but starts with general questions

that may be further refined and that can lead to the creation of more questions as ideas develop over time. The data generated are analysed and tentatively linked to theoretical concepts, new or existing. Later in the process, core aspects and relationships between these and their associated theoretical underpinning are identified.

4 **Phenomenology**. This is an observational technique that involves longer-term, detailed study of small groups of people. Several schools of thought exist regarding this approach, but the common focus is on philosophical thinking about the essential questions of how to define being and knowledge. In its practical application, the phenomena studied relate to participants' subjective interpretations of experiences and the world surrounding them, sometimes called their 'lived experience'. The phenomenologist tries to reach a better understanding of these experiences.

These four approaches have their origins in the sciences, anthropology, sociology and philosophy respectively – although they are now widely used across academia.

> **Learning more about qualitative research theory**
>
> It is beyond the scope of this book to examine the theoretical underpinnings of qualitative enquiry in detail, but you may find it useful in making your decision about the best 'fit' for your study to consult one of the seminal works on aspects of qualitative research. Frequently recommended texts are: Cohen *et al.* (2007), Denzin and Lincoln (2005), Robson (2011) and Strauss and Corbin (2007).

Your supervisor may suggest a well-established approach to your research, possibly following common practice in your discipline. In this case, planning for research methodology can be done at the outset. In other instances, the qualitative research approach to be adopted may not become clear until background research is under way, and so it may be necessary to delay planning the theoretical methodology. Reaching a deep understanding of these complex approaches can be lengthy and sometimes difficult. While you should avoid delaying the research phase too long, you will need to factor into your time-planning enough time to study and develop an understanding of the options.

13 Using qualitative research methods

KEY FEATURES OF QUALITATIVE RESEARCH

Qualitative research is generally exploratory in nature. It is especially important in the social sciences, where its aim often is to understand the complex reasons for human behaviour. Typical outcomes might be, for example:

- a description of an ecological site: 'The soil at the north-western extremity of the study area was a silty clay loam, grading towards the south-eastern side to be a medium loam.'
- a case study: 'Student X described her experience on her first day at university as bewildering.'

> **i** **Surveys and interviews**
>
> These can have outcomes that are qualitative in nature. Principles of the design and conduct of surveys and interviews are discussed further in **Chapter 15**.

Qualitative research generally involves specific situations, individuals or small samples, in contrast to the large, randomly selected samples favoured in quantitative research (**Ch 12**). These small samples may be carefully selected, and they may not be representative of the population as a whole, but that is not always an issue because, in many cases, the value of qualitative research derives from the authentic and case-specific detail that it can encompass. The information obtained is potentially richer and deeper than that described in numbers and statistics, and can take advantage of the many subtle ways of using language to express opinions, experiences and feelings. On the other hand, these properties may mean that it is less easy to compare different responses and arrive at generalised conclusions.

Qualitative and quantitative research methods (**Ch 12**) are not mutually exclusive and may be used in the same investigation. For example, mixed types of data may be obtained – as in a survey eliciting free-text responses and expressions of opinion on a Likert scale.

> **Understanding the nature of bias in qualitative research** ✓
>
> Qualitative research, by its very nature, implies a degree of bias. However, maintaining objectivity is as important in the conduct of the research as it is in reporting findings. It is important, therefore, to recognise the tensions that can arise between objectivity and bias. This is particularly relevant when selecting cases to study, aspects to report and language to describe observations. Observer preconceptions, value systems and cultural influences also need to be taken into account. Examination of the theoretical bases for this type of research (see above) can help to tease out these issues to achieve an objective appraisal of your research problem.

TYPICAL QUALITATIVE RESEARCH METHODS

This section describes techniques used in the most common types of investigation. If your discipline favours a different or modified technique, then consult relevant texts such as those suggested earlier in this chapter.

Observation and description

This category includes a wide range of approaches where the investigator will examine an artefact, person or location and describe it in words. A narrative (outline of developments through time) might also fall into this classification. Examples of suitable topics include:

- primary source material, such as that found in an historical document
- a biological habitat
- a patient's symptoms
- a drawing, painting or installation
- the acculturation process among immigrants.

The specific detailed features to be reported will depend on your discipline and research area. Discussing these with your supervisor is advisable before proceeding too far with your research. Although description is sometimes categorised as a 'lower-level' academic thought process, the interpretations and generalisations that follow involve higher-level skills (Ch 16). For example, a detailed description you produce may be referred to when you are drawing conclusions about a wider topic.

Sometimes your purpose may involve comparing several sources of information. A useful technique when doing this is to create a matrix or grid, where the columns represent the different sources and entries in the rows summarise the specific features of interest. This matrix can be useful when writing a summary of the key features of the sources for a project write-up (e.g. Figure 10.7). In some cases, it could be adapted for use as a table. When interpreting such a table, you should remember that similarities may be just as important as differences.

> **Example of a matrix approach to comparative description**
>
> The introduction to a student's project report or paper might involve comparing the health systems of several countries. Having carried out background reading and scan-read through selected documents, the student researcher might be able to come up with a list of key aspects to compare (for example, the nature of health care provision, the source of funding, the entitlement to free health care, private health care provision, or the nature of specialist care). This list could form the basis of a matrix (grid) comparing the different aspects, following a more detailed reading of the documents.

Observations can generate large amounts of data. As with references and other source materials (Ch 11), you will need a well-organised system for filing data, constructing databases and recording your analyses. This is best decided upon before starting the research, or perhaps immediately following a pilot or initial research exercise.

> **Can I use photography or scans to record complex information?**
>
> This is often a good idea. Photos might be valuable for a field study – for example, by acting as a prompt when you start to write up. Another use could be recording notes made by a focus group on a whiteboard. Scans might assist when collating large numbers of documents. Note that if photographing people as part of a study, you may need to seek ethical approval (Ch 18) and possibly create a suitable permissions form to be completed by participants.

Case studies are sometimes presented in your final text, each in a self-contained text box. If these are numbered, you can refer to them using the same conventions as figures and tables (**Ch 20**). There are layout rules for presenting quotes from sources in an academic document (**Ch 24**) and these should be adhered to consistently.

Action research

Academic departments often encourage students to undertake studies grounded in 'local' issues. In such instances, action research approaches are popular. These are particularly common in the 'caring' disciplines, such as nursing, social work and teaching. The focus is directed on the context of the researcher's practice and a problem or situation within it which requires better understanding and, possibly, identification of some change to resolve or improve that situation or practice. This approach requires planning of the research approach, perhaps through data collection or observation, analysis and reflection through reference to theory and, ultimately, a recommendation for action.

Value of pilot studies

A pilot study is usually a preliminary study conducted on a small scale. This may require some effort to set up, but it can save time and effort in the long run. It will:

- give you a chance to work through your approach, to identify inconsistencies or weaknesses
- help you to decide which background demographic or geographical information will be required to correlate with your observations
- help you decide how you will analyse the results, and whether you need to adjust the approach because of this.

CODING AND ANALYSING QUALITATIVE DATA

In analysing and presenting qualitative data, a key requirement is to represent the material in a balanced and rational way. Do not be tempted to select only examples, answers or quotes that support your view. One way to prevent this tendency is to 'code' your data. To do this, you need to identify themes or patterns before you begin and allocate a code to each one. As you continue to process the data, other themes, patterns and behaviours may become apparent; similarly assign a code to these. Note, also, that while certain of your coding categories may expand, other anticipated categories may prove to be less significant.

Analysing your data will depend on format, content and time available to do this. In one approach, the process can be divided into two stages. In the first stage, go through the recorded data highlighting coded items and noting the code (and sub-code if necessary) in the margin if appropriate. At the next stage, prepare record cards, a table or spreadsheet columns to note:

1. the code and sub-code for what you are recording (according to the key you have decided upon)
2. description of the source (could be, for example, a *verbatim* transcript, paraphrased transcript, comments, numerical information, photograph details)
3. details of the source's identity (could be, for example, a respondent or location).

This process can be used to analyse a transcript or record, by entering the relevant information as you go through the data. For transcripts and records this process can be time-consuming and it is probably better to go through all the data for one code at a time and repeat for the next code, and so on. Trying to transcribe all the codes for one transcript or record in a single sweep could be extremely time-consuming and complex, leading to error.

Examples of studies where coding can be a valuable technique

Coding can be valuable in diverse investigations across many subjects, including, for example:

- recording subject behaviour on interview
- describing animal mating behaviour
- recording distributions of plant species within quadrats sampled in an ecosystem
- analysis of questionnaire responses (see Ch 15).

Once you have coded your transcript, record or raw data, you will be in a better position to judge the distribution of the data via their coding and thereby create a more balanced summary of your findings; this will also help you to identify 'outlier' events as such, where these occur.

In some cases, the analysis may be aided by a basic summary of the codings and sub-codings, using appropriate descriptive statistics (**Ch 9**), which may be more easily calculated if the codes are first entered on a spreadsheet. In other instances, it will be sufficient to unpack the coding and sub-coding elements as compatible or linked themes or groups that reflect the disparate nature of the data. This will enable you to write a tight and well-balanced report of your findings. Note that you should not discount those categories that transpired to be less significant than you had anticipated, but should consider why this is the case. Where you have used quantitative data collection to obtain parallel or analogous information, compare these findings with the qualitative data – looking for inconsistencies as well as confirmations.

ACTION POINTS

13.1 Seek out and try to learn from 'model' approaches to your topic. Investigate theoretical foundations for qualitative research applications by consulting your library or some of the sources suggested in this chapter. You should be able to find, perhaps with the help of your supervisor, a published study carried out in a similar way. Identify and examine the theoretical approach that has been applied. Consider whether this could be adopted or adapted for your own investigation. Also, study the ways the results have been analysed and presented to see whether these approaches might be suitable for your own data. Note that you need to be able to justify your choice of approach and so you must ensure that you understand it thoroughly.

13.2 List potential forms of bias in your research. Being aware of these will help you to avoid or manage them. Discuss your list with your supervisor to see whether you have missed anything, and to explore methods of avoiding the most important sources of bias in your work.

13.3 Plan and carry out a pilot study for your research. This need not be a lengthy exercise and it could be carried out, for instance, at a convenient location or with a friend or group of friends as the subject of your inquiry.

14

CONDUCTING EXPERIMENTS AND FIELD STUDIES

How to design and perform lab and field investigations

Laboratory and/or fieldwork situations provide opportunities to observe specimens, carry out experiments and take relevant measurements. Good design and working practices are essential to ensure the validity of your results.

KEY TOPICS
→ Designing experiments
→ Sampling
→ Preparing for research activity
→ Working in the lab and field

In many disciplines, research activity is undertaken in the laboratory ('lab') and/or field. You are likely to have experienced lab and field sessions and project work in early years as an undergraduate, so will know what to expect. For a research project, the rigour with which you carry out this work must be of the highest standard: essentially, your methods and results should be of near-publishable quality. This means paying full attention to all aspects of relevant protocols and procedures.

The range of experimental designs and fieldwork approaches is infinite, so it is impossible to provide specific guidance. Precise methods will always depend on your discipline and the nature of the investigation. **Chapter 12** introduced the basic aims and elements of experiments, whose context in hypothesis-testing was also covered in **Chapter 3**. The content of this chapter should help to provide a sound foundation for this work, but you will always need to look at approaches used in recent publications in your area and take the advice of your supervisor.

DESIGNING EXPERIMENTS

Table 14.1 outlines the important stages in designing an experiment. In many experiments, the aim is to gather correlative evidence for causality or evidence of a mode of action to connect two processes

Table 14.1 Five key stages in the design of an experiment. Tips are provided for each phase.

1 Preliminaries
• Read background material and decide on a subject area to investigate. • Formulate a simple hypothesis to test. It is preferable to have a clear answer to one question than to be uncertain about several questions. • Decide which dependent variable you are going to measure and how: is it relevant to the problem? Can you measure it accurately, precisely and without bias? • Think about and plan the statistical analysis of your results. Will this affect your design?
2 Designing
• Find out the limitations on your resources. • Choose treatments that alter the minimum of confounding variables. • Incorporate as many effective controls as possible. • Keep the number of replicates as high as is feasible. • Ensure that the same number of replicates is present in each treatment. • Use effective randomisation and blocking arrangements.
3 Planning
• List all the materials you will need. Order any chemicals and make up solutions; identify, grow, collect or breed the experimental subjects you require; check equipment is available. • Organise space and/or time in which to do the experiment. • Account for the time taken to apply treatments and record results. Make out a timesheet if things will be hectic.
4 Carrying out the experiment
• Record the results and make careful notes of everything you do. Make additional observations to those planned if interesting things happen. • Repeat experiment if time and resources allow.
5 Analysing
• Graph data as soon as possible (during the experiment, if you can). This will allow you to visualise what has happened and make adjustments to the design (for example, timing of measurements). • Carry out the planned statistical analysis. • Jot down conclusions and new hypotheses arising from the experiment.

or events (Ch 12). Thus, if you suspect that x causes y, you would expect, repeatedly, to find that a change in x results in a change in y. Hence, the ideal experiment of this kind involves measurement of y (the dependent, or measured, variable) at different values of x (the independent variable), and subsequent demonstration of some relationship between them. Experiments therefore involve comparisons of the results of treatments – changes in the independent variable as applied to an experimental subject. The change is engineered by the experimenter under controlled conditions.

Controlling variables in experiments

Interpretation of experiments is seldom clear-cut because uncontrolled variables always change when treatments are given.

- Confounding variables increase or decrease systematically as the independent variable increases or decreases. Their effects are known as systematic variation.
- Nuisance variables are uncontrolled variables that cause differences in the value of y independently of the value of x, resulting in random variation.

Confounding variables can be disentangled from those caused directly by treatments by incorporating appropriate controls in the experiment (see below).

The consequence of systematic variation is that you can never be certain that the treatment, and the treatment alone, has caused an observed result. By careful design, however, you can 'minimise the uncertainty' involved in your conclusion. Methods available include:

- ensuring, through experimental design, that the independent variable is the only major factor that changes in any treatment
- incorporating appropriate controls to show that potential confounding variables have little or no effect
- selecting experimental subjects randomly ('sampling') to cancel out systematic variation arising from biased selection
- matching or pairing individuals among treatments so that differences in response due to their initial status are eliminated
- arranging subjects and treatments randomly so that responses to systematic differences in conditions do not influence the results

- ensuring that experimental conditions are uniform so that responses to systematic differences in conditions are minimised.

To reduce and assess the consequences of nuisance variables, you can:

- incorporate replicates to allow random variation to be quantified
- choose subjects that are as similar as possible
- control random fluctuations in environmental conditions.

These approaches are examined further below.

> **Constraints on experimental design**
>
> In most experiments, you will find that there are resource constraints on the design. For example, limits may be set by availability of subjects, cost of treatment or availability or cost of a chemical or bench space. Logistics may be a factor (for example, time taken to record or analyse data). Your equipment or facilities may affect design because you cannot regulate conditions as well as you might desire. You may have to accept a great deal of initial variability if your subjects are collected from the wild.

Use of controls

A control is an additional treatment where a potentially confounding variable is adjusted so that its effects, if any, can be measured and taken into account (**Ch 12**). There are often many potential controls for any experiment, with the simplest usually being no treatment at all. For example, suppose it is known that Drug A is acidic in nature and that the formulation available for testing also contains a synthesis by-product (impurity), Chemical B. A suitable experimental design for testing the efficacy of Drug A might include the following treatments:

1 No treatment (usually involving a placebo, or pill without any added chemicals).
2 Drug A (administered as a pill).
3 Control for the effects of pH (a placebo pill with the same pH or buffering capacity as the Drug A pill).
4 Control for the effect of Chemical B (a pill containing similar amounts of Chemical B as in the Drug A pill, but without any Drug A).

If the results show an effect in treatment 2, but not in 3 and 4, then the confounding variables can be ruled out and Drug A is the sole active agent; if there are also effects in 3 or 4, then the confounding variables may well be important in this situation.

Use of replicates

Replicate results show how variable the response is within treatments. They allow you to compare the differences among treatments in the context of the variability within treatments – you can do this via statistical tests, such as analysis of variance (**Chs 9 and 19**). Larger sample sizes tend to increase the precision of estimates of parameters and increase the chance of showing a significant difference between treatments, if one exists. For statistical reasons, it is often best to keep the number of replicates similar among treatments.

> **? Can sub-samples act as replicates?**
>
> The short answer is 'no'. Sub-samples are derived from the same original specimen, and this could mean readings or specimens. Statistically speaking, the degree of independence of replicates is highly important and sub-samples are not wholly independent. Replicates can tell you about variability in the measurement method but not in the quantity being measured.

Randomisation of treatments

The two aspects of randomisation you must consider are:

1 positioning of treatments within experimental blocks

2 allocation of treatments to the experimental subjects.

For relatively simple experiments, you can adopt a completely randomised design: here, the position and treatment assigned to any subject are defined randomly. A completely randomised layout has the advantage of simplicity but cannot show how confounding variables alter in space or time. This information can be obtained if you use a blocked design in which the degree of randomisation is restricted. Here, the experimental space or time is divided into blocks, each of which accommodates the complete set of treatments. When analysed appropriately, the results for the blocks can be compared to test for differences in the confounding variables and these effects can be separated out from the effects of the treatments.

> **Terminology for experimental design**
>
> Many of the terms used for experimentation originated from the statistical analysis of agricultural experiments, but are now used widely in science. Subjects given the same treatment are known as **replicates** (they may be called **plots**). A **block** is a grouping of replicates or plots. The blocks are contained in a **field** – that is, the whole area (or time) available for the experiment.

A 'Latin square' is an example of a method of placing treatments so that they appear in a balanced fashion within a square block or field. Treatments appear once in each column and row (see Figure 14.1), so the effects of confounding variables can be 'cancelled out' in two directions at right angles to each other.

A	C	B
B	A	C
C	B	A

A	B	C	D
D	B	C	A
C	D	A	B
B	A	D	C

Figure 14.1 Examples of Latin square arrangements for three and four treatments. Letters indicate treatments; the number of possible arrangements for each size of square increases greatly as the size increases.

Pairing and matching subjects

The paired comparison is a special case of blocking used to reduce systematic variation when there are two treatments, and can be used in a number of situations.

1 'Before and after' comparison. Here, the pairing is designed to reduce variability arising from the initial state of the subjects – for example, weight gain of mice on a diet, where the weight gain may depend on the initial weight.

2 Application of a treatment and control to parts of the same subject or to closely related subjects. This allows comparison without complications arising from the different origins of subjects – for example, drug or placebo given to sibling rats, virus-containing or control solution swabbed on left or right halves of a leaf.

3 Application of treatment and control under shared conditions. This allows comparison without complications arising from the different environments of subjects – for example, rats in a cage, plants in a pot.

> **Multifactorial experiments**
>
> These involve applying two or more treatments to the experimental subjects in a predetermined way that allows interactions among the treatments to be analysed by specialised statistics. They are economical on resources because of 'hidden replication' – when two or more treatments are given to a subject, the result acts statistically as a pseudo-replicate for each treatment. Consult a statistical text for further details.

Matched samples represent a restriction on randomisation where the researcher makes a balanced selection of subjects for treatments on the basis of some attribute or attributes that may influence results – for example, age, sex or prior history. The effect of matching should be to reduce the unwanted source(s) of variation. Disadvantages include the subjective element in choice of character(s) to be balanced, inexact matching of quantitative characteristics, the time matching takes and possible wastage of unmatched subjects. When analysed statistically, both paired comparisons and matched samples can show up differences between treatments that might otherwise be rejected on the basis of a fully randomised design, but note that the statistical analysis may be different.

Blind and double-blind trials

These are experimental set-ups where the identity of the treatment is concealed with the aim of reducing or minimising bias due to preconceptions about the results.

- A blind trial is one in which the researcher does not know which treatments have been administered to which subjects.
- A double-blind trial is one where the subjects are human and neither researcher nor subject knows which treatments have been administered to which subjects.

Double-blind trials are the norm in medical drug trials, and act to counter the well-documented placebo effect, whereby a patient may feel or even show signs of an effect if they believe they have been prescribed an active treatment, but instead have received an inactive (placebo) intervention.

For both blind and double-blind trials, the assignment of subjects to the treatments (usually randomly decided) and the key to this arrangement is decided by an independent third party who does not disclose this information until the results are collected.

> **Repetition of experiments**
>
> Even if your experiment is well-designed and analysed, only limited conclusions can be made. Firstly, what you can say is valid for a particular place and time, with a particular investigator, experimental subject and method of applying treatments. Secondly, if your results were significant at the 5 per cent level of probability (**Ch 19**), there is still an approximately 1 in 20 chance that the results did arise by chance. To guard against these possibilities, it is important that experiments are repeated. Many supervisors recommend that experiments are done three times in total.

SAMPLING

When carrying out research, it is rare to be able to observe or measure every individual or location in the population or space in which you are interested. In practice, statistics obtained from a subset (or sample) are used to estimate relevant parameters for the total population or area. Samples consist of data values for a particular variable (for example, sodium ion concentration), each recorded from an individual sampling unit (for example, a core sample) in a sample of n units (for example, $n = 50$ cores) taken from the population or area under investigation (for example, a particular geographical location). The term 'replicate' can be applied either to the measurement or the actual sampling unit.

When estimating population or location parameters from sample statistics, the sample size is important – larger sample sizes allowing greater statistical confidence. However, the optimum sample size is normally a balance between statistical and practical considerations. Sampling is often used in fieldwork where natural populations are to be observed under undisturbed conditions; however, the same principles apply in a laboratory context.

> **ℹ Definitions: parameter and statistic**
>
> **Parameter** – a numerical constant or mathematical function used to describe a particular population or location (for example, the mean height of 18-year-old females).
>
> **Statistic** – an estimate of a parameter obtained from a sample (for example, the height of 18-year-old females based on those in your keep-fit class).

At the outset, it is important to provide a complete description of the population or area being sampled, whatever its nature. Failure to do this will make your results difficult to interpret or to compare with other observations, including your own. You should take great care to minimise selection bias, otherwise population parameters inferred from your samples will be unrealistic and this may invalidate your work and its conclusions.

> **✓ Choosing a relevant population: factors to specify**
>
> The population consists of all those individuals or locations within a specified time or space about which inferences are to be made (**Ch 12**). This must be accurately specified by information such as:
>
> - exact geographical location
> - type of habitat or geology
> - date and time of sampling
> - age, sex, physiological condition and health of sampled organisms
> - other details relevant to your work – for example, an index of pollution or geological background.

A sampling strategy should allow you to obtain reliable and useful information about your particular population(s) or area(s), while using your resources efficiently. Selecting a sample involves the formulation of rules and methods (the sampling protocol) by which some members of the population or locations are included in the sample. The chosen sample is then measured using defined procedures to obtain relevant data. Finally, the information obtained is processed to calculate appropriate statistics. Truly representative samples should be:

- taken at random, or in a manner that ensures that all members of the population or all parts of an area have an equal chance of being selected

- large enough to provide sufficient precision in estimation of population characteristics
- unbiased by the sampling procedure or equipment.

You should decide on a sampling protocol before any investigation proceeds. The main aspects to be determined are the number of sampling units in each sample and, where relevant, the position of samples and the size and shape of the sampling area. Before this can be done, however, information is required about the likely distribution of organisms or other factor of interest. This can be even (homogeneous), patchy (contagious), stratified (homogeneous within sub-areas) or present as a gradient (see Figure 14.2). You might decide which type applies from a pilot study, published research or by analogy with other systems.

When choosing a sampling strategy in the field, the chief options are:

- point sampling, where samples are taken at specific coordinate locations
- quadrat sampling, where samples are obtained within a two-dimensional area
- transect sampling, where samples are taken along a linear track.

Table 14.2 outlines relevant matters to take into account. Regarding sampling position, Figure 14.2(b) illustrates representative strategies mentioned in this table.

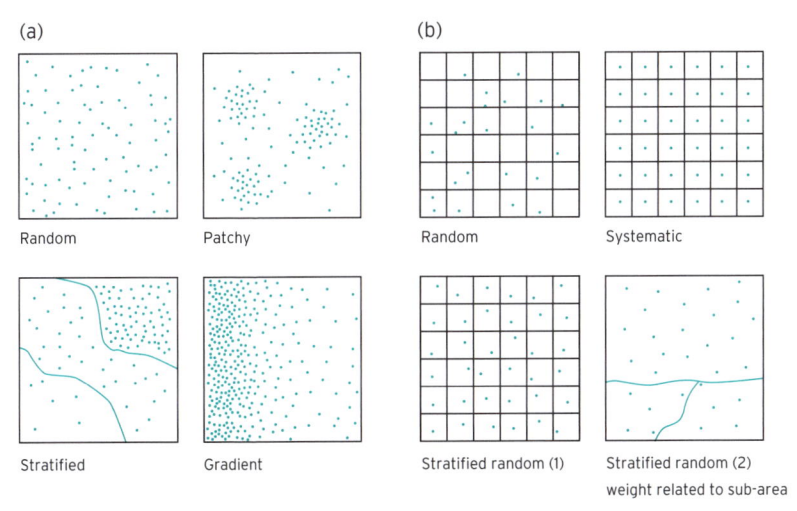

(a) Random, Patchy, Stratified, Gradient

(b) Random, Systematic, Stratified random (1), Stratified random (2) weight related to sub-area

Figure 14.2 Examples of (a) types of distribution and (b) methods of sampling. The terminology here is most relevant to field studies. In (a) the dots represent individuals, while in (b) they represent sampling positions.

14 Conducting experiments and field studies 145

Table 14.2 Issues to be considered when creating a sampling strategy.

The shape and dimensions of the sampling area
• Quadrats are usually circular or square. A circular quadrat has the advantage that its position can be marked as a single (central) point and the area defined by use of a tape measure, whereas a square quadrat may require marking at each corner. Transects are generally used when it is difficult to move through the site to positions.
• When the distribution is truly random, then all quadrat sizes are equally effective for estimating population parameters (assuming the total number of individuals sampled is equal). If the distribution is patchy, a smaller quadrat size may be more effective than a larger one: too large an area might obscure the true nature of the clumped distribution. If the distribution is stratified or graded, then the sampling area is generally less important than the sampling position. However, the size of the organisms must also be considered: it is obvious that you would require different-sized quadrats for trees in a forest than for daisies on a lawn.
• Small sample areas have the advantage that more small samples can usually be taken for the same amount of labour. This may result in increased precision and many small areas will cover a wider range of the habitat than few large ones, so the catch can be more representative. However, sampling error at the edge of quadrats is proportionately greater as sample area diminishes. To avoid such effects, you need to establish a protocol for dealing with items that overlap the edge of the quadrats.
Position of sampling
• In simple random sampling, the coordinates for sampling points are chosen using random numbers. Every organism in the population or location thus has an equal chance of selection, but the area may not be covered evenly. This method works best if the distribution of organisms or factors is homogeneous.
• Systematic sampling involves using some form of pattern or grid to select samples. The advantage is simplicity, but the disadvantage is potential bias if the pattern coincides with some periodic distribution of the population or factor.
• Stratified random sampling ensures that each part of the area is represented. The area is divided into sub-areas within which random sampling is carried out.
Number of sampling units per sample
• When small numbers of sampling units are present, values of sample statistics will be susceptible to the effects of random variation – especially true if the underlying spatial distribution is patchy. You may then be unable to demonstrate statistically that there are differences between populations or areas. On the other hand, measuring very large numbers of replicates may represent an impractical workload.
• If you do not wish to sample the whole of a quadrat, perhaps because the density of sampling units is too high, you can employ sub-sampling by studying a defined part of the quadrat ('two-stage sampling').

> **Sampling in time**
>
> If your samples are taken at different times, this can present problems – especially those related to logistics. In addition, if examining a phenomenon that fluctuates regularly (for example, with a period governed by day and night, or high and low tide), then the frequency of sampling has to be determined with that periodicity in mind.

PREPARING FOR RESEARCH ACTIVITY

If you want to gain the most from your research activity, good preparation is essential. Often lab procedures and field observations are tightly scheduled and you should prepare well for each session. You should, for example:

- know the theoretical background to the methods you will be using
- be familiar with any instructions or protocols you've been given or have developed
- have a detailed plan for what you will be doing, if necessary with minute-by-minute instructions
- make sure you have the appropriate equipment ready to carry out your work
- be ready to record the results or observations – for example, by preparing a table ready to write down data values.

If the methods you are using are new to you, then it may be helpful to discuss them with your supervisor or another student, postdoc or technician familiar with what is involved. If you are trying to replicate materials and methods from a research paper, there may be minor aspects of the procedures that are vital for success. Try to identify and copy these.

Much can be learned from 'trial runs' or pilot studies. These can help you work out where there will be difficulties in procedure and layout, use of instruments and other important limitations on your experimental design. It is also advisable to keep your initial experiments simple. For example, use a design that will provide a conclusive answer to a simple question; this is far better than over-complicating matters, running into logistical problems in setting up the experiment and collecting data. This may mean you end up with inconclusive results.

✓ Reserving shared equipment or facilities

In planning your work, make sure you have identified points in the research process when you may need to reserve specialist equipment or facilities, and so ensure that these are available when you need them.

WORKING IN THE LAB AND FIELD

The rules associated with lab or fieldwork will have your safety as their primary concern, so you must pay attention to them (**Ch 18**). You may have to work with toxic chemicals, dangerous instruments or in hazardous environments, so care is essential. It will be assumed that your early undergraduate training will have familiarised you with basic safety measures and legislation, including fire drills and relevant hazard symbols. Ensure you attend training events, if this is not the case.

✓ Giving priority to safety

Safety rules are common sense and should be part of your normal practice. However, be sure that you keep safety as a priority and do not become slapdash just because you've become familiar with the procedures or working environment.

Carrying out published methods and noting results

As noted above, you may need to follow procedures as indicated from a series of instructions, or detailed in the materials and methods section of a research paper. Always read these instructions right through before starting, as this may help you organise your activities. You may wish to highlight key points or lay out tables ready to record your data. The language of instructions will be very precise and should be followed to the letter or number – for example, success will often depend on the precision with which you measure out reagents, carry out timing or control temperature.

> **Use 'dead' time effectively** ✓
>
> During lab experiments, there may be delays between parts of your work as reactions develop, or as instruments complete a process. Use this time to look ahead to what you will be doing next, to create tables or graphs ready for recording your results, to jot down ideas for your conclusions or to read related literature.

Being able to record accurately what you see and measure is a vital skill in many subjects, but especially in the sciences. The following are key tips for recording your observations:

- don't rely on your memory – write down everything
- never write on scraps of paper (you'll lose them) – use a proper lab notebook
- always date each page and provide full details of the specimen or experiment
- if you are recording numbers, use an appropriate number of significant figures to take account of the precision (or, perhaps more strictly, the lack of precision) of your method (**Ch 9** and **Ch 20**)
- if drawing diagrams, make sure these have a descriptive title and are labelled clearly and comprehensively
- in the field, be prepared for bad weather – buy a special wet-weather notebook or take a clear plastic bag to enclose your notebook, and use a pencil as this will write on damp paper
- draw any graphs or tables according to the normal scientific conventions (**Ch 20**).

Always try to write up your work when it is fresh in your mind. You may be tired after a lengthy session in the lab or field, but if you delay for too long you may forget useful details.

ACTION POINTS

14.1 Read up about your methods before you start work. Having a deeper understanding of what you are doing and why will help you to work safely, make sure you do not waste resources through mistakes in procedure and ensure you obtain more accurate results. For these reasons, don't be tempted to skip this stage and move directly to the procedure itself.

14.2 Think in advance about statistical analysis. Work out how you will analyse your data – this may dictate some aspects of the experimental layout or sampling protocol. If you have some idea of the variability of the data, this may help you to work out how many replicates will be required to demonstrate a significant difference between treatments or samples.

14.3 Create a checklist of potential safety issues. Take into account the safety information provided in the relevant lab handbooks, lab notices and your supervisor's advice. Rehearse safety scenarios: imagine what you would do in different situations, such as if there were a fire, if a lab colleague swallowed a toxic chemical, or if someone cut themselves. This will make you more aware of the dangers of the lab or field environment and might help you react faster if needed.

15 DESIGNING AND CARRYING OUT SURVEYS AND INTERVIEWS

How to obtain relevant information from research participants

Surveys and interviews are useful tools for gaining quantitative and qualitative information from respondents and can be used in many disciplines. However, care must be taken in setting up and carrying out these modes of investigation so that you obtain responses of maximum value for your investigation.

KEY TOPICS
→ Designing surveys and interviews
→ Setting your questions
→ Carrying out a survey
→ Conducting interviews and focus groups
→ Analysing and presenting answers

For many types of research it is necessary to obtain information by asking questions of subjects. On the face of it, this might appear to be a relatively easy process. Find a person or group of people; ask a question; write down the answer or get them to write it down; summarise the results. However, difficulties can immediately be seen by considering the following questions about each of these steps:

1. Who will you select for questioning? Do you want them to be representative of a specific population, or is it appropriate for each person to be a one-off example?

2. What will be the form of the questions? How can you ensure that the answer to the questions will result in information of value for your purpose? Where and how will you ask the question?

3 How will you record the answers? What will you do with them after that? How will you ensure anonymity and data protection (Ch 18)?

4 How will you ensure that your interpretation of the answers, either individually or as a sample, is correct? How will you codify and/or report the different answers?

These and other issues will be addressed in the following sections.

> **Definitions: survey terms**
>
> In the context of this chapter, a **survey** is a mechanism for obtaining information from **subjects** – that is, people or groups of people who are of interest to the researcher. A **questionnaire** is a list of questions designed to do this. An **interview** is a meeting arranged for the purpose of asking questions of an **interviewee** (the subject) or interviewees. A **focus group** or **forum** is a meeting where **participants** discuss questions or issues raised, guided by a **moderator** or **facilitator**. He or she may take notes, or a **scribe** may do this; the interactions may also be recorded and later **transcribed** into written form. **Demographic information** is used to define sub-sets of a population of subjects or participants, such as their age, sex or yearly earnings, and the survey responses may be correlated with this information.

DESIGNING SURVEYS AND INTERVIEWS

The following basic approaches are possible, and you will need to decide which best suits your purpose, facilities and research schedule.

- Surveys – these can be conducted one-to-one, where the investigator usually writes down the responses to oral questions, ensuring legibility and consistency in format, or they can be conducted via a written questionnaire. You can administer this as a paper version or online, with the advantage in either case over an oral survey that it is possible to address a far greater sample of people in a given period of time.
- Interviews – these can be carried out as one-to-one or one-to-few live discussions conducted by an interviewer, usually operating from a script giving the questions to be asked and their order. Although time-consuming, you may find these face-to-face situations produce a more considered response from subjects than questionnaire

answers, and there is the opportunity to clarify the meaning of questions or prompt relevant answers via follow-up questioning.

- Focus groups – these are small discussion groups (four to six members is considered ideal), where participants, led by a moderator, are asked to comment on an issue or, for business purposes, a product or marketing tool. Focus groups allow you to take account of several viewpoints at a time, and to observe the outcomes of free and dynamic discussion among focus group members. A forum or workshop can carry out a similar function, and might consist of more members – often with a wider diversity of views and consequent loss of clarity in answers.

Regardless of the method used to ask questions for academic purposes, common principles apply. In essence, there are six basic rules:

1 Keep your survey or meeting as short as possible. Use the minimum number of questions required to obtain the information you need. You do not wish to waste the time of your subjects nor waste your own time in analysing irrelevant material.

2 Only ask a question if you have a clear idea of how you will use the information obtained. This means thinking through the various possible answers you might obtain and how you will analyse them.

3 Make sure your questions are unambiguous. They may not appear so when first written, possibly because you already have a clear picture of your area of enquiry, but this may not be the case for your subjects.

4 In deciding the order of questions, try to move from the general to the specific. There will then be less chance of early questions influencing responses to later ones. For example, you may run the risk of putting potential answers into a subject's head if you have mentioned certain key words beforehand.

5 Make sure you obtain appropriate demographic information. This will allow you to describe your sample accurately and to draw correlations between subsets of the sampled population and their answers.

6 Always pilot your questions and methods before using them for research purposes. This will iron out some of the problems mentioned above and other logistical issues, such as the time each survey will take.

> **? How can I decide what demographic information to collect?**
>
> This might be clear from the purpose of your investigation (Ch 3), but often can be less easy than it sounds because you cannot always predict how individuals from possible subsections or groups of the population might respond, and it is therefore difficult to predict in advance what categories it might be useful to demarcate. A degree of educated guesswork may be required.

There are both ethical and data protection aspects to surveys and interviews and the reports and case studies derived from them. It is important that you read the material in Chapter 18 and follow your university's rules and regulations carefully, as detailed in your institution's ethical guidelines. You may be required to:

- tell participants about the purpose of your study
- obtain signed clearance from participants to use the information they provide in your research, especially where this may be reported externally
- store participants' personal data appropriately and for a limited time only
- gain agreement of participants before recording their input and give guarantees about confidentiality and destruction of recorded material after transcription.

If children are involved, you may need permission from parents and to have a criminal record check done (the nature of which may be region-dependent). Your supervisor should be able to advise on this.

SETTING YOUR QUESTIONS

Survey and interview questions fall into one of two categories, either closed or open.

Closed questions

These are often used in surveys, but might also be used as an adjunct to more flexible approaches – for example, as an efficient method of collecting demographic data. There are six main types of questions that invite closed answers.

- Categorical. Here, respondents can only select one of the options – for example: 'Gender: M/F'; or 'Do you agree with the above statement? Yes/No/Don't know (delete as appropriate)'. Results are best expressed as percentages of responses in each category.
- Numerical. These request a numerical answer – for example: 'What is your age in years?' Responses can be summarised by appropriate statistics of location and dispersion (**Ch 9**).
- Multiple-choice questions (MCQs). These are useful when there are mutually exclusive options to select. This type of question will be familiar from assessments at school and university. The answers given can be summarised easily as percentages of respondents selecting each option.

> **Example of a multiple-choice question**
>
> Which type of research resources have you found most helpful in your current research? (Tick one box)
>
> ❏ Hard-copy reference books
> ❏ Lecture handouts
> ❏ Electronic encyclopaedia
> ❏ E-journal
> ❏ Textbooks
> ❏ None of the above
>
> Note the use of a 'get out' answer in the multiple-choice example shown.

- Multiple-response questions. These are like MCQs, only respondents are allowed to choose more than one answer. The answers can also be summarised as percentages selecting each option, but note that the total number of options selected may be larger than your sample size. In fact, the average number of options selected may be an interesting supplementary piece of data to report.

> **Example of a multiple-response question**
>
> Which of the following resources have you used in the past month? (Tick all that apply)
> - ❏ Textbooks (hard copy)
> - ❏ Hard-copy journal articles
> - ❏ E-books
> - ❏ Online journal articles
> - ❏ Primary sources
> - ❏ Blogs

- Ranking (ordinal) questions. These ask respondents to place possible answers in an order – for example: 'Place the items in the following list in order of preference, writing 1 for your most preferred option, 2 for the next and so on, down to 5 for your least preferred option'. The results can be presented as the most common selection at each rank or as percentages of respondents choosing each rank for a specific item (perhaps as a histogram). A 'mean rank' is another possible way of expressing the data, but this should be interpreted cautiously.

- Likert-scale questions. These are useful for assessing people's opinions or feelings – typically, respondents are asked to react to a statement, selecting one option to categorise their strength of reaction. Most Likert-scale designs use five categories, but some prefer to use only four categories, missing out the central neutral option (often, 'neither agree nor disagree'), to force respondents to indicate a preference on one side or the other. The results of Likert-scale questions are often treated as ordinal data (see above) and non-parametric statistical tests are applied (Ch 9). Responses to Likert options may be combined, as in the example 'over 57 per cent either agreed or agreed strongly with the statement...'.

> **Example of a Likert-scale question**
>
> 'Smoking is dangerous for your health.' Which of the following best describes your feelings about the above statement? (Circle the appropriate number.)
>
> 1 Agree strongly
> 2 Agree
> 3 Neither agree nor disagree
> 4 Disagree
> 5 Disagree strongly

Open questions

Open-answer survey questions require input from the respondent and are useful when you do not know all the possible answers, or you do not wish to lead the respondent. In a student survey, an example might be 'Why did you choose module P201?', or 'Please summarise your experience in the exam'. The individual text responses often provide valuable (qualitative) quotes for a report or case study. It is possible, however, given a reasonably large sample, to code and/or categorise the answers and present them in a quantitative fashion (**Ch 12**) – for example, in the form of a pie chart (**Ch 9**) showing the proportion of respondents giving each type of answer.

Question-wording and sequencing

The language used in questions is important, as is the order of the words. Questions should be written clearly, using 'simple' English (and with any necessary jargon defined). Make sure your instructions are clear and unambiguous. Not everyone in the sample will make the same assumptions as you. For example, if you write: 'Do you agree with this statement? Yes/No', unless given clear directions, some respondents may circle the answer they agree with, others may score out the one they disagree with, and some may provide other marks that you will find difficult to interpret. A score might look like a tick, for example. It is better to add a phrase such as '(circle your response)' after the question.

> ✓ **Carry out a test run of your questions**
>
> Try out the question set with a friend or family member before using it on real subjects. This may reveal problems with the wording that you may not have appreciated, and is therefore best done with someone relatively unfamiliar with your topic but who is willing to provide you with informal feedback.

You may wish to create a branching structure for your questions – for example, 'if yes, go to question 7…' – in which case, check that all pathways result in a logical series of questions (and potential responses) that ensure you obtain the required information for each possible answer.

Because of the danger that an early question might place a particular idea or concept in the respondent's mind and affect their response to a later question, you should try to move your questions or prompts from the general to the specific. For example, you might ask participants for their opinions on a general issue without prompting, then, later, ask them to comment on specific aspects of interest to you.

You should avoid survey questions that lead or restrict potential answers, unless there is a good reason for doing so. For example, a free-text question in a survey that neutrally asks for the participant's opinion of a political leader does not lead or restrict the respondent in the same way as a Likert-scale question that asks them to grade a leader on his or her response to a specific political issue.

CARRYING OUT A SURVEY

Selection of participants

You will need to consider ahead of time how you wish to select participants for your survey. This is less easy than it might seem. Voluntary enrolment, perhaps in response to an email request, might be biased to those who have the facilities or time to respond, or worse, those who have a 'bee in their bonnet' about the issues you have highlighted. Apparently-random selection methods, such as choosing people from the voters' register by lot, might be biased – not everyone decides to register to vote. Similarly, if you tried to select random passers-by for interview at 9 am, your sample might be skewed towards parents who have just completed the 'school run' and against those who are already at work. You may wish to provide an inducement or reward for responding, so that you attract a large number of answers. This often works but may also bias the sample, say towards those who are motivated by the reward rather than a desire to be open and truthful.

Distributing the survey

The simplest way is to print out and photocopy your questionnaire then hand it out or send it to participants. However, online survey software is often purchased under licence by academic institutions and there may be a specialist survey unit that administers its operation. Their experts can help you to organise your own online questionnaire and analyse the results automatically, according to your wishes. This approach can offer considerable time-saving in data collection and analysis, and a report can be produced in hard copy. Online surveys often result in detailed answers to open questions, possibly because respondents can select a convenient time to complete the answers. This may mean they can spend longer on the responses and can edit and add to them more easily.

> **Provide an estimate of the time it should take to complete your survey** ✓
>
> This will help respondents to feel more at ease and able to give considered answers, rather than rushing through the questions. For this reason, some online surveys incorporate a 'progress bar' so respondents can see roughly how much of the questionnaire remains to be completed.

CONDUCTING INTERVIEWS AND FOCUS GROUPS

Selection of participants

You will need to select your interviewees or focus group participants carefully, since this could bias the results. Choose participants according to a defined set of criteria, having discussed what these might be with your supervisor beforehand. For example, you might wish to interview people involved at all stages in a business process (shop-floor, administrative, management, marketing and customer); or a balanced set of students of both sexes representing different levels of study. You will need to provide details of the selection criteria in your methods section (Ch 23). Note relevant participant details, either by obtaining these beforehand as part of the selection process, or by asking participants to complete a short questionnaire at the start of the meeting.

Setting up the meeting or event

Before your planned interview or focus group activity, ensure that conditions are suitable for the type of research activity you intend to conduct. Make sure the meeting room is in a convenient and quiet location. Offer refreshments where appropriate. For lengthy sessions, include a comfort break. Ideally, an interview should be conducted at a convenient time so that the interviewee(s) will not feel under any pressure.

Think carefully about the seating arrangements, as this could contribute significantly to the success of an interview or focus group. Layouts where people feel comfortable with each other can contribute significantly to the success of the meeting. For one-to one or one-to-few interviews, participants may feel more comfortable sitting at right angles to the interviewer, rather than sitting on opposite sides of a table or sitting side by side.

For focus groups, interactions among participants are said to be better if a 'closed circle' arrangement is used where all members of the group can have full view of and make eye contact with all other participants. There are two schools of thought regarding the position of the moderator (and scribe, if present).

- If a part of the circle, they are in a better position to observe interactions, interpret body language and prompt development of the discussion. However, in this position the researcher may overly influence group members through body language or by making interjections to the discussion.
- If positioned outside the focus group, this may help the group to interact spontaneously. This can encourage the free flow of ideas and reduce influence from the moderator. A disadvantage is that it makes it less easy for the researcher to observe and interpret visual signals among the group members.

Managing the event itself

Begin by introducing yourself. Explain the purpose of the event and confirm the approximate length of time that you envisage the activity will take. When introducing the topic, it may be important to set a context, but try to ensure that this does not influence the participants or lead them to a particular set of answers.

It is essential to have an agenda for the interview or focus group and a list of question 'prompts'; if conducting a series of events, this may help when trying to ensure comparability. You may wish to start with a few questions to put the participants at ease. These might stem from responses in a pilot study, if you have done one, and can serve to produce background information to 'situate' the responses or discussion. The remainder of the question set should be defined by the aims of the project, moving smoothly from general topics to the specific.

> **Start interviews with a few simple questions** ✓
>
> If you start, say, by gathering interviewee or participant demographic details, this will help them relax before you introduce the 'meat' of the interview or discussion. You might wish to develop a short questionnaire for this purpose.

If acting as a focus-group moderator, you should have thought through a list of discussion topics or questions related to your research interest. You should also intervene in the discussion to prompt new topics or bring the discussion back to the point, because a recognised danger is that the group drifts substantially 'off message'. Avoid biasing any comments by leading the discussion yourself, or the tendency for focus-group members to conform to a middle view if they fear exposing a minority opinion. The following suggestions may be useful for a focus group meeting.

- Develop some means of identifying participants. When noting oral data, some researchers prefer to identify participants anonymously (for example, by giving them name tags or sticky label letters A, B, C, etc.), arguing that this emphasises anonymity from the outset. Other researchers feel that this approach is depersonalising and stultifies contributions. Therefore, they prefer to provide students with identifying labels or name tags on which are printed their first names. Either way, identifying contributors allows you to specify in your notes who said what and to link an individual's separate comments together. If appropriate, invite the participants to introduce themselves to each other.

- Use 'question probes' to encourage participants to develop the discussion further. For example, you might ask, 'Could you expand on that point a little?' or 'What do you mean by x?'. One of the strengths of interactive qualitative research lies in the flexibility it offers to explore areas that might be rich in the research context but that might not have been anticipated in a question bank created by the researcher/moderator. Therefore, make sure that your programme allows participants some scope to comment freely but within the time schedule. Otherwise, your interventions should only be made to ensure that you keep to the schedule and that the participants do not digress significantly from the subject – be aware of the danger of 'leading' the group. If a digression does occur, then use your question cues as a means of refocusing the discussion along the lines of your planned prompts.
- Stick to the prearranged end time. You may want to run other interpersonal research activities, and if you earn a reputation for taking up more time than you stated, these or other participants may decline to be involved further in your research.

> ✓ **Always thank participants for their time and contributions at the end of an interview or focus group**
>
> This is more than a matter of good manners: if you fail to observe the courtesy of thanking your participants, they or others in the target category may be less enthusiastic about assisting your research in future.

Taking notes of responses

Careful note-taking and fact-checking are important in interviews, focus groups and case studies. Most people find it difficult to act as both interviewer and scribe. In any case, good secretarial skills would be required to write down every spoken word.

For a focus group, you could ask a friend to act as scribe for you to allow you to focus exclusively on the questions and moderating the session. However, it would be useful to discuss the note-taking strategy with your scribe beforehand to ensure that the data they record is what you require. This might even involve trying a 'dry run' to clarify exactly what both scribe and moderator/researcher expect from the approach, including, for example, a method for identifying which group member said what. Some researchers also encourage participants to record their thoughts on a white board. If you decide to do this, you could photograph the notes as part of the record of the discussion.

Consider using technology to support your interviews or focus groups. With the permission of the participants, some researchers make audio- or video-recordings of the interview or focus group dialogue rather than take notes, preferring to stimulate a more natural discussion by simply observing the participants in the discussion. Some people do appear to relax more in these situations where there is no overt note-taking going on. If you opt to use recording methods, ensure that you:

- know how to operate the technical equipment and have practised using it beforehand
- have checked it out on the day to ensure that you will be able to hear the recording clearly on replay
- have sufficient battery power and recording capacity to last for the whole period of the interview.

Note that when audio- or video-recording, the participant answers might require transcription into printed format. There could be a time and/or cost penalty for doing this.

Confirm details of participant responses ✓

This will avoid you making incorrect assumptions about comments and answers. It might best be accomplished via a staged approach, where checks are made before moving on and supplementary questions are asked if necessary to clarify details.

Responses other than words may be relevant to your investigation, such as facial expressions, eye contact, voice tone and body language. If so, you may be able to develop a coding system for these, and include some record of them in your notes. This information could be important in your interpretation and reportage of the data.

ANALYSING AND PRESENTING ANSWERS

When explaining how your survey was conducted, supply appropriate details.

- Sampling methods. How were the respondents contacted or chosen? What ethical procedures were followed (Ch 18)?
- Details of respondents. You should provide a summary of demographics. However, observe good research practice by ensuring that the privacy and anonymity of your respondents are protected (Ch 18).
- Questionnaire design. The principles and rationale behind the design should be discussed and a copy of the questionnaire provided, perhaps in an appendix.
- Procedure. How was the survey administered?

In some interview situations, the material collected may be suitable to construct case studies. These might include participant information and background to the particular situation discussed, then lead into selected comments taken from your notes. Take care to avoid selection bias (Ch 13) when doing this.

The question types used in questionnaires can be analysed in various quantitative ways (see above). It might prove valuable to use a range of different (appropriate) ways of displaying your data so that your readers maintain their interest.

For approaches centred on open-ended questions, you may find it useful to code types of response using the techniques discussed in Chapter 14. The direct quotation of responses to open questions can be useful to enrich a write-up, with authentic comments illustrating representative points of view or opposing, polarised viewpoints. In some instances, this apparently qualitative material can be converted into quantitative information.

You may need to correct your respondents' grammar and spelling errors. When reporting responses this is generally acceptable practice, because it is true to the spirit of what was written and helps the reader focus on the main points made. You should add a note to the 'material and methods' section of your paper or report to explain that you have done this. Clearly, however, this would be inappropriate if your study were about language, and the inaccuracies in the responses were the main focus of the research.

ACTION POINTS

15.1 If you have a specific question in mind, experiment with different approaches that could be used to achieve a response. For example, you might seek the same information via a multiple-response question or an open question. Think which would be the most effective and efficient means of eliciting answers.

15.2 Plan a set of question 'prompts' and possible 'question probes' for interviews and focus groups. If your investigation involves either of these approaches, it will be worthwhile setting out a sequence of question prompts as the framework for your meeting. If you also note your reasons for asking the question, this will remind you to ensure through appropriate interventions that answers are focused on material that is germane to your research project.

15.3 Investigate potential methods of recording interview and focus-group interaction. Think about the equipment and related facilities that might be available to you personally, or ask about what you might be able to borrow from your supervisor or department. Test it so that you have a clear idea of how it should be used and that you can operate it competently.

16

THINKING IN RESEARCH CONTEXTS

How to apply method to produce valid, original ideas for your investigation

The ability to think critically and with originality is fundamental to project research and the consequent write-up. Your analytical capabilities can improve by studying relevant concepts, employing appropriate methods and watching out for common flaws in thinking.

KEY TOPICS
→ The importance of critical-thinking skills in research
→ Thinking at the appropriate level
→ How to approach a critical-thinking task
→ Being original in research
→ Putting forward a balanced and unbiased analysis
→ Fallacies and other flaws in thinking

Critical thinking can be defined as the ability to analyse a problem and present a solution to it. Your early undergraduate studies will have given you a chance to develop this skill. You will hone it even further both during the research phase of your project and when you write it up. The aim of this chapter is to help you to do this through a deeper understanding of relevant thought processes.

✓ **Always ask yourself questions**

One of the keys to critical thinking is to ask 'why?' when coming across any new fact, concept or theory. Developing this habit of questioning means that you are constantly seeking the underlying reasons for things being the way they are. In research, you must rarely take anything for granted and seldom rely on someone else's views.

THE IMPORTANCE OF CRITICAL-THINKING SKILLS IN RESEARCH

We routinely think without really contemplating what we are doing. It is perhaps only when decisions are particularly difficult, or, in relation to research, when positions and conclusions need to be explained, that writers focus intensely on the logic and evidence behind them. Laying out your analysis or argument in words is thus a key stage in critical thinking. Expressing thoughts in written (or spoken) language requires you to:

- refine and clarify your thoughts
- lay out the logic of your thinking so that it can be followed and understood by others
- understand and make use of the connotations and precise meanings of phrases and words
- find the right expressions to explain your meaning to others
- use language to propose or defend a viewpoint and persuade others to follow your rationale.

Hence, the writing process is important for critical thinking and, in turn, for research.

Contexts for thinking critically

Examples of research activities requiring these higher-level thinking skills:

- making judgements on the reliability of sources and evaluating their content (Ch 8)
- designing experiments, observations and surveys (Chs 12–15)
- arriving at a position and supporting it with evidence (Ch 17)
- selecting and using numerical or statistical methods to analyse data (Ch 19)
- deciding how to present results (Ch 20)
- drawing conclusions (Ch 22).

THINKING AT THE APPROPRIATE LEVEL

In 1956, Benjamin Bloom (a noted educational psychologist), working with several colleagues, identified six different processes involved in thinking within education. These have been popularly termed 'Bloom's Taxonomy'. More recently, some of his co-researchers (Anderson and Krathwohl, 2001) have revised the taxonomy in the following way:

1 remembering
2 understanding
3 applying
4 analysing
5 evaluating
6 creating.

The meaning of these terms is detailed further in Table 16.1. Bloom *et al.* (1956) showed that students naturally progressed through this scale of thought processing during their studies. Looking at Table 16.1, you may recognise that your school work focused mainly on remembering, understanding and applying knowledge, with only some analysing required, while as your undergraduate learning progressed, there was a greater expectation for analysing, evaluating existing knowledge or concepts and creating. Becoming a researcher demands that you refine these more advanced skills yet further. While there will always be elements of remembering facts, understanding and application in any research and research-related writing, what you will be judged upon primarily is your ability to analyse evidence, to evaluate situations, problems and evidential material and to synthesise new ideas.

Thinking about thinking in this way involves an advanced level of insight, known as 'metacognition'. Understanding thought processes at this 'higher' level will allow you to place your activities at a 'lower' level into context. Thus, rather than aimlessly trying to achieve a goal, you become more able to recognise the type of activity necessary to meet your target and then adopt methods that have previously been successful for that sort of task. In short, an awareness of academic thinking at this new level should aid you in performing better in all aspects of your research.

Table 16.1 A classification of thinking processes. This version follows the taxonomy introduced by Anderson and Krathwohl (2001), which was modified from the original organisation of Bloom *et al.* (1956). Those familiar with the latter will note that the term 'synthesis' has been replaced by 'creating' and placed after 'evaluating' in the listing, to provide what is thought to be a better reflection of the general progression of thinking activities.

Thinking process (in ascending order of complexity)	Typical activities characterising each level
1 **Remembering.** Having facts or other material that you can *recall* or *recognise*. This does not mean you necessarily understand it at a higher level.	• Defining • Listing • Identifying
2 **Understanding. *Constructing meaning*** from different sources, both visual and written.	• Comparing • Discussing • Interpreting
3 **Applying. *Using*** learned material in different situations, such as written or oral presentation of information.	• Demonstrating • Calculating • Illustrating
4 **Analysing. *Breaking material into parts*** and differentiating how these components *fit together*.	• Analysing • Comparing • Discriminating
5 **Evaluating. *Making judgements and recommendations*** based on a critique of elements of importance relative to the topic being addressed.	• Arguing • Deducing • Drawing a conclusion
6 **Creating. *Extracting relevant facts*** from a body of knowledge and using these to ***address an issue in a novel way*** or ***create something new***.	• Composing • Deriving • Integrating

> **Definition: metacognition**
>
> **Metacognition** – this has been defined as 'knowing about knowing'. In the context here, it includes understanding how you think and how you might apply different thinking processes to different tasks.

HOW TO APPROACH A CRITICAL-THINKING TASK

Suppose you recognise that critical thinking is required to solve a specific problem within your research, or to arrive at a position on a particular issue. The pointers below should help you to arrive at a logical answer. You should regard this listing as a menu – think about the different stages and how they might be useful for the specific issue under consideration and your own style of work. Adopt or reject them as you see fit, or, according to your needs, change their order.

- Define exactly what the task or problem is. An important early step is to make sure you have identified this properly. It may help to write down a description of the problem or issue – taking care to be very precise with your wording.
- Organise your approach to the problem. You might start with a 'brainstorm' to identify potential solutions or viewpoints. Typically, this might consist of three phases:
  1 Free-ranging thinking. Consider the issue or question from all possible angles or positions and write down everything you come up with. Don't worry at this stage about the relevance or importance of your ideas. A 'spider diagram' or 'mind map' (Ch 10) can be used to lay out your thoughts.
  2 Organisation. Next you should try to arrange your ideas into categories or subheadings, or perhaps group them as supporting or opposing a viewpoint. Arrows on a mind map might accomplish this in a simple way.
  3 Analysis. Now you need to decide about the relevance of the grouped points to the original problem. Reject trivial or irrelevant ideas and rank or prioritise those that seem relevant. This involves several further activities, discussed below.
- Assemble background information and check your understanding of the facts. You will need to gather or rearrange relevant information and ideas to support your viewpoint or position, provide examples or suggest a range of interpretations or approaches.
- Check relevance. Consider the information you have gathered, your thoughts and how these might apply to your problem. Now, marshal the evidence you have collected – for example, for or against a proposition or supporting or opposing an argument or theory. You may find it useful to prepare a table to organise the information and

help you balance your thoughts. Be ruthless in rejecting irrelevant or inconsequential material.

- Think through your argument, and how you can support it. Having considered relevant information and positions, you should arrive at a personal position (**Ch 17**) and then construct your discussion or conclusion around this. When writing about your conclusion, you must take care to avoid value judgements or other kinds of expression of opinion that are not supported by evidence or sources. This is one reason why frequent citation and referencing is demanded in academic work (**Ch 24**).
- Write up your thoughts. Once you have decided on what you want to say, putting this down on paper or screen should be much easier.

A useful strategy for analysis

The 'SPSER method' can be helpful when analysing complex situations. It is also useful whenever you feel that you cannot identify a theme or trend in your material. The approach helps you to 'deconstruct' or 'unpack' the topic. There are five elements or stages:

1 **situation:** describe the context and brief history
2 **problem:** describe or define the problem
3 **solution:** describe and explain the possible solution(s)
4 **evaluation:** identify the positive and negative features for each solution by giving evidence/reasons to support your viewpoint
5 **recommendation:** identify the best option in your opinion, giving the basis of your reasoning for this (this element is optional, as it may not always be a requirement of your task).

BEING ORIGINAL IN RESEARCH

Most original thinking tends to result in small-scale changes in academic understanding. Occasionally, however, major 'paradigm shifts' occur after important new ideas, concepts or discoveries come to the fore. These events sometimes involve a period of intense opposition from proponents of 'established' understanding (**Ch 3**). Even with small-scale changes in thinking, differences of opinion are part and parcel of academic debate and often aid the development of an idea by requiring the proponents of different interpretations to defend the logic of their position.

> **? How can I produce creative, original thoughts?**
>
> This kind of thinking proceeds best when you:
>
> - have a good all-round understanding of the topic – making it possible to create something new from these building blocks
> - make connections – for example, using approaches from one discipline in another
> - are not afraid of failing – and approach your subject with confidence
> - are willing to take risks – and be unconventional in your approach
> - have a personal technique for generating ideas – and for overcoming being 'blocked'
> - do not act as a perfectionist – and are willing to build on imperfect starting points
> - do not procrastinate – and find a way of starting.

Do not allow thoughts about practicalities to stifle your initial thoughts. What is required for originality is an initial focus on the generation of ideas, without these being constrained by theory or feasibility. You should delay the process of selecting those ideas that are viable as a secondary process. Table 16.2 describes some methods for producing ideas.

Table 16.2 **Six methods of stimulating fresh thinking.**

Brainstorming
This is probably the most-used technique for generating ideas. It means coming up with a range of thoughts about a topic before trying to make sense of it. The advertising executive and theorist on creativity, Alex Osborn, who coined the term, proposed that the four keys to effective brainstorming are: • think of as many ideas as possible – the more you generate, the greater the chance of finding an answer • encourage seemingly eccentric lines of thought – even your wildest ideas might give rise to further ideas and even solutions • resist evaluating the ideas until later – the process of judgement may stifle your creativity • look for associations between your ideas – this may give rise to new patterns of thinking. Most people use a mind map or similar diagram to capture their ideas, and this method can also incorporate visual concepts. A brief description of the topic should be written out in the centre of the page so it can continually be referred to.

Finding connections

This method is essentially a more focused approach to brainstorming. It involves three main phases. First, write down a short description of the topic. Second, try to tease out the different aspects of the subject. Ways of doing this include:

- focusing on each key word or phrase of the topic description in turn, to see what thoughts arise
- addressing the traditional six journalists' queries 'Who?' 'What?' 'When?' 'Where?' 'Why?' 'How?' to the topic
- viewing the topic from a range of different perspectives – for example, the different subdisciplines of your subject, different places, ages, protagonists and so on.

The third phase is to review and select from the ideas you have produced.

Free writing

This approach aims to get ideas flowing by making you write spontaneously, quickly and continuously about your topic. It particularly helps those with writers' block. First, find an undisturbed location and decide on a specific period of time to spend on the exercise. Now, write down your current theme and then start writing about it. Don't stop, just keep going, and write as speedily as you can. The idea is to capture a stream of consciousness. Don't worry about what you are writing or why, nor its neatness, grammatical correctness or spelling. If the text seems to drift off-subject don't be concerned – just keep writing (but try to return to the main theme if you can). Finally, after your allocated time is up, review what you have written and select the interesting points. Use these ideas within a further free-writing or brainstorming exercise.

Going on a 'thought walk'

This is meant literally – going on a solo walk to focus on thinking. Perhaps surprisingly, many great thinkers have used this simple method, including Sigmund Freud. Several aspects of the approach may be valuable:

- it gives you undisturbed time and space to think
- it gets blood circulating to your brain
- it seems that while part of your brain focuses on the repetitive motor action of walking, another part is released to think
- you may see random things or events on your walk that stimulate new thinking.

There are other variations on this theme, such as meditation, walking a labyrinth or having a workout in the gym.

Keeping ideas notebooks, sketchbooks, mood boards and inspiration boards

The straightforward reason for keeping an ideas notebook is to prevent valuable ideas being forgotten. For written notes, a pocket- or bag-sized book is best, so it can be carried with you for use at any time – for example, to note ideas that come when day-dreaming on public transport. Laptops, notepads and phones can also be used if preferred. You might also position a pen and pad near to your bedside to capture any ideas that come at night; inspiration at these times is easily forgotten.

Making random associations

This technique seeks to stimulate chaotic, unpredictable new thoughts about your topic. First, write down the topic. Now find 5–10 random words (nouns are best). You could do this, for example, by flicking through a dictionary, a thesaurus, a newspaper, a series of websites, or via an online random word generator. Now try to incorporate each word into a sentence about your topic. This forces you to think in spontaneous ways about it.

Many new ideas involve 'lateral thinking' – a concept first coined by Edward de Bono, a prolific researcher and trainer on the themes of thinking and creativity. This phrase means jumping out of past thought patterns and concepts ('thinking out of the box'). It involves challenging the assumptions or limitations that apparently define a situation, and choosing a new perspective on the problem. Unsurprisingly, then, it is important to support free and unfettered thinking. This involves resisting or moving away from the influences of others' prior arguments or work, one's own preconceptions or apparent boundaries. Finding a personal route to liberate your thoughts is essential for turning on your creativity. However, thinking with freedom should not be confused with being ignorant about your topic. New ideas rarely arise independently from a framework of understanding. This mental 'scaffolding' is important to understand the problem, the underlying principles and the language in which a solution might be described. You need to find a balance so your fresh thoughts are not overly constrained by these influences.

Your brain needs stimuli to come up with ideas. You can select these stimuli and try to focus your thoughts or set up conditions that support unpredictable new thinking. However, the results may not be immediate; sometimes original thoughts come in unusual places and at unexpected times.

✓ Reading and note-making as adjuncts to originality

Sometimes when you have no ideas, it is because you lack the seed to grow them. You might need to read around the subject to find out more about it. If stalled, finding a new source with a fresh approach might kick-start your own thinking. It is important not simply to read: you need to make notes (**Ch 10**), so you can keep things active and retain your thoughts. Your notes should contain three main elements:

1 notes about the subject material (**Chs 8 and 10**)
2 details of the sources, so you can cite these and avoid plagiarism (**Ch 24**)
3 your own ideas, as they appear through association as you read.

It is a good idea to keep a brief written summary of the problem alongside these notes and refer to it from time to time, so that your mind remains connected with the problem.

PUTTING FORWARD A BALANCED AND UNBIASED ANALYSIS

In academic situations, the outcome of critical thinking should always be balanced. This means that due consideration must be given to all sides of a topic. 'Bias' is the opposite of this even-handedness and arises because a person's views are affected by such factors as:

- a specific past experience or their life experience in general
- their culture or ethnicity
- their gender
- having a strong political stance
- looking at a small or skewed sample of sources
- having a vested interest in a particular outcome.

Propaganda is a rather more insidious form of bias that uses incomplete or even false information to garner support for a particular political or moral view. It may also appeal to base emotion rather than logic – for example, to sustain a racist or xenophobic stance.

Awareness, especially self-awareness, is important in minimising some of these sources of bias. This is not always easy to achieve. However, if you try to read widely around the topic, you may become aware of a greater variety of possible viewpoints on relevant issues, and some of these sources will also draw attention to bias in others. This will help you become more alert to this possibility in your own position. Discussing issues with others is another way of gaining a wider perspective.

When writing up your project, it is important to arrive at a position (Ch 17) and not remain undecided. However, you must balance your discussion. You should mention the conclusions of others, but also provide well-argued reasons why you disagree. At the same time, you should always strive to be open-minded and receptive to the ideas of others. If you really feel there is not enough evidence to support any conclusion, be prepared to suspend judgement.

Language can help you to achieve balance. In particular, try to avoid 'absolutes'; be careful with words that imply that there are no exceptions – for example: 'always', 'never', 'all' and 'every'. These words can only be used if you wish to imply 100 per cent certainty. Instead, it may be better to use the 'hedging' language typical of academic writing, such as 'this suggests', 'it may be' or 'it seems that', and 'may' or 'might', 'can' or 'could' rather than the more certain 'will' or 'would' (**Ch 22**).

> ### Definitions: bias, fallacy and propaganda
>
> **Bias** – a focus on a particular viewpoint or set of evidence, often at the expense of others.
>
> **Fallacy** – a breakdown in logic leading to an invalid conclusion.
>
> **Propaganda** – a (biased) selection of information or misinformation, used to persuade and so modify opinion in support of a particular cause.

FALLACIES AND OTHER FLAWS IN THINKING

The ability to dissect arguments is a key aspect of critical thinking. In some cases you will be trying to understand and counter a viewpoint, while in others you will be trying to construct a coherent view of your own. In both instances you need to assess whether the argument is logical or whether it involves a fallacy – a breakdown in reasoning. A fallacy occurs where an argument initially seems to be valid, but is logically flawed or is based on hidden assumptions that may not be true.

We can sometimes be bamboozled by a multitude of facts, complex arguments or strong rhetoric. You must look beyond the superficial and analyse the basic line of reasoning that is being used. Sometimes you will sense something is wrong and spot it immediately; at other times an error will only become apparent after close scrutiny. One of the best ways to detect fallacies is to study the basic types of fallacy and then, by analogy, extend this understanding to the argument that you face.

There are many different types of logical fallacies – one internet source recognises over 70. Here we focus on some of those you are most likely to encounter (see Table 16.3). Once tuned in to this way of thinking, you should observe that faulty logic and debating tricks are frequently used in areas such as advertising, politics and newspaper opinion columns. Analysing the methods being used in these presentations can be a useful way of developing your critical thinking skills.

Equally as important as understanding the characteristics of deeper thinking is an awareness of the hazards of shallow thinking. Apart from bias, propaganda and fallacy, discussed above, here are some of the common bad habits and errors that we all make from time to time.

- Rushing to conclusions. In the context of research, this means basing a view on very little or unbalanced reading around the subject.
- Generalising. This means drawing a conclusion from one (or few) case(s). An awareness of other possibilities is important to avoid this mistake. Also included in this category might be situations such as relying on too few observations or experiments, or not carrying out the necessary statistical analysis of results.
- Oversimplifying. This means arriving at a conclusion that does not take account of potential complexities or other possible answers.
- Unthinkingly adopting the approaches or conclusions of others. This can involve a lack of originality or a lack of belief in the validity of your own thoughts.
- Personalising. This means drawing conclusions based solely or largely on your own experience or being subjective about an issue.
- Thinking in terms of stereotypes. Here, the danger is of thinking in terms of 'standardised' ideas, especially about groups of people. This 'received wisdom' may come about due to one's life experience, gender, ethnicity and so on, and involves basing an opinion on superficial appearances, rather than the underlying facts.
- Making value judgements. These are statements that reflect the views and values of the speaker or writer, rather than the objective reality of what is being assessed or considered. Value judgements often imply some sense of being pejorative (negative).

Examples of value judgements

In the example, 'Australian wines are the best – they are full bodied and smooth', the assumption is made that the listener/reader will share the view that a good wine needs to be full bodied and smooth – a value judgement. Similar assumptions may be inherent in descriptive phrases. For example, if a person is sympathetic to a cause they may refer to those who support it as members of a 'pressure group', if they disagree with the cause, then its members become 'militants'; similarly 'conservationists' versus 'tree-huggers' and 'freedom fighters' versus 'insurgents'.

Table 16.3 **Some common examples of faulty thinking found in arguments.**

Type of argument	Description	Example	How to counteract this approach
Ad hominem (Latin for 'to the man')	An attack is made on the character of the person putting forward an argument, rather than on the argument itself. This is particularly common in the media and politics.	'The president's moral behaviour is suspect, so his financial policies must also be dubious.'	Suggest that the person's character or circumstances are irrelevant
Ad populum (Latin for 'to the people')	The argument is supported on the basis that it is a popular viewpoint. Of course, this does not make it correct in itself.	'The majority of people support corporal punishment for vandals, so we should introduce boot camps.'	Watch out for bandwagon and peer pressure effects and ignore them when considering rights and wrongs
Anecdotal evidence	This is the use of unrepresentative exceptions to contradict an argument based on statistical evidence.	'My grandmother was a heavy smoker and she lived to be 95, so smoking won't harm me.'	Consider the overall weight of evidence rather than isolated examples
Appeal to authority	An argument is supported on the basis that an expert or authority agrees with the conclusion. This is often used in adverts, where celebrity endorsement and testimonials are frequent.	'My professor, whom I admire greatly, believes in Smith's theory, so it must be right.'	Point out that the experts disagree and explain how and why. Focus on the key qualities of the item or argument
Appeal to ignorance	Because there's no evidence for (or against) a case, it means the case must be false (or true).	'You haven't an alibi, therefore you must be guilty.'	Point out that a conclusion either way may not be possible in the absence of evidence
Biased evidence	This is a selection of examples or evidence for or against a case.	A writer who quotes those who support his/her view, but not those against	Read around the subject, including those with a different view, and try to arrive at a balance.

Type of argument	Description	Example	How to counteract this approach
Correlation used to imply cause	A correlation between two events (that is, they appear or disappear or rise and fall together) is taken to imply that one causes the other.	'Whenever I wear this lucky jacket my football team wins.'	Point out that the two things are in no way connected, or that there may be other factors causing the event
Euphemisms and jargon	This involves the use of phrasing to hide the true position or to exaggerate an opponent's position – stating things in mild or emotive language for effect. It also involves the use of technical words to sound authoritative.	'My job as vertical transportation operative means I am used to being in a responsible position.'	Watch for (unnecessary) adjectives and adverbs that may affect the way you consider the evidence
False dilemma	This is offering a choice of alternatives when other options may be available.	'The patient can be treated with Drug A or Drug B. Drug B has side effects, so we should choose A.'	Demonstrate that there are other options
Repetition	This involves saying the same thing over and over again ('*ad nauseam*') until people believe it.	Common in politics, war propaganda and advertising – e.g. 'Beanz meanz Heinz'	Look out for repeated catch-phrases and lack of substantive argument
Slippery slope	This is the notion that a step in a particular direction will start a chain of events leading to an undesirable outcome.	'If we let one property become a house of multiple occupancy, soon the whole street will be full of them.'	Point out that progress along the chain of events is not a foregone conclusion
Straw man	This is where a position is misrepresented in order to create a debating point that is easily accepted or rejected, when in fact the core issue has not been addressed.	'Asylum seekers all want to milk the benefits system, so we should turn them all away.'	Point out the fallacy and focus on the core issue

As with bias, many of these errors of judgement can be avoided by reading more widely around your subject – either to take account of a greater selection of views, the way they have been presented, or the methods used to analyse findings. You will also need to look beneath the surface of what you read. It is important to decide whether sources are dealing with facts or opinions, examine any assumptions made, including your own, and think about the motivation of the writers. Rather than restating and describing your sources, focus on what they mean by what they write.

> ✔ **Being descriptive rather than analytical**
>
> This is regarded as a symptom of shallow thinking. Overly descriptive work relies too much on quotes, facts or statements. Being analytical, in contrast, involves explaining the importance and context of information and showing an understanding of what it means or implies (Table 16.1). Note that while some extensive description may be required at certain stages in research writing, this should only provide the foundation for making deeper critical analyses. Striking a balance between the simpler description and the more demanding analysis, synthesis and evaluation, is an important skill – especially at the writing-up stage.

ACTION POINTS

16.1 Practise seeing different sides of an argument. Write down the supporting arguments for different sides of the issue, focusing on your least-favoured option. This will help you see diverse aspects of a debate as a matter of course. Draw on the ideas and opinions of your peers, lecturers and supervisor. Discussions with others can be very fruitful, revealing a range of interpretations that you might not have thought about yourself. You may also find it useful to test out your own ideas via informal debate.

16.2 When quoting evidence, use appropriate citations. This is important as it shows you have read relevant source material and helps you to avoid plagiarism (**Ch 24**). The conventions for citation vary among subjects, so consult course handbooks or other information and make sure you follow the instructions carefully, otherwise your work may be downgraded on assessment.

16.3 Explore different types of fallacies and biased arguments.
There are some very good websites that provide lists of different types of these, with examples. Investigate these using 'fallacy' or 'logical fallacies' in a search engine. Not only are the results quite entertaining at times, but you will also find that your increased understanding improves your analytical and debating skills.

17
ARRIVING AT A POSITION AND SUPPORTING IT

How to sift fact and opinion and express your conclusions

As part of many research investigations you will need to arrive at a position on a topic, and express an opinion on it. This requires skills of research, thinking and argument, and an understanding of related concepts.

KEY TOPICS
→ Dealing with fact, opinion and truth
→ The nature of evidence and proof
→ Arriving at a position and supporting it
→ Putting forward your views

When analysing complex issues for any research project, arriving at a personal viewpoint, or position, is rarely easy. It requires that you:

- read and understand sources
- judge other interpretations or arguments being put forward
- check facts and assertions
- place your own results or thoughts in the context of the work of others
- arrive at a position
- express your position clearly
- support your view with appropriate evidence
- review and reappraise your position in light of emerging publications and your developing understanding.

You may have to do this not only to arrive at an overall 'position' for your research project, but also when considering narrower elements of the topic, such as your 'take' on a particular research publication or result. This is a multi-faceted activity, requiring elements of critical thinking combined with skills of originality, argument, academic writing and referencing (**Chs 16, 22 and 24**). There can be no formula for arriving at a position, as each specific issue must be judged on its merits. However, understanding some concepts relevant to opinion-making should help you to analyse what you read with greater clarity and thereby help you to form a view.

DEALING WITH FACT, OPINION AND TRUTH

When coming to terms with a wide diversity of viewpoints, you can easily become confused and lose sight of the differences between fact, opinion and truth. You need to establish what conclusions can be regarded as valid and what constitutes an unsupported viewpoint. Do not avoid the issues, but be clear about the facts, the truth and your opinion of the evidence, as well as potential flaws in your argument and the counter-arguments of others (**Ch 16**).

Examples of fact, opinion and truth

The world record for the 100-metre sprint in athletics was set at 9.58 seconds on 16 August 2009. This is a fact. The record may change over time, but this statement will still be true. Some claim that many world records are created by athletes who have taken drugs to enhance their performance. This is an opinion. There may be evidence to back up this position, but recent controversies have highlighted the problem of proof in these cases. Claims about a specific athlete's drug misuse are open to conjecture, claim and counter-claim, not all of which may be true.

A fact is a statement generally acknowledged as valid, and knowledge is built from a body of facts. In the context of scholarly thinking, fact or knowledge is the basis for further theorising or discussion. Typically, you might find a fact in a textbook, encyclopaedia or website. Not all 'facts' are true – they may change with time as new information is uncovered, and some may be hotly disputed. In academic contexts, therefore, it is often important to establish the reliability of the source of a fact (**Ch 8**) and vital that you quote the source of your information (**Ch 24**).

In many branches of learning, the concept of repeatability is important in relation to facts. Thus, it should be possible to repeat an observation or experiment that established a fact (**Ch 3**). This is one reason why scientists, for example, take such care to describe their materials and methods – results can sometimes depend on these factors. The unreliability of facts is often acknowledged: the error associated with a value is calculated, or an estimate made of the probability of a hypothesis being wrong or right (**Chs 9 and 19**). This information should be taken into account when assessing facts in a discussion.

> **i** **Definitions: objectivity and subjectivity**
>
> In any realm of research, concepts of truth and fact involve the notions of objectivity and subjectivity.
> **Objectivity** – involving a balanced consideration of the facts.
> **Subjectivity** – taking a stance on the basis of a personal opinion.
> Understanding the distinction is important for research work. The key is to produce valid reasons for holding your opinion.

Most academics aim for a detached, objective piece of writing, and your write-up will need to follow that notion – especially when analysing results or dealing with emotive or controversial issues, as in some arts subjects. Additionally, this may be difficult at some stages because you may be impassioned by your subject and the thrust of your findings. Of course, it will be important to state your own view at some point in the work, but you should couch this appropriately, using objective language (**Ch 22**).

An opinion is a view about a matter that is not wholly confirmed by the current state of knowledge or on a topic that may be regarded as a matter of judgement. Thus, in many fields – for example, in the arts and the social sciences – there is often no 'right' or 'wrong' answer, simply a range of stances or viewpoints. It is therefore possible that your position may differ significantly from the viewpoints of noted authorities and possibly even that of your supervisor. When your project write-up and the views expressed in it are examined, you will be assessed on your ability to argue your case and to support it with evidence.

Truth is usually defined in relation to reality – our current state of knowledge. That is, something can be designated as true if it corresponds to known facts. However, the concept of truth involves a host of philosophical concepts (including perception, for example) which may complicate the issue. In debate, something is only true when those on all sides of the argument accept it. If a particular line of argument can be shown to lack credibility or to be in some way unacceptable, this will add weight to the counter-argument.

> **Always try to maintain a healthy, detached scepticism**
>
> You should remain aware that, no matter how reliable the source of a piece of information seems to be, you need to retain a degree of scepticism about the facts or ideas involved and question the logic of the arguments (**Ch 16**). Also, try not to identify too strongly with a viewpoint, so you can be detached when assessing its merits and failings. In the research process, there is always the risk that you might pick out the material that supports your personal view without critical appraisal. It is important to be aware of such a tendency in your own approach.

THE NATURE OF EVIDENCE AND PROOF

The nature of evidence and proof differs according to discipline.

In the sciences, evidence will most likely be quantitative in nature, such as numerical or statistical summary data. This evidence will be the result of an observation or experiment. The data might have been obtained with the aim of testing some hypothesis about a situation (**Ch 3**). If statistics are used, it may be possible to assign a probability to whether the hypothesis is true or not (**Ch 12**). Even apparently 'on or off' qualitative results, as obtained, say, in molecular genetics, rely on assumptions and are capable of multiple interpretations.

> **Scientific method and falsifiability**
>
> The notion of falsifiability is central to scientific method, which involves continually updating our understanding of the world through provisional notions of reality – hypotheses (**Ch 3**). Falsifiability means that, at least in theory, the evidence can be tested by observation or experiment. Thus, whether the Higgs boson exists is a falsifiable notion; however, the idea that extraterrestrial beings have visited Earth and erased all the evidence is not.

The word 'proof' often carries a connotation of certainty that is unsatisfactory in such contexts. Unsurprisingly, therefore, to most scientists there is no such thing as proof: there is always a possibility, however remote, that an alternative explanation is true.

In the arts and humanities, evidence is more likely to be (but not exclusively) qualitative in nature; that is, a description of an event, an interpretation or an opinion. Here, proof is still an elusive concept, because it involves the presentation of 'convincing' evidence (a matter of degree) and notions of persuasion. This explains why many conclusions are couched in tentative 'hedging' language (**Chs 16 and 23**).

> **i** **Definitions: categories of evidence**
>
> **Anecdotal evidence** – that which relies indirectly on the experience of others, such as hearsay.
>
> **Circumstantial evidence** – indirect evidence.
>
> **Intuition** – personal feelings (hunches), obtained without the direct use of fact or reasoning.
>
> **Personal evidence** – obtained by one's own observations or experience.
>
> **Scientific evidence** – observations or data obtained or testable by experiment.

ARRIVING AT A POSITION AND SUPPORTING IT

During the literature-search phase for your project writing, you should make careful notes of information and other material you might like to quote at some stage (**Ch 10**). In addition, you should also be appraising the viewpoint of the writer(s). You will find yourself naturally attracted to some positions rather than others. This 'gut feeling' is a starting point for forming your own stance.

Before consolidating your position, however, you should carry out an analysis of points for and against all the viewpoints you have encountered. When reviewing this, you should try to be as objective as possible. Does the evidence support your initial feelings? If not, then perhaps you should re-consider your opinion. However, you should not necessarily be swayed simply by the extensive volume of literature in support of a particular viewpoint; it is the strength of the argument and the nature of the supporting evidence that should guide you. Here are some other factors to take account of when trying to arrive at a position.

- The guidance that you have received from your supervisor. Of course, you don't have to follow this, but there will usually be a very sound rationale behind his or her advice.
- The writings of noted authorities in the field. Again, you don't have to follow their viewpoint, but you should take account of the strong likelihood that it is likely to be carefully considered, based on research and defensible. In many instances, however, you may be faced with opposing positions.
- The views of your peers. This is not the most reliable of sources, but discussing the topic with other students may assist you in forming an opinion, either by being swayed by an argument or by feeling the need to respond with an alternative view.

In scientific subjects, you may model scientific method by setting up an experiment specifically to test a hypothesis (**Chs 3 and 14**). The data you obtain will then lead you to a position related to the hypothesis. You may need to demonstrate confidence in your own results in the face of contradictory findings elsewhere. You must take care, however, to consider alternative explanations or reasons why your results might not be as clear-cut as they superficially appear to be. It is always valuable to support your conclusion with reference to an appropriate statistical test (**Chs 9 and 19**).

In other subjects, you may find that the information you glean from observations through action research, grounded theory or phenomenology, for example, allows you to identify trends pointing towards certain conclusions. Continuing observational research might then strengthen your commitment to these conclusions.

In either case, how convincing your argument is may depend on the evidence you use to support your position. Evidence comes in many forms: from statistical/numeric sources, from structured argument, from quotations, from experiments, or from observation. You should assess all potential evidence for relevance and value, and you must make sure you cite the source of the information in your own writing, otherwise you may be accused of plagiarism (**Ch 24**).

Above all, you should try to produce a balanced conclusion. This is one where you are open about counter-arguments and counter-evidence that does not, at least on the face of it, support your case. You must explain what others think or might think, then explain why you have arrived at the conclusion you have reached yourself.

> ✓ **Taking care with concepts of evidence and proof**
>
> Adopt the following principles:
>
> - provide evidence to support an assertion or statement of fact
> - account for the nature and reliability of all evidence
> - cite references to back up an assertion or statement of fact (**Ch 24**)
> - be clear when something is an opinion rather than a fact
> - take care when using the noun 'proof' or the verb 'proves'
> - use hedging language (**Chs 16 and 23**) to avoid implying certainty.

PUTTING FORWARD YOUR VIEWS

Argument through discussion, and its more formal partner debate, is a vital part of scholarship. A valid position on any subject should be capable of being defended. Similarly, you should feel able to attack a position with which you disagree. In some cases, the acts of defence and attack are artificial devices to explore a position. The ground rules for this are as follows.

1 State your viewpoint. Of course, this requires that you have first arrived at a position on the topic, as discussed above. This view should be explained clearly – demonstrating, where necessary, the steps in logic you have taken to arrive at your view. A certain amount of background information may be important here.

2 Provide reasoning and evidence. As part of arriving at a view, you should have researched the topic (**Chs 7–9**), and this is your opportunity to summarise the key evidence.

3 Outline briefly the counter-arguments and your points against them. This forces you to identify and confront the potential weaknesses in your position, and is an essential part of arriving at a coherent viewpoint. If you have thought things through carefully, it should not be difficult to point out the flaws in other arguments, but remember again to use evidence to support this side of your case.

4 **Conclude.** This is where you summarise the key evidence for and against your position, the implications or consequences of taking this line of thought, ending perhaps with a final restatement of your case and why you consider that it is valid.

Various linguistic devices can be used to promote a point of view. General guidance on the structure, language and presentation of scholarly writing is provided in **Chapter 22**. Here, the focus is on persuasive speech or writing, sometimes called rhetoric. These methods are important because a poorly constructed argument will fail to convince.

> **Keeping attention and focus when writing your argument**
>
> When writing about a complex issue, it is easy to become mired in detail and run the risk of 'losing' your intended reader. Avoid this by returning to your key theme from time to time. You can use 'reminding' wordings, such as 'in relation to the theme of...' or 'this shows that...', which give you the excuse to repeat or summarise your position from time to time. Another approach is to 'number' your points ('Firstly,...; then secondly,...; and finally,...'), so readers will know where they are in your argument.

Table 17.1 outlines ten methods commonly used to persuade. It is easy to overdo some forms of rhetoric, and if used wrongly they may even be the source of fallacies (**Ch 16**). Moreover, certain methods commonly found in politics, advertising and bar-room arguments are regarded as unacceptable in scholarly work. These include:

- use of emotive or pejorative wording
- implication of certainty when this is unjustified
- making opinion sound like fact
- selective use of information
- unjustified simplification and generalisation
- use of exaggeration and melodrama
- unsubstantiated anecdote or invented examples.

Some of these approaches may be associated with propaganda techniques – that is, providing strongly biased or partial information (**Ch 16**). Using any of these methods will almost certainly lead to strong questioning of your conclusions.

Table 17.1 **Ten techniques for persuasion.** These are phrased for a written argument, as in project writing, where for 'reader' you might substitute 'examiner', but they also apply for oral argument – the word 'reader' here could apply to listeners.

1. **Provide evidence.** Back up your argument with relevant information that supports your case. Query the status of evidence that is used by those who oppose your view.

2. **Create a problem – and help solve it.** Convince your reader that there is an issue at stake and that your preferred solution is the best available. The more they identify with the problem or its consequences, the more they will be inclined to connect with your argument and, potentially, to accept your answer. This method is much used in advertising.

3. **Create a consistent and logical route to your answer.** Start with an initial point that is easy for the reader to agree with, and then move step-by-step towards your conclusion, with each element moving on from the previous. Make the connections clear. It will be difficult to escape from your logic.

4. **Give reasons for agreeing.** Explain the advantages of agreement with your line of reasoning and the disadvantages of disagreement. This will reinforce your position in the mind of the reader. Help the reader imagine the consequences under different scenarios. Explain why things are likely to turn out as you predict.

5. **Repeat your case in different words.** Restate your argument several times in the hope that it hits home. However, do not overdo this or the repetition may antagonise the reader.

6. **Get your reader thinking your way.** Why not use rhetorical questions to do this? These are queries that you go on to answer for the reader. They are a good way to engage readers and can be used to lead them to your preferred answer.

7. **Deal with potential objections.** Lead the reader through any objections that they might come up with, then try to counter each of these objections. There will be only one path remaining: to agree with you.

The following methods are generally *not* suitable for academic writing:

8. **Help the reader identify with your argument.** There are several methods for this: you could establish common ground and by extension a common goal; let the reader feel they are in on a secret; use humour; or personalise the issue and its solution.

9. **Mix up the way you express your argument.** Employ metaphor, simile and analogy to restate your points in ways that will engage different sorts of reader.

10. **Illustrate your argument.** Tell a story. Lead the reader via an interesting anecdote. This will help them imagine the issue and the solution. Use visual images, if this suits the situation.

One way to practise your analytical powers is by dissecting the arguments of politicians, pundits and seminar speakers. For example, when watching a televised debate, news report or sports programme, listen carefully for the ways in which the participants' points are made – look out particularly for fallacies, methods of persuasion, or the incorrect use of evidence. Also, when attending talks, pay particular attention to the techniques speakers use when presenting their views.

> **What's the value of understanding techniques of persuasion?**
>
> Not only will awareness about these methods help you structure your own case, it will help you to think about the way others' points are being made – particularly useful if you wish to counter their argument.

ACTION POINTS

17.1 Think further about the nature of opinion and evidence in your own subject. For example, how do authors present their views in academic papers and how do lecturers state their conclusions in formal lecture contexts? What types of opinion are expressed, and how? What types of supporting information are generally used? What can this tell you about the origins of facts in your discipline?

17.2 Reflect on the origin of your position on a specific issue. Think of a situation where you have had little problem in deciding where you stand. This could be a moral issue, a political issue or an academic debate. Why do you think the way you do? Think back to influences such as people, events or books. Why were you persuaded to have a particular viewpoint? How much is this supported by evidence, or is it, at least in part, intuitive? Would you have a problem in defending it in an academic scenario? What does this tell you about the way you should arrive at viewpoints for your research project?

17.3 Look at a specific issue from all possible angles. Choose one in which you are not yet certain of your views. The idea is to test whether your initial stance might be the result of unwitting bias (Ch 16), and whether consciously trying to see things in different ways changes or hardens your position. One way of doing this would be to imagine what the different 'stakeholders' in an issue would think or say. Even the act of thinking who these groups could be might open up possible 'takes' on the topic.

18

FOLLOWING GUIDELINES ON ETHICS AND SAFETY

How to observe good research practice in your investigation

For many research topics and methodologies, it is important to consider the ethical and safety aspects regarding your study. The precise details differ according to the discipline and the nature of the investigation.

KEY TOPICS
- → Ethical principles
- → Consent and confidentiality
- → Obtaining ethical approval
- → Plagiarism
- → Safe research

In a research context, the term 'ethics' refers to the principles, rules and standards of conduct that apply to investigations. Most disciplines have self-monitoring codes of ethical practice and your institution will operate its own internal research governance policy.

The types of ethical requirements vary among disciplines and your study must comply with recognised practice in your field, as well as the regulations that apply in your university.

You have a duty to familiarise yourself with relevant codes and be able to bring that understanding to discussions with your supervisor. He or she will be responsible for ensuring that your research proposal (**Ch 4**) complies with ethical practice in your institution, but you have an important part to play. Where necessary, your supervisor will help you prepare an application to conduct the research for submission to your institution's ethics committee. There may be different committees and rules for clinical and non-clinical research.

Ethics committees

These bodies comprise academics from within your institution and they monitor all research activity, including that at undergraduate and postgraduate levels. In addition to approving applications to conduct research, they also hear appeals where approval has not been granted, provide guidance on cases that are unclear and refer cases of research misconduct to higher institutional authority. Their procedures are recorded in writing and are available for public scrutiny.

ETHICAL PRINCIPLES

Any research project involving human beings should be characterised by protection of the human rights, dignity, health and safety of participants and researchers. This is achieved by observing three fundamental tenets:

- the research should do no harm
- consent should be informed and voluntary
- confidentiality should be respected throughout.

Research involving humans might require interactions with people of certain groupings – for example, people in their roles as patients, clients, pupils, parents or peers. The list is boundless. Regardless of whoever is involved and in whatever respect, these ethical principles must be recognised and followed, in practice as well as spirit.

Codes of practice for human research

These principles are enshrined in the Universal Declaration of Human Rights (1948) and in the Nuremberg Code (1947–9). These agreements have provided the basis for ethical research practices in academic research involving humans.

Ethical considerations may relate to non-human as well as human research activity. Important areas include the use of animals in research, cloning, human embryo research, stem cell research, *in vitro* fertilisation and nuclear research. In the UK, experiments involving animals are subject to Home Office approval. If this is required for your work, your supervisor will assist. Similarly, experiments involving genetic manipulation must comply with relevant legislation and you will be guided through relevant procedures if necessary.

CONSENT AND CONFIDENTIALITY

Participants may need to be informed in writing about certain aspects of your research. This is usually provided as a 'Participant Information Sheet', which generally includes the following information:

- outline of the purpose of the study
- invitation and reason for being selected
- explanation of the voluntary nature of participation and of the freedom of the subject to withdraw from the project at any time
- explanation of the procedure to be followed in the research and the time commitment involved
- advantages and disadvantages of participation
- assurance of confidentiality and anonymity
- information about outcomes
- information about the funding source
- names of the researcher and any assistants
- information about any sponsorship or affiliation connected to the project
- information about refunding of expenses, if applicable.

❓ How ethical is your research?

Unethical approaches to research can be inadvertent and unintended. For example, vulnerable groups may feel pressured into participating although individual members of such groups may not express this to the researcher – a hospital patient may feel that they will receive better treatment if they participate in a study and risk a poorer level of treatment if they don't. Consequently, your research design and consent forms must reflect your awareness of such potential perceptions. If you have any doubts at all about the ethical dimension of your study then you should discuss these with your supervisor to ensure that neither you nor your subjects are compromised by the research activity.

Particularly in the clinical area, a 'template' is often adopted to frame the explanation for participants. However, in many instances this is often unsatisfactory because the language used and the format and layout are often unclear to the non-specialist. Therefore, every effort should be made to inform participants about the project as concisely as possible and in 'plain' English – that is, in language that can easily be assimilated and understood by people in all walks of life. In response to this information, participants are then requested to complete an 'Informed Consent Form' that requires their signature. In some instances, a debriefing form will also need to be completed once the data-gathering phase is concluded.

Human participants – for example, those completing a survey – must be assured that their identities will be protected by the security of anonymity. This means that the confidentiality of any representation of data, whether in aggregated forms (for example, mean value) or as qualitative material that might be obtained from individuals (for example, opinions expressed through questionnaires, interviews or focus groups), is protected in any printed format. It is essential that written permission to quote informants be sought from them at the time of participation in the enquiry, with the proviso that identities will be protected when findings are reported.

Data protection

The storage and use of personal information is an ethical issue. In the UK, the Data Protection Act (1998) covers procedures that must be adopted. Consult your university's Data Protection Officer or relevant web pages for information and guidance on local procedures if you plan to store information either in paper files or electronically. Legislation apart, it is simply good practice to time-limit the period for which data will remain on your records – and to inform participants how their data will be stored, and when it will be deleted or destroyed.

OBTAINING ETHICAL APPROVAL

You should first read the guidance notes provided by your university's ethics committee or department. Consult your university's website for up-to-date and detailed information on approaches to research ethics. In addition to the ethical policy, there may be general guidance, information, discipline-specific advice and links to useful websites.

Once you have satisfied yourself that you have made arrangements to cover the ethical dimensions of your research project, you will be in a position to frame your proposal for ethical approval. Institutions will vary in the formats required. In general, you will need to provide information on:

- the names and other details of the researchers, one of whom (it may be your supervisor) will be nominated as the 'principal investigator', with certain responsibilities
- the title, purpose and duration of the project, and the location of the study
- the methodological approach to be adopted, and information on how data will be stored securely
- if appropriate, the way in which participants will be recruited, plus information as to age, gender and any inclusion/exclusion criteria
- measures taken to ensure that all ethical dimensions are covered in compliance with the appropriate research code of practice in your institution, including confidentiality in reporting results
- if appropriate, identification of the involvement of any funding body.

When preparing your research proposal and planning your research programme (**Ch 4**), you should make due allowance for the time taken to obtain ethical approval (your supervisor can advise on likely delays). Anticipated time delays may influence your topic choice. Where you decide to pursue your topic and need to wait for approval, make sure that you carry out some relevant work, such as a literature review, in the waiting period.

> ✓ **Consult appropriate texts and websites related to ethics**
>
> If you wish to know more about this area, potential starting points are Sana (2000) and Shamoo and Resnik (2009), but also consult the library catalogue or ask at your library for holdings specific to your discipline. Websites for the learned societies in your discipline will include up-to-date information about ethical aspects that may impact on your research study.

PLAGIARISM

Academic knowledge is produced after extensive study of the existing publication and developed through applied or theoretical research into the topic. The convention has developed that academics in their own writing cite the work of others to respect the original thinking and consequent ownership of that work – in effect, the intellectual property behind it. All academic authors are expected to follow this convention, including those writing project reports or papers. To fail to do so is regarded as unethical. Institutions and the departments or schools within them have come to recognise the need to mark out their ethical position in this area by having a formal code of practice on plagiarism, while some require students to sign a declaration to the effect that the work is entirely of their own making. A statement of this kind might be required at the start of your write-up (**Ch 23**).

> **Definitions: plagiarism and to plagiarise**
>
> **Plagiarism** (noun) – the process of taking another person's work, ideas or words and using them as if they were your own.
>
> **To plagiarise** (verb) – to take someone else's work, ideas or words and use them as if they were your own.

Regrettably, intentional plagiarism occurs at all levels of study. Some notable cases have been reported where the use of search engines, for example, has exposed instances years after the plagiarism occurred. Whatever the circumstances, the negative consequences can be seriously damaging – shame, loss of professional status, loss of job, loss of marks, loss of degree and even expulsion from an institution.

Avoiding a potential allegation of plagiarism should therefore be a concern of all researchers. The main ways to avoid the risk of unintentional plagiarism are to cite others' work and ideas correctly, to provide attributed quotes where this is necessary and to paraphrase rather than copy when using sources. These techniques are discussed in detail in **Chapter 24**.

SAFE RESEARCH

A fundamental tenet of ethical research activity in the spirit of international codes of practice is that the health and safety of all those involved should be a priority at all times. This applies to both participants and researchers. All research approved by the appropriate committee must follow defined protocols exactly. Any modification to the original proposal has to be referred back to the ethics or safety committee. For the purposes of undergraduate and postgraduate research proposals, although the student is acting as the main investigator, the actual principal investigator responsibility remains with the supervisor.

Those researching in laboratory- or field-based subjects, or in the workplace, will be familiar with the general regulations for safe research from their early undergraduate days. Any local rules associated with lab, field or workplace, even if familiar, will have safety as their primary concern, so you must pay attention to them. However, in some cases as a researcher you may be expected to take responsibility for acting safely. You may need to work with toxic chemicals, dangerous instruments, or in hazardous environments, so care is essential. At an initial meeting with your supervisor, you will be introduced to relevant safety measures and legislation, told about the fire drill and reminded of the relevant hazard symbols (Figure 18.1).

When working in a laboratory, you will be expected to wear a lab coat – which should always be buttoned up – and, if you have long hair, asked to tie it back. Eye-protection goggles may be necessary for some procedures, and those who normally wear contact lenses may be subject to special rules because vapours of corrosive laboratory chemicals may become trapped between the lens and the cornea of the eye. You should never eat or smoke in a lab. You should also keep your bench space tidy and quickly dispose of specimens or sharps as instructed. Where hazardous materials or procedures are involved, you will be told about the COSHH risk assessment and you have a duty to read this carefully.

Explosive   Oxidising agent   Extremely or highly flammable   Toxic or very toxic

Corrosive   Harmful or irritant   Dangerous for the environment

Figure 18.1 **Some of the main EU hazard symbols.**

> **Definition: COSHH**
>
> **COSHH** – an acronym standing for 'Control of Substances Hazardous to Health' – a UK regulation that came into force in 1999. This lays out the legal framework for risk assessment whenever hazardous chemicals, agents or procedures are used. Normally the person in charge of your lab work or field visit (your supervisor or a senior lab technician) will carry out a COSHH assessment, which should be displayed prominently and/or communicated to you.

When working with chemicals or live organisms, such as bacteria, take appropriate precautions:

- be aware of all possible modes of ingestion, including inhalation by nose or mouth, ingestion by mouth, absorption through exposed skin or inoculation through skin
- take special care with procedures such as pipetting or transferring samples between vessels
- note where eye washes and emergency showers are located in your lab and understand the appropriate procedures when you come into contact with chemicals
- know what to do to contain or remove accidentally spilt chemicals (you will also probably need to report such events)
- make sure you know what type of fire extinguisher or fire blanket to use for the reagents being used, and where these are located
- always wash your hands thoroughly after each lab session.

> **Always follow safety procedures, including COSHH requirements**
>
> Your university will have a safety office and policies in place for potentially dangerous procedures or to cover risks such as exposure to hazardous chemicals. Ignoring these would be regarded as a serious disciplinary offence. Completing paperwork, such as Control of Substances Hazardous to Health (COSHH) forms, should be regarded as an opportunity to learn about the risks associated with your work, rather than a chore.

For field research, you will be advised about appropriate clothing. You should take special care to use appropriate footwear and be prepared for a change of weather conditions. If in a group, you should stay close to the main body of people; otherwise, try always to work alongside another person, rather than alone. Any fieldwork researcher should:

- take a first aid kit (and know how to use it, following basic first aid procedures)
- leave full details of where they are going and when they expect to return
- consult a weather forecast before they leave and, if working on the seashore, find out about the state of the tides and plan accordingly.

Similarly, if researching in a workplace, you should follow local rules and be sensitive to the specific dangers associated with the environments you will enter.

ACTION POINTS

18.1 Brainstorm the ethical and safety dimensions of your research. Using this chapter as a guide, elaborate on these aspects and any others you should be taking into account – then research them fully. Where possible, discuss ethical and safety dimensions of research with peers and academic staff. This will raise your awareness of issues that can arise and may also provide you with some benchmarks against which to judge your own study.

18.2 Address ethical and safety issues as soon as you can. If there are likely to be significant ethical and safety dimensions to your project, ask to meet up with your supervisor at an early stage to discuss these issues and how they should be handled.

18.3 Familiarise yourself with the wider ethics guidelines that govern research activity in your specialist field. Often the guidelines are provided in the literature of the relevant professional association. Look also at the 'Materials and Methods' sections in relevant research papers to establish the norms for ethical behaviour in your field of work. Use a search engine to identify any major cases that have raised ethical issues in the research context.

DATA ANALYSIS AND PRESENTATION

19 ANALYSING DATA

How to manipulate and interpret your results with simple, effective techniques

Assuming you have obtained data as a result of observation or experiment, this will need to be summarised and analysed so that you can extract meaning from it. Typically, you may wish to summarise your results using descriptive statistics, carry out statistical hypothesis tests or perform database functions.

KEY TOPICS

→ Data capture and storage
→ Simple manipulations of data
→ Ordering, classifying and filtering data
→ Testing statistical hypotheses

This chapter covers a range of basic techniques that you can use to record, transform, order, classify and analyse the data you have collected as part of your research project. The tools required all exist within readily available word-processor and spreadsheet programs and the examples presented will refer mainly to Microsoft Word and Excel commands[1]. A complete tutorial cannot be provided, but the aim is to indicate the possibilities these products offer for those unfamiliar with their valuable features.

There are many specialist software products for analysing data, including databases and statistics programs that offer more advanced data analysis options. If these relatively sophisticated programs are required for your research, then it is likely that your supervisor will be able to make a recommendation; there may also be training courses to introduce you to the finer points of their operation.

---

1   Syntax and menu hierarchies as used in Office 9 versions of both software programs

Again, lack of space precludes a detailed treatment in this book – nor does it allow a detailed discussion of statistical methods. You should consult introductory texts, such as those in the '…for dummies' series (published by Wiley), or the companion titles *How to Improve Your Maths Skills* (Lakin, 2010a) or *How to Use Statistics* (Lakin, 2010b).

> **i Counterpart functions**
>
> Many of the Word and Excel commands or functions described in this chapter will have their counterparts in other software. The syntax and formatting may vary, but the operations carried out will essentially be similar.

DATA CAPTURE AND STORAGE

Data can come from many sources and be accumulated in many different ways. Examples include:

- written notes, perhaps from research papers or records of interviews (**Chs 10 and 15**)
- observations, perhaps from environmental or behavioural studies (**Ch 13**)
- questionnaire results, perhaps from an online survey (**Ch 15**)
- experimental results, perhaps showing results from replicates within treatment (**Ch 14**)
- numerical output, perhaps from lab instruments or environmental sensors (**Ch 14**).

Unmodified original information is sometimes referred to as 'raw' data. At some point such data must be 'captured' – that is, recorded so they are available for the investigator to analyse. This normally means stored digitally within a computer file.

In some situations, data may be accumulated in a 'low tech' format, such as handwritten notes or an audio recording of a meeting. There are considerable benefits for typing these up in word-processor or spreadsheet format. This will greatly facilitate ordering, searching for key phrases or coding for further analysis, as described in **Chapter 13**. Care should be taken with the arrangement of data, as this may need to be in defined arrays for some software functions. Additionally, suitable space may need to be left in the file (say at the top of the sheet) for the output of a given function.

> **Organise qualitative data in a spreadsheet** ✔
>
> If using a spreadsheet to store data, such as responses to an open-answer question, use initial columns to note demographic information about the respondent, then place the relevant text alongside. This will allow you to sort data according to the demographic information. It may be useful to use the first column or columns to provide respondent identifiers – perhaps their number in a sequence, or their names. The same principle applies to other qualitative information, where initial columns might store, for example: date, location, dose, height and so on.

As to 'high tech' data harvesting approaches, many modern instruments offer the facility to output accumulated data in spreadsheet format. This might mean, for example, a list of machine readings taken at specific times. Likewise, many software programs, such as those used for online surveys (**Ch 15**), can provide output in spreadsheet-compatible form – such as a file of typed responses to open questions. The advantage of this is that the spreadsheet can be used to order, analyse and graphically display the data. It can also be used to format the data for analysis in more specialist programs.

> **Organise your data files** ✔
>
> Some studies will have the potential to generate lots of data. These need to be stored using a naming and filing system that identifies the data set and allows easy retrieval at a later date. A system for copying and/or backing up these files is essential.

SIMPLE MANIPULATIONS OF DATA

Once data have been recorded digitally, it is possible to manipulate them efficiently.

Simple operations and transformations on numerical data

A spreadsheet is excellent when routine and repeated calculations are required. Examples would be finding sums or means of columns, rows or arrays, or entering source data into a standard formula. If the format of these calculations is likely to be similar each time, then it may be worthwhile to build a spreadsheet template for entering the data in the form of an 'empty' table with preconfigured formulae in relevant cells.

> ✓ **Use dummy data to test your spreadsheet formulae**
>
> These entries can be simplified to provide an easily calculated check on any formula used. You can also evolve a better design by testing on dummy values. Perfect the output so it is arranged to suit your needs – for example, for creating a graph of the data.

Often, you may wish to carry out some mathematical operation on a datum or to all the data in a data set. At its most basic level, this could mean multiplying numerical data by some factor, so they are in appropriate units. For example, you may also need to convert data in non-SI units into their SI equivalents (**Ch 20**) using an appropriate conversion factor.

Where raw data have been downloaded to a spreadsheet file page (or 'sheet'), you might carry out a mathematical transformation by creating a new 'mirror' sheet in which all the original data have been subject to a mathematical operation but appear in the same relative position. For example, the function **'=Sheet2!A1*0.9144'** placed in cell A1 in sheet 1 would convert a number in yards into one in metres, and this formula could be copied to other relevant cells. In this situation, it might be a good idea to give the different sheets appropriate titles rather than accepting the Excel default.

Other transformations may involve using data within a mathematical formula to achieve a new value of interest. This might involve multiplying by a constant stored in a relative address, or using cells in different arrays. Spreadsheets are extremely valuable for carrying out this type of analysis, which would otherwise involve tedious calculator work with a high possibility of human error.

Another type of transformation is used in statistics where the frequency distribution of the data set can be manipulated to follow more closely a 'Normal' distribution (a feature often assumed in statistical tests). This means that a mathematical function is applied to each datum. For example, the square root function might be applied to a set of data where there is a positive skew about the mean by using the function **'=SQRT(Sheet2![cell address])'**. However, extreme care should be taken when using transformations as they can sometimes lead to violations of other assumptions of the statistical test.

One benefit of using a spreadsheet is that detailed numerical data can be shown with an appropriate number of decimal places or significant figures (Ch 20), which can aid interpretation. The exact number will effectively be hidden from view, but will always be used in any calculations referencing the relevant cells.

> ### Data presentation in Excel
>
> The following are ways in which you can simplify data presentation:
>
> - store raw data in background sheets and calculate 'display' data in an appropriate format within the top sheet
> - 'hide' certain rows or columns of data
> - 'freeze panes' to show headings for columns and the rows you are working on underneath – for example, this allows you to scroll through multiple rows of data while still viewing the heading in an early row.
>
> Consult the 'help' menu for assistance with these functions.

Standard statistical functions

Data stored in an array in a spreadsheet are amenable to various statistical functions. Some useful Excel examples, assuming a data set stored in an array (for example, **A1:F15**), include:

- '**=AVERAGE(array)**', which would return the mean of the data in the array
- '**=STDEV(array)**', which would return the sample standard deviation of the data set
- '**=VAR(array)**', which would return the sample variance of the data set
- '**=COUNT(array)**', which would return the number of cells in the array with data present
- '**=MIN(array)**', which would return the lowest value
- '**=MAX(array)**', which would return the highest value
- '**=MEDIAN(array)**', which would return the median value.

Under the Data>Data Analysis>Analysis Tools menu within Excel, there is also an option to output a set of descriptive statistics for a single vertical array of data or sets of data arranged in columns or rows. The output can be placed in specified cells, sheet or workbook, as desired. This function provides 13 automatically generated statistics, including mean, standard deviation, median, mode, range and so on (for an example, see Figure 19.1). These can then be accessed for use in other calculations.

	A	B	C	D	E	F	G	H
1	My data set		Descriptive statistics			Frequency distribution		
2	10		My data					
3	12					Bins array	Classes	Frequency
4	14		Mean	14.33333		8	6.1-8.0	0
5	11		Standard error	0.673772		10	8.1-10.0	1
6	13		Median	14		12	10.1-12.0	3
7	13		Mode	16		14	12.1-14.0	4
8	16		Standard deviation	2.609506		16	14.1-16.0	5
9	14		Sample variance	6.809524		18	16.1-18.0	1
10	16		Kurtosis	0.151593		20	18.1-20.0	1
11	15		Skewness	0.329824		22	20.1-22.0	0
12	17		Range	10				
13	16		Minimum	10				
14	12		Maximum	20				
15	16		Sum	215				
16	20		Count	15				

Figure 19.1 Descriptive statistics and frequency distribution produced from an array of source data using Excel (Office 9 version). This screenshot shows the source data entered under the heading 'My data set' in cells A2:A16. The 'Descriptive statistics' command on the Data>Data Analysis>Analysis Tools menu was then used to produce the table under the header 'Descriptive statistics', with the data output array selected as cell C2. Note that the source data must be in a vertical column or horizontal row for data entry. The output as shown is uncorrected for appropriate significant figures (**Ch 20**). The frequency distribution was produced from the same array of source data using the Excel function =**Frequency(data_array, bins_array)**. The values under the 'Bins array' heading were user-defined beforehand and show the desired upper limits of the frequency classes – for a more complex data set this could be decided with reference to the 'Range, Minimum and Maximum' values following a similar descriptive statistics analysis. The 'Classes' array was also user-defined as text entries and would provide suitable *x*-axis values for a histogram representation, if desired. Next, the output array cells (H4:H11) were selected and the formula typed with data_array selected as A2:A16 and bins_array as F4:F11. To complete the output this was entered as an array formula by keying <Ctrl> + <Shift> + <Enter>. The output indicates, for example, that four data values were found in the class 12.1–14.0.

ORDERING, CLASSIFYING AND FILTERING DATA

One common means of simplifying large data sets is the frequency distribution, which indicates the number of values within a data set appearing within a designated value range. The function **'FREQUENCY(data_array, bins_array)'** in Excel creates a frequency distribution for a data array (for an example, see Figure 19.1). These summary data can then be used in a graphical representation – for example, using a histogram chart.

Simple alphabetical and numerical sorting is possible, within both Word and Excel, with options for ascending and descending order. The Word sort function (A↓Z) can be used at multiple levels – for example, to sort tabulated data firstly by one column's entries and then by another. Excel has a 'sort and filter' function that allows basic database operations to be carried out (Home> Sort & Filter). The 'sort' option allows data in a specified column to be sorted by value (A being low and Z being high), a cell or font colour or a specific icon, if these have been used in a preliminary classification of the data. The 'filter' option allows, for example, only entries with a particular key word to be visible within the spreadsheet – a particularly useful feature when reviewing complex data sets.

Database or spreadsheet?

If you are tempted to use a standard database for storing your data, it may be worth exploring whether the functions you need can be carried out within a spreadsheet, which might be much simpler to set up.

Conditional functions in Excel can be useful where the data stored are in words or are alphanumeric. For example, the function **'=COUNTIF(A1:A20, 'painful')'**, would return the number of cells containing the word 'painful'. When using these functions, care needs to be taken that all original entries are spelt correctly. This might be ensured via a quick spell-check on the data before starting.

Text formulas

Excel allows a number of useful functions to be applied to text entries – for example: 'LOWER' converts uppercase letters in text strings into lowercase; 'REPLACE' allows a given text string to be substituted with another.

Excel offers opportunities for organising the coding exercises described in **Chapter 13** that allow aspects of qualitative data to be treated as quantitative data. The coding can be entered in adjacent columns to the qualitative data in hierarchical fashion (ideally to the left). Thus, in column one, codes 1, 2, 3 and so on might be used to refer to different aspects of the data, whereas in column two each of these codes might then be further sub-classified numerically 1, 2, 3 and so on. This system allows the coding system to develop 'organically' as the data are reviewed, and a sub-category might even be elevated to higher status if enough values were recorded. The number of values with a specific code can be found by using **=COUNTIF(array)** functions in an Excel formula, and these functions can be nested using the conditional **=IF function** for finding data with specific sub-codes. For example, the formula **=IF(COUNTIF(D1:D7,1),COUNTIF(E1:E7,2))** returns the number of rows in which 1 appears in column D and 2 also appears in column E.

TESTING STATISTICAL HYPOTHESES

All the common types of hypothesis-testing statistical methods (**Ch 9**) can be carried out within Excel. Depending on the test, the output either provides an exact probability associated with the result found, or some statistic that can be compared with a reference value generated using a spreadsheet function.

> **✓ Always check the assumptions of any statistical tests you use**
>
> A danger when using spreadsheets and other statistical software is that the assumptions underpinning the test may be invalid (**Ch 9**). Parametric tests assume that data are distributed according to the Normal distribution, and some parametric tests assume that the variances of compared data sets are similar. There are methods of testing whether these assumptions are correct, and a statistical text should be consulted if you need to do this. If the assumptions are likely to be unsound, then a non-parametric test (**Ch 9**) may be used instead.

Student's *t*-test

This is used to compare two means, where the samples they are derived from are thought to differ in some way – perhaps in a simple experiment with a control and treatment. In Excel, the function '**=TTEST(array1,array2)**' returns the probability of the difference between the two samples arising by chance, assuming they came from the same original population (the null hypothesis, **Ch 9**). If this is less than 0.05, then by convention the null hypothesis can be rejected and the alternative – that there is a genuine difference – may be accepted.

Chi-squared test (χ^2)

This is used to compare observed against expected values – for example, where there is some theoretical reason for expecting a particular value or ratio (such as in Mendelian genetics). In Excel, the function '**=CHITEST(Actual_range,expected_range)**' returns a value for the test of independence, whose significance can be found from tables or calculated using the Excel function CHIDIST.

Analysis of variance (ANOVA)

This test is used to compare means among several groups and is suited to situations where, for example, there are more than two treatments. In Excel, the relevant tool is available under Data>Data Analysis. In some versions, this is an 'add-in' that has to be downloaded.

Other tests are available using Excel, including tests for correlation, and of course it is possible to use your own formulae to carry out a test – for example, a non-parametric test relevant to your study, say by applying formulae obtained from a statistical textbook.

> **ACTION POINTS**
>
> **19.1 Seek out and attend relevant training sessions.** If the information in this chapter prompts you to learn more, you may find that your university organises training sessions for people in your position. Time spent learning about advanced features of word processors or spreadsheets could save time in the long run, and if you feel you may need to use specialist software, such as a database, this might also be a route to learn about their functions and use.
>
> **19.2 Explore the functions available on your spreadsheet.** A trawl through the menus under the 'Formulas' tab in Excel will reveal many functions of potential interest. Usually there is a relatively user-friendly explanation of how to use these.

19.3 If your research requires you to carry out statistical tests routinely, check out the options in Excel. The program may already incorporate the exact test you wish to use as a function, but otherwise it is not too difficult to lay out a spreadsheet to carry out the underlying calculations of any test, with the advantage that once this has been created it has the potential to be used repeatedly.

20 PRESENTING DATA

How to display information, graphs and tables to academic standard

The expectation is that you will present your research data to the high standards and style adopted in publications within your research discipline. This requires both an understanding of the principles involved and great attention to detail.

KEY TOPICS
- Presenting simple numerical and qualitative data
- Creating effective graphs
- Using spreadsheet charts
- Creating effective tables

A number of academic conventions apply to the presentation of data, including often rigorous standards for displaying graphs and tables. These rules have arisen, in the main, so that results can be assimilated easily by the readers of reports and research papers. You will need to know and apply these conventions, otherwise you may lose credit. Moreover, when producing graphs and tables using standard 'office' software (usually a spreadsheet and word-processor program

> **Create figures and tables as you go along**
>
> Figures and tables can be extremely time-consuming to produce to the required standard, so avoid leaving this task until the end of your research period. If you store the source data for graphs in spreadsheet form, then you can experiment with and perfect their presentation during gaps in your research programme. Similarly, tables can be formatted ahead of time as separate word-processed files and can be transferred to your report or paper later.

respectively) you will need to understand what is expected so that, where necessary, you can adjust the default output for incorporation in your project write-up.

PRESENTING SIMPLE NUMERICAL AND QUALITATIVE DATA

The simplest forms of numerical data are usually integers or real numbers. An integer is a number with no fractional element. It can be positive, negative or zero. A real number can be positive or negative but can have a fractional element, and this includes numbers with digits after a decimal point.

In academic writing, adopt the following conventions when reporting numbers:

- for integer values up to ten, express in words ('No more than three treatments were used…')
- for integer numbers above ten, figures should be used ('In this survey, 35 people were interviewed')
- spell out integer numbers at the beginning of a sentence ('Thirty-five people were interviewed…')
- spell out high numbers that can be written in two words ('six hundred'); with a number like 4,200,000, you also have the choice of writing '4.2 million'
- always spell out indefinite numbers ('hundreds of soldiers') or fractions ('seven-eighths')
- always use figures for dates, times, currency or to give technical details ('5-amp fuse')
- hyphenate numbers (twenty-five) and fractions (three-fifths) appropriately.

Real numbers may arise if you have measured something accurately or calculated a mean or similar descriptive statistic (**Ch 9**) from replicate measurements.

Particularly in the latter case, the resulting data may include more significant figures (digits) than is justified by the method of measurement. In these instances it is important when reporting data to reduce the number of significant figures after the decimal point appropriately. The number of significant figures chosen should reflect the precision of measurement techniques and tolerance of measuring equipment. To reduce the number of significant figures you must 'round' your data up or down as appropriate. Table 20.1 provides examples and further explanation.

Table 20.1 **Tips for dealing with significant figures, decimal places and rounding.**

Tips	Examples
When choosing an appropriate number of significant figures to use, consider the accuracy of your original measurements. Round up or down to the nearest whole number of your finest measurement division.	If you measured a specimen using a Perspex ruler, you would quote a length (say) of 134 mm rather than 133.8, which would imply an accuracy probably not possible with that device; on the other hand, it might be possible to measure to that level of accuracy using Vernier calipers.
Sometimes it may be appropriate to present data with a particular number of decimal places (the number of digits after the decimal point). Round up or down as appropriate.	• 56.78478 to two decimal places is 56.78 • 56.78478 to three decimal places is 56.785
To round a number to a particular number of significant figures (or decimal places), pay attention to the number immediately to the right of the last relevant position: • if this is less than 5, cut off all the digits to the right (rounding down) • if it is greater than 5, cut off all the digits to the right and add one to the number in the last relevant position (rounding up) • if it is exactly five, then the convention is to round to the nearest even number (but if your data include both positive and negative numbers, the latter should be rounded to the nearest odd number to avoid bias).	• Imagine that your calculations give you a reading of 5.46192. To round this to give three significant figures, this becomes 5.46. It would become 5.462 with four significant figures. • If the original number were 5.675, this would become 5.68 to two decimal places; however, 5.685 would also become 5.68 to two decimal places. • If the data set included negative numbers, then −5.685 would become -5.69 to two decimal places.
Always round after you have done a calculation, not before.	The area in cm^2 of a rectangular piece of carpet where the sides have been measured to the nearest mm as 1286 x 1237 would be 15,908 cm^2, not 129 x 124 cm = 15,996 cm^2.
When carrying out a calculation using values with differing accuracy, the one with the least number of significant figures should be used to define the number of significant figures used in the answer. Note that mathematical constants such as π are assumed to have an infinite number of significant figures.	• 12.232 − 9.2 = 3.0 (*not* 3.032) • 176 x 1.573 = 277 (*not* 276.848) • Converting 1456 m to km, this is 1.456 km, *not* 1 or 1.5 km
Take care where zeros are involved: • for numbers with no leading zeros, the number of significant figures is equal to the number of digits • with leading zeros, the significant figures start after the last leading zero • 'internal' zeros count as significant figures • trailing zeros are not regarded as significant figures in whole numbers • trailing zeros can be significant if they come after the decimal point, as they imply a certain accuracy of measurement.	• 94.8263 has six significant figures • 0.0000465 has three significant figures • 0.00044304 has five significant figures • 2300 has two significant figures • 10.10 cm has four significant figures.

> **? When should I carry out rounding?**
>
> Always round after your calculations are complete, as doing this at an intermediate stage can introduce a 'rounding error' when information is lost from the component numbers, as illustrated in Table 20.1.

Most academic work adheres to the SI for presentation of dimensions and units. The SI follows the principles of engineering notation – very large or small numbers are given as a number between 0.1 and 1000, multiplied by an appropriate power of ten – normally one divisible by three.

> **i Example of SI notation**
>
> Instead of writing 0.0005638, you should write 563.8×10^{-6}. However, sometimes SI prefixes are used instead of exponents. If the number above referred to a number of moles of a chemical, for example, you could write 563.8 µmol.

Although simple qualitative data can normally be presented in words (for example, 'the patient stated a preference for an operation rather than continued drug treatment'), more complex presentations of such data involve the use of tables.

For quantitative data, you may be faced with a decision whether to present in tabular or graphic form, but in general you should not include the same data in both a chart and a table. In choosing between these modes of presentation, consider what you are trying to achieve. For example:

- a visual presentation in a graph may help readers to assimilate your points
- a graphic presentation may not be suitable for some or all of the data (for instance, when some are qualitative)
- there may be too many data sets or variables to include in a chart, in which case a table may actually be clearer
- your audience might be interested in the precise values of some of your data, which can be given in a table
- you may wish to place large amounts of your data on record, for instance as tables within an appendix to your write-up.

CREATING EFFECTIVE GRAPHS

A good graph will allow the reader to understand the meaning of your data in visual form. For example, it will typically illustrate trends through time or differences between treatments.

The basic components of a graph were covered in **Chapter 9** (especially Figure 9.1). When creating a graph from your own data, you should follow a logical process, as detailed below. This is naturally a generalisation, but the sequence will suit many circumstances.

1. Think carefully about what you want to plot and why, then choose an appropriate type of graph. You may have in mind a particular graph type for your data, possibly adopting a model from previous research. Otherwise, review the common options shown in Figures 9.1 and 9.2 or use the 'Chart' function in a spreadsheet to explore possibilities. For several forms of chart, you will need to decide which variable will appear on the x-axis (generally the 'controlled' variable, **Chs 12 and 14**) and which on the y-axis (generally the measured variable). If you have selected an unfamiliar form of graph, you may wish to sketch out how this will appear for your data set. A spreadsheet can be a valuable tool when working through this phase.

2. Consider the range and units for the axes, where appropriate. What are the upper and lower limits of your data? Should you start each axis at zero, and, if not, will this act to distort the presentation, as in Figure 9.3(a)? Will your axes be linear? Will they be in the same units as your measurements, or might you wish to work out ratios, percentages or other transformations before graphing the data? Once you have settled on these aspects, and adjusted the chart settings, you can write the descriptive label for the axis, which should first state what is presented and then, usually in parentheses ( ) or after a solidus /, the units used (Figure 9.1 provides an example). Other forms of graph, such as a pie chart, may require a descriptive label for each segment, or you may prefer to use a legend or key.

3. Choose aspects of presentation. For example, if you are using a pie chart, select colours and/or shading for the segments. Note that the distinction between some colours and shade types may be lost if photocopying in black and white – this is one reason for choosing different shades or patterns based on black and white as the base

colours. If your graph has axes, decide how frequently you wish the tics and associated numbers to appear: too many and the axis will seem crowded, too few and it becomes less easy to work out the approximate values of data points. Decide which symbols will be used for which data sets, and if presenting several graphs in sequence, try to be consistent on this. If measures of location (Table 9.1) are plotted, consider whether you wish to add error bars to show the variability in the data.

> ### ✓ Adding trend lines to graphs
>
> Take special care when adding a curve to a graph, because any trend line you add indicates that you have assumed an underlying relationship between the variables (**Ch 9**). If the points carry no (rare) or very little error, then you may be justified in drawing a straight line or curve between each point. If, however, the points do carry error, then the curve should take an 'average' line between them. Many calibration graphs are expected to demonstrate an underlying straight-line relationship, but most other plotted relationships are complex, so the line should probably be a smooth curve rather than a straight line.

4 Write the figure title and caption. Your aim should be to ensure that the figure is 'self-contained' and that its essence can be understood without reference to detail normally given elsewhere, such as the 'material and methods' section of a scientific report. Titles should be short, but allow the reader to grasp immediately what is shown. There is no need to use the words 'figure' or 'table' in the title (for example, 'Figure showing effect of x on y'); instead just summarise the content ('Effect of x on y'). The caption can be used to provide additional detail relating to methods or statistics. Items to include here are:

   – the figure number and title

   – a caption indicating what the symbols and error bars mean (a legend or key within the figure may or may not be acceptable, so check this first)

   – if appropriate, the caption should also indicate how the plotted curve was chosen and provide any brief details about the data (for example, differences in the treatments) that will help your reader understand the figure better without having to refer to another section.

> **Make your graphs clear and straightforward** ✓
>
> Chapter 9 covered the ways in which certain graphic presentations can be misleading. Avoid confusing your audience by using these forms of misrepresentation when constructing your own figures.

USING SPREADSHEET CHARTS

Spreadsheets such as Microsoft Excel are useful for collecting data and for creating graphs ('charts'). These can also be embedded easily within written text, especially if using a word-processor program within the same suite of software. However, most spreadsheets use business models for chart designs and these are rarely appropriate in academic contexts. In addition, the chart automatically produced may incorporate features that you do not want (such as a non-zero axis, or unwanted symbol type). Therefore, if you wish to take advantage of the convenience of this method of producing charts, you will also need to learn how to modify the default versions. Typically, you will wish to:

- modify the axes – so that start and end points, and tic marks, are in the required place
- add appropriate axis labels – to include variables and units in a suitable format
- change the default fonts used for axis labels and numbers – to suit your own (consistent) style
- change the chart background and/or plot area boundary lines – the standard for academic work is clear (i.e. white) or non-existent
- remove gridlines – these are rarely used when presenting formal academic work (although they may be useful for some calibration curves)
- change the symbols – so that these are of the required size and shape
- add error bars – to show the variability in the source data (these can be calculated within the spreadsheet)
- modify trend lines and associated data – so that these meet your requirements
- remove headings and any boxes showing the symbol key – this information will normally be put in the title and caption, which you should embed in the word-processed document rather than the chart itself.

An example of changes made to a default chart is shown in Figure 20.1. There will be a software-dependent menu system for carrying out these changes, and, in addition, each aspect can usually be altered using the pop-up options that appear if you right-click when the mouse cursor is over the relevant feature (or equivalent for different control systems).

(a)

(b)

$y = 0.893x - 0.287$

Measured variable (units)

Controlled variable (units)

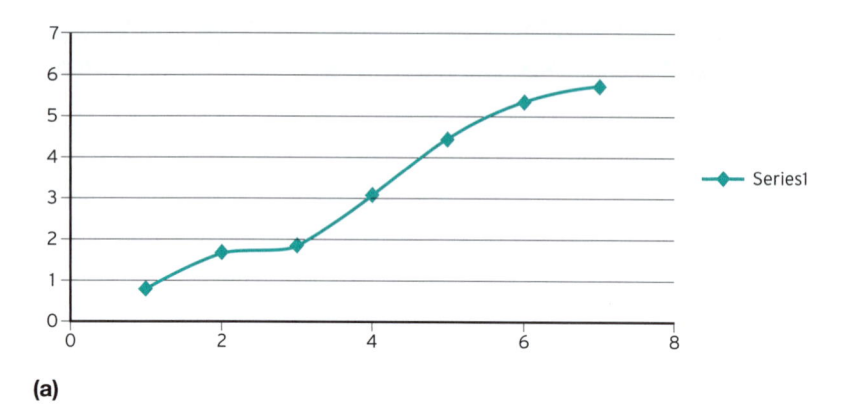

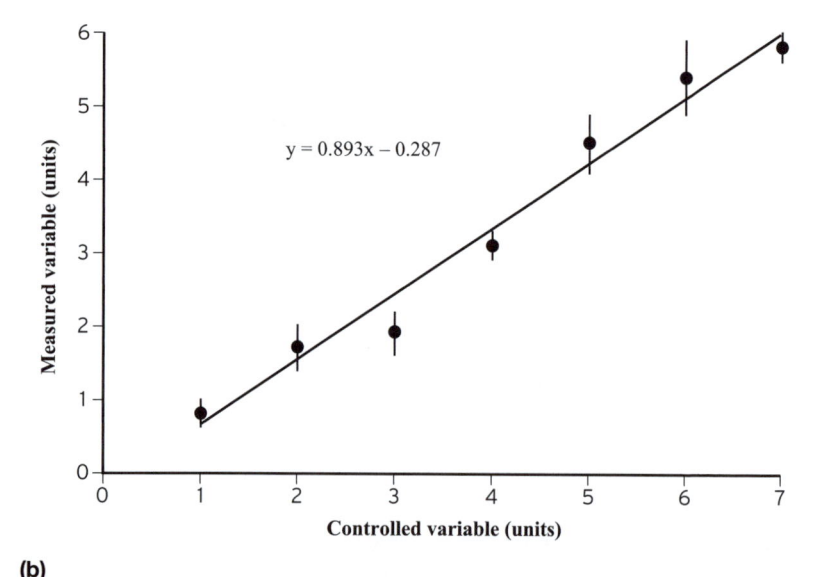

Figure 20.1 Example of modifications to a 'plotted curve' produced in Microsoft Excel. The chart (graph) in (a) was produced using the default settings. The chart in (b) shows this default version modified to suit the style expected in academic writing, by changing aspects as noted in the text. Many relevant menu options for achieving this can be accessed from the 'Layout' tab, which appears when the chart is selected within the spreadsheet.

> **Title and caption positions for figures and tables**
>
> **Figures** – the title and caption should always appear **below** a figure
> **Tables** – the title and caption should always appear **above** a table

CREATING EFFECTIVE TABLES

The basic components of a table were covered in **Chapter 9**, especially in Figure 9.4. A good table presents data in a compact, readily assimilated format. Think about and draw a rough design for your table before constructing a final version:

1 Decide what will appear in the columns and what in the rows. If in doubt, the equivalent of the 'controlled' variable (**Ch 12**) would normally appear in the column headings and the 'measured' variable in the rows. Do not forget to include the units of the information listed if this is relevant.

2 Choose where the rulings (gridlines) should go. The default in word-processing programs such as Microsoft Word is to create lines around the perimeter of each cell in a table; however, the modern style for research reports and publications is to minimise the use of lines – often restricting their use to horizontal rulings only (Figure 9.4).

3 Each vertical column should display a particular type of data, and the descriptive headings should reflect these contents, giving the units where data are quantitative. Each row might show different instances of these types of data. Rows and columns should be arranged in a way that helps the reader to compare them if this is desirable.

4 Numerical data values should be presented to an appropriate number of significant figures. An indication of errors, if included, should be given in parentheses, and the heading should make it clear what statistic is being quoted.

5 Qualitative data should be presented in as short a form as possible for easy assimilation and to save space.

6 The justification of data within the cells should be consistent. In general, use left-only justification for qualitative data, as double (left and right) justification can lead to excessive spacing where column widths are narrow; for quantitative data choose an approach that aligns the last significant figures or the decimal point, as appropriate.

7 Footnotes can be used to explain abbreviations or give details of specific cases. Use superscripts (for example, 79.35[a]) to denote

the reference, and in the footnote give an explanation (for example, [a] there were only five replicates in this instance).

> **Basic rules for the numbering and positioning of figures and tables**
>
> ❏ Tables and figures must be numbered sequentially in order of appearance
> ❏ The numbering scheme for tables is independent from that of graphs
> ❏ Tables and figures should appear at the earliest possible position after their first mention in the text
> ❏ The position of tables and figures is normally at the top or bottom of a page (avoid 'sandwiching' them between portions of text)
> ❏ 'Wide' tables may be better suited to presentation in landscape orientation, with the top of the table always to the left of the page if held in normal portrait position.

ACTION POINTS

20.1 At an early stage, decide on your personal figure and table styles. In making your choices, look for good examples from publications and previous write-ups, adopt any specific departmental or university rules and discuss representative examples with your supervisor. Once your format is settled, note down all the font, pattern and other settings and 'rules' in a personal style sheet. Refer to this each time you draw up a new figure or table.

20.2 Decide on the correct way to present quantitative data in your text and tables. You will need to present numerical data in a manner appropriate to such factors as measurement error (**Ch 12**). This need not be the same in every case, but has to be thought about each time and should be consistent between similar cases. If necessary, refresh your understanding of SI units and the associated rules to ensure your data presentation adopts the appropriate discipline standard.

20.3 Refresh your knowledge of software functions. Drawing up graphs and tables to the required standard may stretch your skills in using word-processor or spreadsheet commands. If this is the case, study appropriate online or published guidebooks, or attend any courses on their use that are offered in your institution.

THE WRITING PROCESS

21
PLANNING THE WRITING PHASE
How to organise your work effectively to produce the best-quality product on time

The formal writing up of the project may be the longest and most detailed piece of writing you have attempted thus far as a student. Therefore, you will need to plan carefully to ensure that your project is of high quality in its written format and that it is submitted on time.

KEY TOPICS
- Creating an effective timetable for writing
- Deciding on the final theme or direction
- Getting started on your writing
- Keeping on track

People and their thought processes are different, and so individual approaches to planning an outline for a piece of writing will vary. For some individuals, this can be a highly detailed process; for others, it may be a minimal exercise. Too much detail in a plan can be restricting, while too little can fail to provide enough direction. Therefore, a reasonably detailed plan should give some guidance while leaving you the flexibility to alter the finer elements as you write.

CREATING AN EFFECTIVE TIMETABLE FOR WRITING

As noted in **Chapter 5**, it may be useful to consider research project work occurring in a number of phases (see Table 5.1). Ideally, you should try to avoid a sequential approach to the investigation and drafting phases and try to tackle these partly in parallel, if you can.

Figure 21.1 illustrates how this might look in diagrammatic form. For example, some of your initial work in the scoping phase (**Chs 3, 5 and 13**) may be of value when drafting your text. There is much that you can do in the early stages of a project, and this includes some of the time-consuming chores that otherwise eat up the available time at the end.

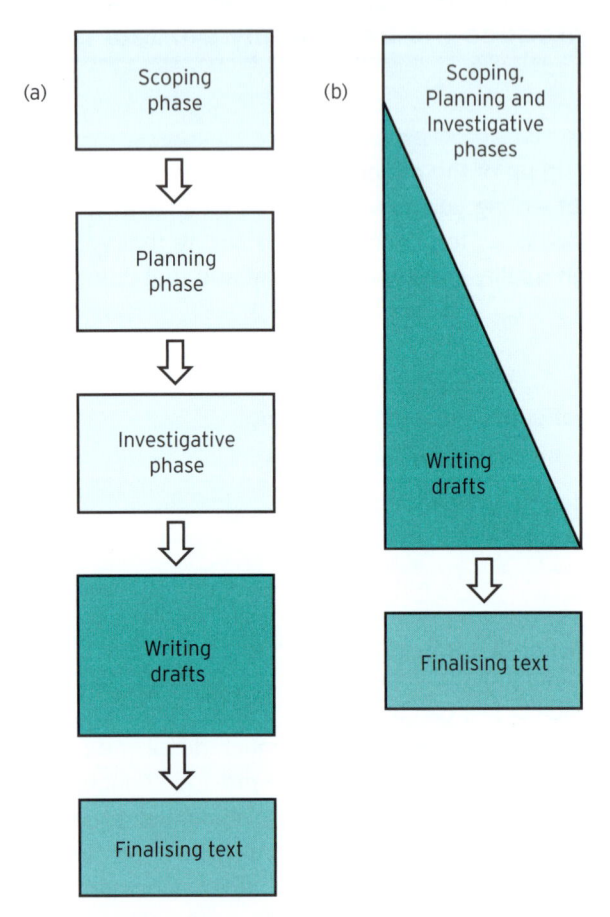

Figure 21.1 Models of the process of the writing-up phase of a project: (a) 'sequential' model, where each phase is completed in sequence; and (b) 'part-parallel' model, in which some drafting is carried out at the same time as the scoping, planning research/investigation phases – likely to be more efficient as an approach in many, but not all, disciplines.

> **Aspects of the write-up that can be worked on during the early stages of a project**
>
> The following can be drafted during the research/investigation stage:
>
> - calculations on raw data (**Ch 19**) – formatting can be decided later
> - figures and tables (**Ch 20**) – order and numbering can be settled later
> - 'Materials and Methods' or 'Methodology' (**Ch 23**) – a check for completeness can be made after the research/investigation phase is completed
> - sections of introductory text (**Ch 23**) – these can be adjusted once conclusions are made
> - references (**Ch 24**) – these can be entered into referencing software and later formatted, or typed up and manually formatted
> - elements of 'Conclusions' section ('mini-conclusions', **Ch 23**) – collate with main conclusion near to end of writing phase.

Even if you take this 'parallel working' approach, you can anticipate a time when nearly all of your study time will be devoted to the writing. At this point, review your initial timetable (**Ch 5**) and create a new, more detailed one leading up to the completion date. This will help you to:

- provide a realistic estimate of the writing that needs to be done, lowering the risk of running out of time
- ensure you balance your effort between the different sections of the writing, promoting uniform quality throughout
- devote adequate time to proofreading and editing, which will help you to improve your writing in the final stage
- avoid any mark or grade penalties for late submission.

A similar approach can be taken to that used for timetabling the whole project (**Ch 5**), although at this later stage it would almost certainly be better to use days rather than weeks as the 'working unit'. The obvious end-point for your work is the submission date, which should be reconfirmed at this point. As noted in **Chapter 5**, there is a strong argument for planning to complete your work a week or so before the deadline. This will reduce the feelings of tiredness and stress near the end of the writing phase because there will be space for some slippage in the timetable. It will also allow you to let your writing 'settle' before a final proofread (**Ch 25**).

The elements of the manuscript should now be separated out and an estimate made of the time required for each section. Divide the available time into convenient working periods and decide how much you wish to allocate to each aspect of the task. Map these time allowances onto the available time, taking account of your other commitments. An example related to a scientific project is shown in Table 21.1; however, in the arts/social sciences the sections of a project paper might be constructed in a way that would be unique to that project and so would not necessarily follow the standardised order presented here. This might be a point for discussion with your supervisor.

The order of tackling each part should be decided – as noted above, there is no need to write sequentially. If appropriate, it may be beneficial to split each element into a 'draft' and 'completion' period. This will allow you to get going on an 'achievable' part, leaving the final touches until nearer the end.

Table 21.1 Example of an outline timetable for the writing-up phase of a project. This model follows the structure of a report in the sciences. The norm would be to substitute days for percentage figures in the 'time allocated' column. The sections are shown as they might appear in the final product, but there is no need to work in that order, nor, in some disciplines, to these precise headings.

Report section	Percentage time allocated	Complete by
Preliminary material	5	
Introduction	15	
Materials and methods	12	
Results	18	
Discussion	20	
Conclusion	10	
References	10	
Incorporating supervisor's feedback and final editing	5	
Printing and binding	2	
Allowance for slippage	3	
Submission		

DECIDING ON THE FINAL THEME OR DIRECTION

In many cases, there will be a breakthrough event or moment when the overarching theme of your account of your research becomes clear or self-evident. If a research method under trial works well, then this may open up a clear avenue of investigation – leading to obvious content and structure. Analysis of survey results might reveal a majority view on an issue that orientates your conclusions. You might find a sudden understanding following a meeting or when finding a particular research source. Often, making an intellectual connection between ideas or findings will lead you to inspiration for your writing.

Many students write draft material and notes as they proceed and may then accumulate so much work and so many ideas that they struggle to see how it might appear as a coherent, cohesive piece of writing. This is where your supervisor's experience and wisdom will be valuable. He or she should have a wider view of the subject area and know what is likely to be judged significant, and what not.

You can start the process of exploring your topic by creating a brainstorm 'mind map' (Ch 10). At this stage, include as many related aspects as you can within a free-flowing diagram. If you have already produced a project proposal (Ch 4), your map will be strongly influenced by this, as well as any research sources you have read. It is important to exercise your critical thinking skills (Ch 16) as you analyse the topic and to think about potential content and approaches.

When you have a clear idea of how the text reporting your project should be arranged, it is wise to plan out the framework as far as you can before you meet with your supervisor. This gives you a starting point for your discussion. You should take this draft framework further than a listing of the common elements – introduction, literature review, methods and materials, results, discussion and conclusion. You will need to include specific sub-headings under each of these elements and this means thinking through the detail of what you intend to write and where. Only by doing this will you be able to recognise that some pieces of information or work need to precede others; some may need to be analysed and explained in greater or less detail; and some chapters may potentially be overloaded while others may be 'light' on content.

> **? When should I stop researching and start writing?**
>
> There is no comprehensive answer to this question. There are, however, a number of ways of answering it, any of which may be relevant:
>
> - when you know more or less what the theme of your analysis will be (you can then start writing drafts with a purpose)
> - when you feel your findings or results are of significance or a high standard
> - when you are running out of time
> - you should begin writing draft material right from the start (that is, do not partition the investigation and writing phases).

GETTING STARTED ON YOUR WRITING

By the time you read this section, you may already have made significant contributions to the writing. This is because the notes you took of sources during the scoping and investigation phases will help as an initial point for your drafts (Ch 10). These short pieces can form the basis for further development once you have undertaken further reading and may fit within a structure that is decided at this point (Ch 23). There is the added advantage that note-writing may have provided you with the opportunity to explore your position in relation to the topic (Ch 17).

Engage with the formal writing as soon as possible. Finding a way to start is a very common problem because of the perceived need to begin with a 'high impact' sentence that reads impressively. This is unnecessary, and starting with a simple definition or restatement of the issue or problem is perfectly acceptable. In fact, there is no need to start at the beginning of any given section if you feel this would potentially hold you back. If no inspiration is forthcoming, get going on the substantive part of the work. Once that is written, it may be far more obvious what you should say in this initial piece.

If you simply feel overwhelmed by the size of the job and this prevents you from starting it, break the task down to manageable, achievable chunks. Then, try to complete something every day. Maintaining momentum in this way will allow you to whittle away the job in stages.

Be clear about your purpose and what you need to achieve (**Ch 23**). Revisit your proposal (**Ch 4**) and decide on the direction you wish to take, given the research you have done. Unless you do this, your writing will lack direction – a common reason for stalling.

> **Clear the decks**
>
> Your mind may find it difficult to function when it is distracted, so:
>
> - quickly finish other tasks that are outstanding
> - tidy your work area
> - make it clear to others that you may not be available for socialising
> - make sure you have a good stock of stationery and other requirements.

Avoiding procrastination

People agree that one of the hardest parts of project work is getting started on the larger tasks. Putting things off – procrastination – is all too easy for a lengthy task such as a project write-up, and can involve the following symptoms:

- convincing yourself that other, lower-priority activity is more important or enjoyable
- switching frequently among tasks, and not making much progress in any of them
- talking about your work rather than doing it
- 'helping' others by discussing their project rather than getting on with your own
- planning for too long rather than writing
- having difficulty starting a piece of writing
- spending too long on presentational elements (for example, how a graph looks), rather than the 'meat' of the project.

If you admit to any of these warning signs, you may subconsciously be procrastinating. Becoming more aware of how you might be falling into this trap is the first stage in consciously avoiding it.

Delaying completion of a task, in itself a form of procrastination, is another aspect of time management that many find difficult. It may be that you are avoiding moving on to another, more difficult task. Another possibility is that you are subconsciously anxious about the quality of the final submission and therefore reluctant to produce the final version. In this situation, 'worrying' the text instead of moving on simply wastes time. It is far better to leave a piece of text and move on to the next task, perhaps returning to edit it later with fresh eyes.

> ✓ **Don't be a perfectionist**
>
> Procrastination is a special problem for perfectionists. Good time managers recognise when to finish tasks, even if the task is not quite in a 'perfect' state. Recognising that you should leave one task and move on to the next can mean that the sum of multiple tasks making up the written account of your project is better all round.

KEEPING ON TRACK

Once you become immersed in writing, it is easy to lose track of where you are in your timetable. That's one reason why it is a good idea to put it on a planner or whiteboard so you can see it each day. Crossing out the days as they go past is one way of keeping in touch with your progress and any forthcoming end-points for the completion of sections.

Work through writer's block. Some days go well; some just do not. Accept that this is simply part of the process – a feature of the human condition. As an academic author, you will find that sometimes the words will flow almost effortlessly. At other times, every paragraph, sentence or even word is a struggle. That's all part of the thinking process and will eventually contribute to a fresh stream of high-quality writing. If feeling blocked in parts where you need to be creative, carry out some routine but productive work that will save time later, such as writing up and formatting references.

> ✓ **Review each day as it passes. You should ask yourself:**
>
> ❏ What have I achieved?
> ❏ What went well?
> ❏ What could have gone better?
> ❏ Am I keeping up with my timetable?
> ❏ What do I need to do next?
> ❏ What do I need to do to ensure the next session is better?

If you find you are keeping on track, or are even ahead of schedule, keep up your efforts – problems and delays can appear from anywhere and it is good to have time in reserve for adding quality touches near the end. If, on the other hand, you find that the schedule is slipping, you need to try to understand why this is the case. You may need to review your work-rate or hours, or cancel recreational activity. Better to do this sooner rather than later, when a 'mad rush' will surely affect the quality of your submission.

One final reminder is necessary – ensure you keep frequent and secure back-up files of your work. Few things could delay your progress more than losing a file or having a computer malfunction, meaning that you had to go back to square one and rewrite a section from scratch.

Working back from your submission date

Sometimes it is easy to be lulled into a fall sense of security by thinking that there is plenty of time until the deadline date for any big task. In the case of your submission date, a reality check may be needed, and this can be achieved by working backwards from that date, factoring in all remaining tasks – such as the time needed to:

- finalise your remaining research (**Ch 5**)
- personally edit and proofread your final version (**Ch 25**)
- obtain final feedback from your supervisor (**Ch 26**)
- print and, where necessary, bind the work (**Ch 27**).

The list could go on, but these examples are sufficient to show that there are many steps in the process leading up to final submission and it would be wise to outline all that apply in your case.

ACTION POINTS

21.1 Take time out to consider where you are and what you still need to do. Find an hour or two where you can be alone to think clearly. If necessary, distance yourself from your normal working environment. Critically review your achievements so far and work out what you think you can achieve realistically in the time that remains. Use this to adjust an existing timetable or to set up a new one.

21.2 Review your work patterns. If you have created a new timetable for the writing phase, you may be apprehensive about the amount of work you still need to do. This might be a good time to review how much time you are able to devote to the task, and perhaps to explain to friends and family how you may be less available in the near future owing to this responsibility.

21.3 If you are having difficulty in writing, try the 15-minute 'block breaker'. If you are having difficulties with writing on a specific topic, remove all distractions, sit down with an empty notepad or screen and force yourself to write about the relevant topic for 15 minutes only. Don't worry about the content, the accuracy of facts or the grammar – just write. The aim is to try to find an 'entry' into the topic that you can later refine. Even if this would not be the first aspect sequentially, or even if it requires substantial modification, you can top and tail it or adjust it later on; at least you may have broken the barrier that was holding you back.

22

WRITING UP IN THE APPROVED FORMAT

How to report on your research using standard structure and content

The format of the finished written project document differs across the disciplines, and especially across the arts/sciences divide, but there are some common or similar components that adopt comparable principles of content and presentation.

KEY TOPICS
→ Options for formatting a project write-up
→ The focus of the main elements of a research document

Different models of research lead to different processes and outcomes. In general, however, a written document is required that summarises the research you have done. This write-up may be termed a report, dissertation, paper or thesis. The discipline 'standard' for structuring this differs across subjects, and especially between the arts and sciences. In some cases the prescribed format must be followed rigidly, whereas in other instances/disciplines there is scope and greater flexibility allowed for the researcher to organise the structure of their manuscript, often at their own discretion. In general, there tends to be greater flexibility in the arts domains about how the work should be explained.

OPTIONS FOR FORMATTING A PROJECT WRITE-UP

Table 22.1 shows possible listings that include standard elements for both the sciences and the arts, although not all parts will appear in all cases.

Table 22.1 The key sections used when reporting research in the arts and sciences. This shows two possible listings that illustrate typical elements for either area.

Arts	Sciences
• Title	• Title
• Preliminary material	• Preliminary material
• Abstract or Summary	• Abstract or Summary
• Introduction	• Introduction
• Literature review	• Methods
• Methodology	• Results
• [Investigation]	• Discussion
• Discussion	• Conclusions
• Conclusions	• References
• References	• Appendices
• Glossary	
• Appendices	

From Table 22.1, it can be seen that sections/chapters may carry different names in different academic disciplines: for example, 'Materials and Methods' is common in the sciences; 'Analysis' may be preferred to 'Results' in the arts. Sometimes sections may be combined (the 'Literature Review' being part of the 'Introduction', or the 'Conclusions' appearing as a final part of the 'Discussion', for example). Whatever the sections or chapters are called, the elements described in Table 22.1 can be seen as generic content of any document reporting research.

> ✓ **Look into the structures previously used for writing up in your subject**
>
> At an early stage, compare the structures adopted by other students in your research area or department, if available. A consistent model may be used, which you can adopt, or there may be variety – in which case you can decide which model might be best adapted to suit your research.

For a lengthy report on your research, composed of work in different areas or using divergent approaches, the following model is an option:

- Preliminary Material
- Abstract
- General Introduction

- General Methods (or General Materials and Methods, or Methodology)

Then the elements in brackets, repeated as often as necessary:

{
Chapter x
- Introduction
- Method (or Materials and Methods)
- Results
- Discussion
}

- General Discussion
- Conclusions
- References.

This model allows very specific approaches and their methods to be outlined closer to the relevant results and discussion. Again, some elements may carry different names or be combined. Note the use of a 'General Introduction' and 'General Discussion' before and after the chapters. These introduce and discuss the content of the document as a whole, whereas the chapter 'Introduction' and 'Discussion' deal primarily with the theme of each specific chapter. In some cases, you may only need one Materials and Methods (or Methodology) section before the first results/analysis chapter, especially where these are essentially common to all parts of the investigation.

One advantage of using this type of design is that any figures and tables can be made independent among chapters by adopting a numbering system relative to each chapter (that is, Figure 3.4 would be the fourth figure in Chapter 3). This means that you can add figures and tables to a chapter at any stage without disrupting the numbering system for the whole document. It also means you can write the chapters in any order – thus avoiding a tedious renumbering exercise.

In general, the institution will dictate the content, and sometimes presentation of the preliminary material (see below), but you will have some freedom to decide options for presenting the sections unique to your work – your methods, results and discussion. The style of citation and the reference section usually need to follow discipline norms or department/university regulations (**Ch 24**).

Some disciplines – especially those that are relatively modern, such as computing and design, and professional subjects such as teaching and nursing – have adopted different approaches to presenting research findings, using structural models that fit with the norm for research papers in their disciplines. In these cases, always follow the course documentation or your supervisor's guidance in the first place.

> ✓ **Check the rules about document structure and length at an early stage**
>
> Access your department's regulations at an early stage and print and file the section on structure and presentation. You may wish to create folders and files for mandatory sections so that you can draft these as you go along. If there is a prescribed or recommended length, create a provisional target length for each section so you can give appropriate attention to each part.

THE FOCUS OF THE MAIN ELEMENTS OF A RESEARCH DOCUMENT

The following sub-sections discuss content and approaches for each of the elements outlined above, and in Table 21.1. For each case this is necessarily a general outline, as disciplines and writers may have different expectations and wishes respectively. To accommodate the wider differences in practice, the discussion is sometimes divided into parts for 'sciences' and 'non-sciences'. Before committing words to paper or getting too far down a particular avenue, always discuss your plan with your supervisor and respond to any feedback received.

The title and title page

Despite its short length, the title of your report or paper may be one element you wrestle with because of the need to encapsulate your investigation succinctly. The first version of your title may have been created at an early stage in the research process, perhaps when writing your research proposal (**Ch 4**). However, as your investigation proceeds you may find that this draft title no longer reflects your findings or thoughts.

The general principle is that the title should be a concise yet informative description of what the study or research is about. It might help to think about key words first, before framing the title – that is, those words you would expect another researcher to input into a database search program when trying to find out about work such as your own. The convention is not to write 'An investigation of…' or 'Studies on…', as this is assumed. In the sciences, titles would normally encompass wider topics than those of research papers and might be more analogous to those of research reviews. In the arts, the possibilities are wider ranging, but you still may find that your original title is honed to a much simpler wording by the end of the writing process.

The title page usually includes the title, the author's full name and existing qualifications, the name of the degree for which the report or paper is submitted, the department (school or centre) and university, and the date of submission (usually just month and year).

The preliminary material

There are many technical parts that need to be included before the full text. Depending on departmental or institutional rules, these may include the following components, sometimes with different titles but usually in the order given below.

- The table of contents. This is a sequential list of the sections or chapters of the text, with page numbers. Clearly, this can only be completed properly after the text is written, although a 'shell' document can be constructed ahead of this without the final page information.
- List of figures and tables. This is exactly what the title implies, with numbering and page numbers. The aim is to allow an examiner or reader to find a specific piece of information quickly. In shorter documents, this may not be required.
- Acknowledgements. This is a list of all those who have helped and supported you and to whom you wish to pay tribute. It may include thanks to a funding body.
- Declaration. This is effectively a statement that the content of the write-up is all your own work, except where indicated. This normally follows an institutional format; Figure 22.1 provides an example.
- Abbreviations. This is a comprehensive list of the shortened forms used in the text. Normal practice is always to introduce the abbreviation at the first point of use, but if a reader sees a later use but has forgotten the meaning, it can be found in this early section. The abbreviations with expanded versions are listed in strict alphabetical order.

> 'Following the acknowledgements, if any, there shall be: a signed declaration, that the candidate is the author of the thesis; that, unless otherwise stated, all references cited have been consulted by the candidate; that the work of which the thesis is a record has been done by the candidate, and that it has not been previously accepted for a higher degree: provided that if the thesis is based upon joint research, the nature and extent of the candidate's individual contribution shall be defined'

Figure 22.1 An example of a typical regulation for an 'all my own work' declaration. Taken from The University of Dundee Code of Practice for Supervised Postgraduate Research (2006). Available at: ***www.somis.dundee.ac.uk/calendar/senate/hdtheses.htm*** [Accessed 6 November 2013].

Abstract (or Summary)

This is an outline of the content of the report or paper, often between 100 and 300 words in length but this may vary according to discipline or regulations. The Abstract should allow a reader to understand quickly what you did, why you did it and what you discovered or think about the topic. This is usually quite difficult to write because of the length restriction. It should cover: the aims of the investigation or research, the methods, the findings and the conclusions. The language should be general rather than technical, wherever possible.

Introduction

The aim of the Introduction should be to provide a rationale for your work. Thus, it needs to include background information leading to a description of the issue under investigation and the reason for the study. For most situations, it would normally incorporate a review of past work (the literature) in the area, leading to the aims of your own work (see also **Chapter 23**). Possible topics to be addressed in an Introduction might include:

- general and current importance of the (wide) research area
- a review of the wider subject area and the context of your particular field, including its potential importance
- a review of recent findings from the literature in your (narrow) field
- a description of the hypothesis or hypotheses you intend to test (in the sciences especially)
- identification of the 'gap' in knowledge or understanding that suggests the need for investigation, which will be addressed by this study and described in your paper (both arts and sciences)

- comments on novel aspects of experimental design, materials or methods to be adopted
- a brief description of the structure of the write-up, where this might assist the reader.

In some cases, an outline of the content of the report or paper and its conclusions might be included in the later parts of the Introduction; in others, this would not be accepted style.

Literature Review

In the sciences, reviewing and appraising the literature may be a component feature of the introduction. However, in some disciplines, including those in the arts, reviewing the literature might require an independent chapter. In some instances, the Literature Review might fit more appropriately within separate chapters, with only a general mention of seminal work in the literature provided in the introductory chapter.

Finalising your Introduction

The Introduction is the first detailed explanation of the context and purpose of your study. It sets the scene and whets the appetite of the reader; it also helps your examiner to understand the context and possibly how you intend to tackle the problem. That said, while your Introduction is of considerable significance, it can only reflect the content of the full work. This means that you should not waste time trying to achieve a perfect Introduction before you have completed all the other chapters. Until you have finished the Conclusion, you should see your introduction as 'work in progress'. Only when everything else is written should you reread your Introduction and remodel it, so that it does, indeed, reflect the content of the full work.

Methods (or Materials and Methods, or Methodology)

Sciences – in these disciplines, your aim is to describe what you did in sufficient detail to allow a competent lab worker in your field to carry out exactly the same research as you. This is a key part of any scientific communication, because the essence of all science lies in its repeatability (**Chs 3 and 12**). There is no need to go into unnecessary detail. For example, a competent technician would be able to work out how much of a specified chemical to use to make a solution of defined concentration, or would know to use a stirrer bar to dissolve a chemical when making up a solution. However, the precise supplier, purity and concentration of the chemical might be crucial to the results, and should, therefore, be specified. Structure the Materials and Methods into sections in the order in which they are presented in the manuscript (which may not be the order in which they were done). For example, you might start with how the experimental material was obtained. Crucial at this point is an adequate description of its origins and nature (in the life sciences, for example, this would include the binomial Latin name plus authority of any organisms studied). You might then move on to describe how each experiment was carried out. Finally, you might have a section on data analysis (and presentation).

This section should be written in the past tense – for example, 'The drying board was positioned at an angle of 45°', or 'The leaves were dried out overnight'.

- Do not separate materials from methods (unless otherwise instructed); as you describe what you did, incorporate information about what you did it to.
- Do not include any results: there are rare occasions when (say) a calibration might be included, but in general, experiments that validate your methods should come in the first section of the results.

Non-sciences – a Methods or Methodology section in arts-related subjects can relate to both the theoretical approaches that underpin the research activity and the way in which the research was conducted. The former part may require an in-depth scrutiny of theoretical, often qualitative, approaches to research (**Ch 13**) and an explanation of why one particular approach is best suited to your study over other options. It follows, therefore, that the description of the conduct of the research will derive from these theoretical parameters. The increasingly technical approaches being used in research in the arts and social sciences may mean that this chapter is a lengthy one.

Results (or Findings)

Sciences – the Results section should consist of a clear sequential description of your findings. The exact sequence need not be the order in which you did the thinking or carried out the experiments, but it should be logical. You need to guide the reader through the figures, pointing out the main points. Refer to them in sequence, numbered strictly in the order of first mention. For example, 'Figure 1 shows that treatment x had a greater effect on z than treatment y'.

> **✓ Construct the figures and tables before you start writing the results**
>
> As a result of the dynamic nature of results analysis, figure and table numbers and numbering may change frequently because you are creating new representations, or even feeding in new results as you complete a chapter. When this process is complete, lay them out in the order you wish to describe them and this will dictate their numbering.

Data should be simplified and presented clearly (see Ch 20). Include information about statistical hypothesis tests (for example, values of P – the probability of getting your result by chance).

- Do not repeat data in more than one form, unless this is crucial to your conclusions.
- Do not present all the replicate data you have obtained.
- Do not include textual analysis of the data: put this in the Discussion section. If you find it difficult not to discuss the results, consider using a combined 'Results and Discussion' section.

Always carry out any statistical tests before you start writing up the results. These analyses could materially alter your perspective on the data and affect the subsequent discussion dramatically.

Non-sciences – in these disciplines, a section labelled 'Results' or 'Findings' may not exist, although this does not mean that there are no findings in the account you are presenting. Much will depend

> **ℹ The sequence of writing**
>
> Writing is a dynamic process and you can write the sections whenever you feel ready. This means that you can jump around in the sequence. This can be helpful because there will be moments when you just do not feel like writing about a particular aspect of the study. At such times, choose an area where you feel that you can write fluently and accurately with a good chance of being productive. For scientists, one such area might be the Methods and Materials section because this more descriptive writing may be easier to construct. Conversely, those in arts subjects may find that their Methodology section presents a challenge in the writing process that is best left to a more favourable moment. Here, starting at the Literature Review might induce more fluent writing.

on the discipline, the topic and also, perhaps, on the regulations, but the findings may suitably be introduced in the main body of the paper, where analysis of the issues and the related literature may be divided into individual chapters. Gradually, as the dimensions of the research problem are examined and the data are introduced to amplify understanding, the 'finding' element will be revealed. For those conducting research in the arts and social sciences, this allows a valuable flexibility to compartmentalise analyses and their corresponding findings.

Discussion

Sciences – here, you should state the significance of your results. This is an important section, because it shows that you understand what you have done. The Discussion should be critical – that is, mentioning both good and bad points about your study. Be prepared to reject your original hypothesis, but state what others you might now adopt in its place. Be aware that there will always be an alternative (possibly low-probability) explanation, which should be discussed. You may also wish to state the main conclusions, compare your results with other published data, indicate what future studies might be undertaken and mention the significance of the work in a wider context.

- Do not extend the Discussion too much – it can easily degenerate into waffle.
- Do not simply repeat the Results section; you should be analysing your results rather than describing them.

Non-sciences – as with the above explanation of the positioning of Results/Findings in these disciplines, it can follow that the Discussion is subsumed in each of the sections/chapters that comprise the main body of the text. However, there may also be a separate chapter that brings together these discussion points and relates them to the conclusions reached regarding the study.

Conclusions

This is not always a separate section and may be combined with the Discussion. An option to consider is to state your main conclusions in a numbered list or logical sequence of paragraphs. You might also wish to present some clear notions of further directions that could be followed arising from your study, or provide indicators of recommendations that you might make for further action and change.

This might especially be more likely in a work based on case studies, action research or a business analysis.

> ### Cohesion in your writing – making links
>
> The nature of the writing process may mean that chapters and sections have been written at different stages in the study period; they may also have been written when you were unsure of what would precede or follow them. When reviewing your early writing late in the process, you may find that some of the introductory or closing paragraphs in your chapters seem awkward and even inelegant in the way that they were written. To smooth out this roughness, you should make time to review your manuscript as an entity – ensuring that there are clear 'backward' and 'forward' links between the chapters as they appear in the final sequence. You can enhance the cohesion of your work by ensuring that you relate your activities, findings, conclusions and recommendations to the literature that you introduced earlier in the text. Substantive new literature should not be introduced in the final sections; if new material has been published, then you should revisit the earlier Literature Review section of the work and update it appropriately.

References (or Bibliography, Literature Cited or Works Cited)

This section (all the names above effectively mean the same thing but depend on the referencing style you follow – **Ch 24**) gives the details for any articles cited in the text. There will be a precise format for doing this, depending on the rules adopted by your department or discipline. Even if you select a referencing style yourself, you will need to adopt it accurately and consistently. **Chapter 24** and McMillan and Weyers (2013) should be consulted for further information.

Glossary

This lists all specialist terms or terms that have been used in a way that is unique to your work, and so may require definition. The inclusion of such a listing allows the non-expert to understand the content of the thesis without recourse to specialist dictionaries.

Appendices (or Supplementary Material)

An Appendix (plural: appendices) is a section at the end of a piece of academic writing consisting of information closely related to the content of the main body of the work. Nevertheless, it is usually material that, while adding further understanding, might clog up the main part of the work with distracting detail and would inhibit the flow of the key issues in the discussion. Appendices are usually listed as Appendix A, B, C... or as Appendix 1, 2, 3... and so on. The pages are usually numbered with lower-case Roman numerals – that is, (i), (ii), (iii) and so on.

Supplementary Material may be required in some disciplines – for example, when involving discussion of an artefact. This could be shown via material on a CD/DVD. Your departmental or university regulations should give you guidance on this, but if not, then ask your supervisor for advice.

> **When should I stop writing?**
>
> Obviously, you need to follow your plan to completion, including all relevant sections and chapters. You may then wish to refine your text, perhaps via successive editing 'sweeps' (Ch 25). You will then need to seek feedback on this material from your supervisor, discuss this and incorporate any agreed changes (Ch 26). If you are a perfectionist, you may still wish to tinker with the text. Unless you are well ahead of the submission date, this is probably not a good idea. So long as your supervisor is happy with the product, start the submission process.

ACTION POINTS

22.1 Ensure you file your progress reports, notes and early drafts in a well-organised way. These will be very useful sources when you come to write the final version of your work. Good filing will mean that you should be able to find relevant material easily. Files should carry meaningful names and a version number or date should be noted.

22.2 Ensure your references are well-organised from an early stage. This is a very tedious part of writing up if you do not tackle it as you go along. Programs such as EndNote may be helpful in organising and presenting this information in the appropriate manner (Ch 24).

22.3 Keep back-up files (including print-outs) at all stages. There are heartbreaking tales of students who lose all their files near to the end of a write-up. Printing out hard copy as you complete chapters is another way of ensuring that you have a working text, should electronic disaster strike. This can always be scanned if required.

23 WRITING UP IN THE APPROPRIATE STYLE

How to use academic language and well-organised discourse to express your ideas and findings

Some students find it easy to write about their research, but others struggle to organise their thoughts and express them in a style that is suitable for reporting their research project. This requires an understanding of the key principles that lie behind academic discourse and style.

KEY TOPICS
→ Fundamentals of good scholarly writing
→ Writing objectively
→ Taking account of genre, register and audience
→ Organising your discourse
→ Grammar conventions in academic writing

At all stages of project writing, you must exert control over both the content and the way in which it is expressed. It is important to recognise that writing at this level requires more than simple reproduction of facts (Ch 16). You need to be able to construct an argument and to support this with evidence (Ch 17). You must draw on the data you have produced or the literature that you have read in order to support your position. You need to present a tight, well-argued case for your viewpoint or conclusions, and write this up using a suitable, scholarly style. This requires that your writing follows a sequence of sound logic and argument and is grammatically correct.

FUNDAMENTALS OF GOOD SCHOLARLY WRITING

Scholarly writing is an expression of higher-order thinking (Ch 16). In terms of a research project, the text you write should explain the research journey. It must incorporate the following qualities:

- accuracy – giving a precise and detailed account of the research process and findings
- clarity – writing in a style and format that are easily comprehended
- balance – providing a considered appraisal of the issue by taking account of opposing views, real or imagined
- originality – reporting research or ideas that introduce new knowledge to the field
- objectivity – avoiding bias
- principled methods – reporting work conducted following established methodologies based on ethical and safe procedures for the collection of data
- referencing sources – affording recognition to other contributors in the research field by attributing their work following a recognised citation and referencing model
- tentativeness – acknowledging that findings are rarely definitive by explaining the uncertainties that exist in the research.

Academic style involves the use of precise and objective language to express ideas. It must be grammatically correct, and is more formal than the style used in novels, newspapers, informal correspondence and everyday conversation. This should mean that the language is clear and simple. It does not imply that it is complex, pompous and dry.

Academic writing should promote objectivity by using language techniques that maintain an impersonal tone and a vocabulary that is more succinct, rather than involving personal, colloquial or idiomatic expressions. Some of these topics are discussed below, and Table 23.1 provides some examples. However, space prevents a fully detailed discussion, and the companion volume to this book, *How to Write for University: Academic Writing for Success* (McMillan and Weyers, 2014), is suggested as a source for more information.

WRITING OBJECTIVELY *

When writing academically, it is vital that your personal involvement with your topic does not overshadow the importance of what you are commenting on or reporting. The main way of demonstrating this objectivity and lack of bias is by using impersonal language. This means:

- avoiding personal pronouns – try not to use the following words: I/me/one, you (singular and plural), we/us
- using the passive rather than active voice – try to write about the action and not about the actor (the person who performed the action).

Examples are provided under 'Voice' in Table 23.1.

You can use other strategies to maintain an impersonal style in your writing. For general statements, you could use a structure such as 'It is...', 'There is...' or 'There are...' to introduce sentences. However, beginning a paragraph with 'It' is not advised as, by definition, this word has to refer to a preceding word or idea; a new paragraph introduces a new point. To avoid the initial 'It' here, change the sentence around so that, for example, 'It is important to note...' becomes 'An important point to note is...'.

For more specific points relating to statements you have already made, you could use the structures 'this is...' or 'these are...', 'that is...' or 'those are...', with appropriate tense changes according to the context. When you use words such as 'it', 'this', 'these', 'that' or 'those', there should be no ambiguity over the word or phrase to which they refer. Hence, to ensure clarity, it is better to use this/these/that/those followed by a noun (often defining a generic group) – for example, 'this evidence suggests...' or 'these data imply...', rather than 'this suggests...' or 'these imply...'.

Another way in which you can maintain objectivity by writing impersonally is to change the verb in the sentence to a noun and then reframe the sentence in a less personal way. You can see how this works in the information box on verb- or noun-led expressions.

23 Writing up in the appropriate style

Table 23.1 **Conventions in language use and grammar in academic writing.**

Absolute terms
In academic writing, it is important to be cautious about using absolute terms, such as: ❏ *always and never* ❏ *most and all* ❏ *least and none* This does not mean that these words should never be used; simply that they should be used with caution – that is, when you are absolutely certain of your ground.
Acronyms
These are formed by taking the initial letters of a name of an organisation, a procedure or an apparatus and then using these letters instead of writing out the title in full. Thus, **W**orld **H**ealth **O**rganisation becomes **WHO**. The convention is that the first time that you use a title with an acronym alternative, you should write it in full with the acronym in brackets immediately after the full title. Thereafter within that document you can use the acronym. For example: *'The European Free Trade Association (EFTA) has close links with the European Community (EC). Both EFTA and the EC require new members to have membership of the Council of Europe as a prerequisite for admission to their organisations.'*
Clichés
Living languages change and develop over time. This means that some expressions come into such frequent usage that they lose their meaning; indeed, often they could be replaced with a much less long-winded expression. For example: *First and foremost* (firstly,...); *last but not least* (finally,...) *This procedure is the gold standard of hip replacement methods.* (This procedure is the best hip replacement method.)
Colloquialisms
This form of language is regarded as informal and more common in spoken than in written language. Colloquialisms would generally not be used in academic writing. For example, the following would be inappropriate: *'Not to beat about the bush or mince my words, that is a load of rubbish!'*
Contractions
Generally, in spoken English, contractions such as 'don't', 'can't', 'isn't', 'it's', 'I'd' and 'we'll' are used all the time. However, in academic written English, they should not be used.
Gender-free expressions
Try to use gender-free expressions by using plurals. For example, instead of writing: *'Students asked each colleague to give his or her time to the project.'* the alternative plural construction would be preferred: *'Students asked colleagues to give their time to the project.'*

'Hedging' language

Often in academic writing it is impossible to state categorically that something is or is not the case. There are verbs that allow you to 'hedge your bets' by not coming down on one side or the other of an argument, or allow you to present a variety of different scenarios without committing yourself to any single position:

- ❏ *seems that*
- ❏ *suggests that*
- ❏ *looks as if*
- ❏ *appears that*

This involves using a language construction that leaves the reader with the sense that the evidence presented is simply offering a hypothetical, or imaginary, case. To emphasise this sense of 'hedging', the use of a special kind of verb called a *modal* is introduced. These verbs are called modal auxiliary ('helper') verbs:

- ❏ *can/cannot*
- ❏ *may/may not*
- ❏ *could/could not*
- ❏ *might/might not*

These can be used with a variety of verbs to increase the sense of tentativeness. For example:

> 'These results **suggest** that there has been a decline in herring stocks in the North Sea.'

More tentatively, using the modal, this could be:

> 'These results **could suggest** that there has been a decline in herring stocks in the North Sea.'

Idiom and slang

These are usually colloquial and are used in different ways. For example, where:

- ❏ the language is used in such a way that the meaning is difficult to interpret because there is no apparent link between the words – *to give someone short shrift*
- ❏ the literal sense is only partial in explaining the meaning – *to strike while the iron is hot*
- ❏ the whole meaning can be guessed from the parts – *as the crow flies*.

Thus, idioms should be avoided in academic writing because they are sometimes unclear or simply in vogue for a short time. Their use in academic text might be perceived as inappropriate to the genre and register.

Impersonal language

Impersonal expression is encouraged in many disciplines, and this means that the passive voice is the standard (see under 'Voice'). However, in other disciplines, especially those that embrace reflective writing, the active voice and use of the first person is expected. If you are unsure, speak with your supervisor about this.

Continued overleaf

Jargon

Some technical terms (sometimes called jargon or argot) are inevitable when writing academic text. However, they can act to obscure meaning if overused. There is usually a simple alternative, as shown in the slightly exaggerated example below.

Complex, jargon-rich text:

> 'These neophyte cognitive developers have innate resistance to the inculcation of cerebral processing in relation to technological ramifications of knowledge acquisition. Absence of verbal intercourse in cognitive fora aggravates their detachment from reality and reinforces isolationism.'

Clear and simple version:

> 'These new students have a natural fear of using technology in learning. Their silence in lectures adds to their isolation from the learning process.'

The first version comprises 36 words, while the second uses only 24 words. The difference in word count provides another good reason for simpler writing.

Personal pronouns

Experiment with other language structures so that you avoid the personal pronouns – *I/me, you, we/us* and *one*. Generally, these are avoided in academic writing, although there are instances in which they may be appropriate – for example, in reflective writing or writing about group research.

Rhetorical questions

Some writers use direct rhetorical questions as a stylistic vehicle to introduce the topic addressed by the question. However, although this is a good strategy if you are making a speech, it does not have the same power in academic writing. Therefore:

> 'How do plants survive in dry weather?' becomes

> 'Understanding how plants survive in dry weather is important.' (Question mark not needed.)

Signposting

You can guide your reader through your text by using appropriate 'signpost' words. For example, if you are presenting a point of contrast, then you would use 'however'; or if you are presenting a list of points, then you might use 'firstly,...'. Other common 'discourse markers' like these include: 'nevertheless'; 'in contrast'; 'for example'; 'accordingly'; 'in other words'; and 'in conclusion'. A fuller list is provided in McMillan and Weyers (2014).

Pronouns that 'demonstrate' some reference to something already mentioned are 'this', 'these', 'that' and 'those'. In academic writing it is often better to back-reference to the concept or thing being represented by such words. For example, rather than writing the following in relation to the plan of a new motorway:

> '*This* will take ten years to complete.'

you should consider writing:

> '*This project* will take ten years to complete.' This addition ensures clarity and precision.

Tense
This grammatical term describes how verbs are used to indicate the time of the action. In general, tenses can be divided into three categories – past, present and future. The tense you need to use will depend on the context of your work – for example, whether you are narrating a sequence of events in the past, whether you are discussing concepts, or whether you are conjecturing about events in the future.
Voice: active or passive
'Voice' is used in grammar terms to explain the relationship between an action and the person who performs the action (the actor). In English these are the passive and the active voices respectively. The difference between these two forms is perhaps best shown in two examples: 1 **Passive voice**: *'The plants were deprived of water for six days.'* 2 **Active voice**: *'We deprived the plants of water for six days.'* The passive voice focuses attention on the action rather than the actor and helps to maintain objectivity in an impersonal style. Some would argue that the second example is clearer, but their opponents would counter-argue that the use of 'we' takes attention away from the action. Note that some referencing styles require the active voice, being simpler and easier to understand (see McMillan and Weyers, 2013). The rules are not hard and fast, but many academics have strong views in favour of one voice or the other. It is advisable to consult your supervisor to find out if they or your department have any stated preferences.

Can I trust my word processor's 'advice' when it comes to academic writing?

The answer to this question is to approach spelling and grammar checking with caution. For example, you may find that the grammar checkers in some word-processing packages suggest that passive expressions should be changed to active. However, if you follow this guidance you will find yourself having to use a personal pronoun, which is inconsistent with impersonal academic style. Recommended spellings, too, might adhere to American English style rather than British English, and hence be unsuitable in many situations.

Example: verb- or noun-led expressions

- Verb-led: 'We **applied** pressure to the wound to stem bleeding' (verb in bold)
- Noun-led: 'The **application** of pressure stemmed bleeding' (noun in bold).

TAKING ACCOUNT OF GENRE, REGISTER AND AUDIENCE

Three fundamental factors influence all academic writing. These are:

- genre – the precise writing task to be completed
- register – the conventional tone and style of the text
- audience – the intended readership.

These aspects are discussed below.

Genre

This term describes types of writing for particular contexts. Each genre requires a subtly different approach to the writing. This might mean level of detail, it could mean verb tense, and it might include vocabulary. Some typical examples could occur in the Abstract, Materials and Methods and Conclusion sections of your document. It will be necessary to adopt different forms of language as you write these components (**Ch 22**).

For example, the Materials and Methods section in a scientific report will be almost note-like, use very precise technical terms and will generally adopt the past tense (describing what you did). On the other hand, the Conclusion of a paper in the arts and social sciences might be less rigid in style, include some personal viewpoints (albeit expressed impersonally) and might use the present tense (as the findings are current at the time of writing).

> **✓ Find models for the genre in which you are required to write**
>
> When writing up your work in a particular genre for the first time, find a model you can follow. This might be one of your supervisor's papers, a section of a previous student's well-received submission, or a publication from your field. Use this as a template for your own writing. This does not mean copying it, but rather adopting a similar style.

Register

Register (or tenor) in scholarly writing is important. Traditionally, writing in a formal tone is expected. Language should follow the standard rules of grammar, including sentence and paragraph structure, punctuation and spelling. For example, it would not be appropriate to use contractions or slang expression. Therefore, the sentence 'We ain't gonna spend too long banging on about this' would be entirely out of place in scholarly text and would perhaps be expressed more formally as 'Little time will be spent considering this point'.

That is, of course, an extreme example, and modern approaches in some disciplines are less stringent with regard to some aspects of language use, such as passive voice, first person singular/plural and a more conversational register. However, the academic world is generally rather conservative in its practices. If you are in doubt, it is best to opt for the more formal option. Scholarly writing should never replicate spoken language.

> ### British English (BE) versus American English (AE)
> Academic writing in the UK nearly always adopts BE. The differences are most evident in spelling; for example, 'colour' (BE) and 'color' (AE). However, there are also differences in vocabulary, so that in AE people talk of 'professor' for 'lecturer'; and in language use, so that in AE someone might write 'we have gotten results', rather than 'we have obtained results'. In some disciplines, there is an attempt at standardization – for example, in chemistry the spelling of 'sulphur' (BE) has become 'sulfur' (AE) as the international standard.

Audience

In terms of writing about your research, you should write as if the primary audience was the examiner. He or she will expect the text to be written as if it were for academic readers from your discipline area. Thus, in your writing you must use not only the language structures, but also the argot (jargon and idiom) of the discipline for this expert audience. Each discipline, and even sub-discipline or school of thought, has its own jargon. In certain cases, the same word may mean different things in different subjects.

However, if your writing is too complex and jargon-rich then the examiner may simply discard it as impenetrable. Conversely, if it is too down-to-earth, then it could appear simplistic. The two examples under 'Jargon' in Table 23.1 show, firstly, an overly complex piece of writing that would confuse many readers and, secondly, a simpler text that is clear, neutral and understandable by most audiences. The measure of good writing is its clarity to the reader.

ORGANISING YOUR DISCOURSE

Good writing requires organisation. It must fit within an appropriate format (**Ch 22**), but within each section of your text there must be a logic and flow to what you write.

Chapter 16 examined some of the approaches to thinking critically about the material you gather. Essentially, you need to decide for yourself what you think is important about the topic, and why. Your initial thoughts will develop as you move into the reading and research phase that follows. Next, you need to develop a plan for the text, as discussed in **Chapter 21**. Understanding how academic text is organised will help you to create this plan.

> ### ✓ Thinking and writing, and more thinking
>
> Even the best of plans for your writing can alter as you begin to write. Thinking inspires writing but writing, in turn, stimulates further thinking. This can mean that, as you compose a structure for your writing and then write following this plan, your ideas may change, new ideas may emerge and even the thrust of your argument might shift in direction. Being aware that this can happen is significant, because your writing may take longer and may need a revision of your plan involving a major rethink of what you have written already.

The basic model for academic text

Once you have gathered the material and established the direction of your text as part of your plan, you need to be able to set this within a framework for each section or chapter. This can be simplified if you follow the model common to text in most academic disciplines – namely, one that involves just three fundamental elements: introduction, main body and conclusion. Superimposed on this is the principle of leading readers from general to specific points and after that back to general points (see Figure 23.1). This organisational structure can be applied to the formats of many different types of academic writing – essays, reports, dissertations and theses – as well as to individual chapters and even to paragraphs. The focus is on the different elements in terms of discourse that you will need to apply in the different sections of your text, as outlined in **Chapter 22**.

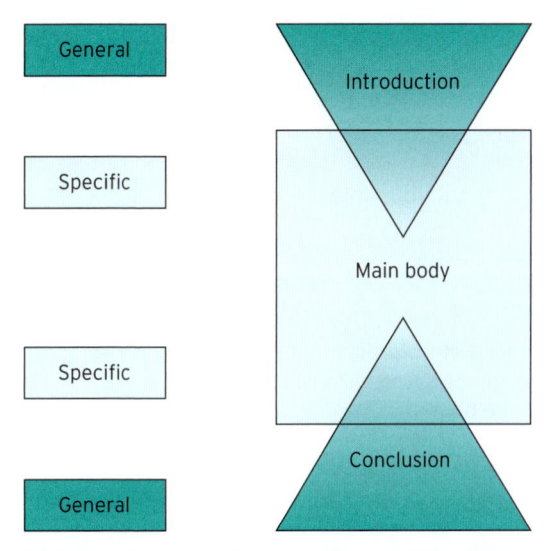

Figure 23.1 The basic structure of academic text. This diagram shows the fundamental structure of a typical piece of academic text, working from the top to the bottom of the figure. Note that each section in the diagram will comprise a number of paragraphs.

Figure 23.2(a) shows the introductory element of Figure 23.1 as a scene-setting section covering:

- the general context of the text or topic – what the text is about, defining the parameters of the discussion within the wider field
- the specific issue to be examined – what particular aspect will be examined and possibly what will be excluded from that examination, giving reasons for this choice
- the 'statement of intent' – how the examination of the topic will be addressed in detail so that the reader is provided with a 'map' of the writer's thought process and an insight into what to expect in the main body of text
- the transition to the main body – preparing the reader for the later detailed discussion of the topic.

23 Writing up in the appropriate style 257

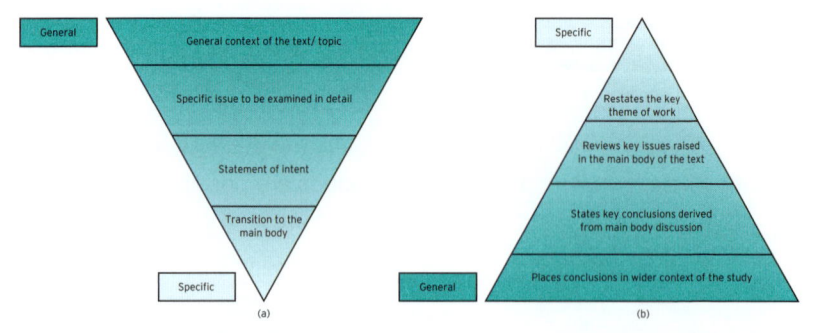

Figure 23.2 Typical structures, (a) of introductory paragraphs and (b) of concluding paragraphs. The writer would normally cover these topics in order, from the top to the bottom of the diagram.

Diagram (a) – inverted pyramid, General to Specific:
- General context of the text/topic
- Specific issue to be examined in detail
- Statement of intent
- Transition to the main body

Diagram (b) – upright pyramid, Specific to General:
- Restates the key theme of work
- Reviews key issues raised in the main body of the text
- States key conclusions derived from main body discussion
- Places conclusions in wider context of the study

> ✓ **Moving from lower- to higher-order thinking**
>
> Writing about your project gives you opportunities to demonstrate advanced thought processes of critical thinking (**Ch 16**). Often, each component initially contains a description of the context or process in order to outline the background to the topic. This is then followed by in-depth consideration of the topic, using more analytical or critical approaches.

The final section, modelled in Figure 23.2(b), draws the work to a conclusion by:

- restating the key theme of the work – outlining the main focus and purpose of the text
- reviewing key issues raised in the main body of the text – reminding the reader of the main aspects, explaining these in a concise way by using more technical/professional language
- stating key conclusions derived from the main body of the discussion – providing an assertive stance on the conclusions reached within the text
- placing conclusions in the wider context of the study – re-situating the topic within the broader body of knowledge.

There may seem to be a degree of repetition between the introductory and concluding sections. However, in practice, the difference is that the introductory section is expressed using simpler language formats and less specialised terms. By contrast, the concluding paragraphs use more sophisticated expressions and the terminology already introduced in the main body. The concluding text will also refer to the results or arguments described in the main body, whereas the introductory section involves scene-setting.

The main body of the text should present a reasoned explanation of individual points, following recognised steps of logic as part of the greater whole. However, different approaches are possible, using either inductive or deductive logic. These can be explained as follows:

1. inductive model of text structure: the writer begins by presenting the supporting information and concludes with the main point
2. deductive model of text structure: the writer moves from the key idea and follows it with supporting information or evidence.

These models may be deployed according to customary discipline style. Some disciplines favour the inductive approach while others use the deductive approach.

> **Establishing the model of logic for constructing discussion in your subject**
>
> The way that academics write about their research follows conventions within disciplines, using the logic of either inductive or deductive reasoning. If you fail to recognise which is the norm in your subject, then your writing may be perceived as woolly and lacking rigour. Thus, analysing the logic that is used by writers in your subject area may help you construct your writing. You could start by looking at some of your supervisor's publications.

The role of paragraphs and sentences

Having a clearer idea of the role of paragraphs and sentences can help to improve your writing. A paragraph is a unit of text usually comprising several sentences. Each paragraph should cover a specific topic. This topic is outlined in the first sentence; it is developed further within the paragraph, and the paragraph concludes with a sentence that terminates the topic or, possibly, acts as a link to the topic of the next paragraph. In good writing, the paragraphs 'flow' in an organised and logical way, leading the reader through the theme of the writing.

The building blocks of paragraphs are sentences, each performing a particular role, such as introducing a topic, developing it, linking between ideas, terminating a discussion or making a transition to the next paragraph. Again, the sentences in a paragraph should 'flow', developing its logic for the reader.

Some organisational approaches for text

Table 23.2 shows eight model frameworks that help set out the logic of analysis and argument. In different ways, these all allow a situation to be presented coherently. Note that it may sometimes be necessary to incorporate one of these models within another. For example, within the common denominator approach, it may be necessary to include some chronological description within the discussion.

Table 23.2 The eight most common structural approaches for academic writing. The examples beneath the headings describe relatively simple examples of each approach.

1 Chronological: description of a process or sequence
Example: describing a developmental process, such as outlining the historical development of the European Union. This kind of writing is likely to be entirely descriptive.
2 Classification: categorising objects or ideas
Example: you could discuss modes of transport by subdividing your text into land, sea and air modes of travel. Each of these could be further divided into commercial, military and personal modes of transport. These categories could be further sub-divided on the basis of how they are powered. The approach provides a means of describing each category at each level in a way that allows some contrast, and is particularly useful in scientific disciplines. The rationale also assists an approach of starting from broad generalisation to the more specific.
3 Common denominator: identification of common characteristics or themes
Example: for a project looking at the high levels of infant mortality in developing countries, you could investigate whether there is a common denominator of deficiency or lack. This topic could therefore be approached under the headings, for example, of: • Lack of primary health care • Lack of health education • Lack of literacy.
4 Phased: identification of short-, medium- and long-term aspects
Example: discussing the impact of water shortage on flora and fauna along river banks. You may wish to organise this by considering, in order: • Short-term factors, such as drying out of the river bed so that annual plants fail to thrive • Medium-term factors, including damage to oxygenating plant life and reduction of wildlife numbers • Long-term factors, such as the effect on the water table and falling numbers of certain amphibious species.

5 Analytical: examination of an issue in depth, for example: • situation • problem • solution • evaluation • recommendation

Example: evaluating potential solutions to the problem of identity theft. You could perhaps adopt the following plan:
- define identity theft, and perhaps give an example
- explain why identity theft is difficult to control
- outline legal and practical solutions to identify theft
- weigh up the advantages and disadvantages of each
- state which solution(s) you would favour, and why.

This approach is useful for complex issues.

6 Thematic: commentary on a theme in each aspect

Example: taking different situations and looking at specific aspects in each case. Precise details would depend on the nature of the topic, but possible examples could be:
- social, economic or political factors
- age, income and health considerations
- gas, electricity, oil, water and wind power and their relative merits.

This approach is similar to the phased approach, but in this case themes are the identifying characteristics.

7 Cause and effect: analysis of events or processes linking cause(s) with corresponding effect(s)

Example: explaining the influences of poverty on poor diet in modern urban society. You might examine or propose causal relationships – sometimes termed cause and effect, sometimes reason and result – using a themed approach of short–medium–long effects, as shown above. At other times, the time dimension is less relevant.

8 Comparative/contrastive: discussion of similarities and differences (often within a theme or themes)

Example: discussing the arguments for and against the introduction of car-free city centres. You might approach this by creating a simple table that notes positive aspects (Column A) and negative aspects (Column B) for the major stakeholders and use this to structure your text. For an example considering three stakeholders, there are two potential methods of constructing text in this comparative/contrastive approach:

Method 1.
- Introductory statement on the topic
- Follow Column A vertically (A1 + A2 + A3)
- Follow Column B vertically (B1 + B2 + B3)
- Concluding statement about the merits and demerits of one over the other.

Continued overleaf

8 Comparative/contrastive: discussion of similarities and differences (often within a theme or themes)

Method 2.
- Introductory statement on the topic
- Follow row 1: discuss positive point A1 then negative point B1
- Follow row 2: discuss positive point A2 then negative point B2
- Follow row 3: discuss positive point A3 then negative point B3
- Concluding statement about the merits and demerits of one over the other.

This is a derivative of the themed approach. Each method of structuring the points has advantages and disadvantages, according to the context. Method 1 has the advantage that it allows for a continuous appraisal of allied aspects (in this case, the positive and then negative aspects). This can suit some topics where it is important to establish the case in its entirety before considering counter-points. For long and complex topics where there are many points of comparison/contrast, Method 2 offers greater integration of each aspect under consideration.

Once you have decided what kind of approach is required to cover your written assignment, then you can formulate this as the main body of your essay and frame an introduction and conclusion that will 'top and tail' your writing. In this way you can create the outline plan based on the introduction–main body–conclusion design.

> ✓ **Explain your approach**
>
> Although the models outlined in this chapter are fairly standard approaches to tackling academic issues, it is still necessary to identify for your reader which approach you intend to adopt in the piece of text. Your reader should learn at an early point in your writing of the route you intend to follow. In most cases this would be included in your Introduction.

GRAMMAR CONVENTIONS IN ACADEMIC WRITING

There are many conventions – often unspoken – that are expected to be observed in academic writing. Table 23.1 defines some relevant concepts and terms and outlines some simple rules that will help you to develop as an academic author.

ACTION POINTS

23.1 Analyse good writing. Find a textbook or research paper by an author whose style you admire, or who you find explains complex matters clearly. Look closely at the structure of the writing at different levels of scale, from chapter to paragraph to sentence. Try to identify what makes the writing attractive to you, and see if you can use this as a model for your own writing.

23.2 Invest in reference books to support your writing. Online versions are available, but they generally lack the authority and detail of the standard printed works. As a minimum, you should have the following ready for consultation near your desk: a good dictionary, a detailed thesaurus and a book on English usage.

23.3 Review academic conventions for language use and grammar. Read through Table 23.1 and see if you tend to be guilty of any of the errors described there. You might find that these have been noted in feedback on previous work. Experiment with the methods suggested for expressing yourself more appropriately.

24 CITING, REFERENCING AND AVOIDING PLAGIARISM

How to refer appropriately to the work and ideas of others

The ability to cite and quote sources correctly in your text and create an appropriately formatted reference list is essential for any form of project writing. You will need to understand the principles behind these processes so that you can, from the outset, apply them correctly in your own submission.

KEY TOPICS

→ The rationale for correct citation and referencing
→ Avoiding plagiarism
→ Methods and styles of citation
→ Quotation techniques
→ Summarising and paraphrasing
→ An outline of referencing styles

With the advent of digital archiving and searching systems, today's researchers have at their fingertips a wide array of accessible material to support their learning and writing. Clearly, the ability to search, copy, paste and adapt that material has many advantages, but it also brings the risk of plagiarism closer. That risk can be avoided via the processes of citation, referencing, quotation and paraphrasing, when these are carried out in an appropriate way.

> **Definitions: citation and referencing**
>
> Some terms connected with citation and referencing are used loosely. Here are the definitions adopted for this text:
>
> **Citation** (noun) – a quotation (a book, its author, or a passage from the book) as an example or a proof; a mention as an example or illustration.
>
> **To cite** (verb) – to use a phrase or sentence from a piece of writing or speech, especially in order to support or prove something.
>
> **Reference** (noun) – a direction to another passage or another book where information can be found; a book or passage referred to; the act of referring to a book or passage for information.
>
> **To reference** (verb) – to mention a particular writer or piece of work; to create a list of all the books that are mentioned in a piece of academic writing.
>
> **Chapter 18** includes a definition of plagiarism.

THE RATIONALE FOR CORRECT CITATION AND REFERENCING

Several citation and referencing systems exist and, over time, some have been modified to create a wide array of similar and sometimes competing systems. When choosing and/or using one of these, the focus is often on the mechanics – the complex and exacting layout and punctuation rules that cause so much angst to novice academic authors. However, there is more to following the conventions than sprinkling your writing with citations or pressing the punctuation keys in the right places. The rationale behind the rules and conventions of citation and referencing can be approached via explanations of the key terms involved.

Plagiarism

Academic authors demonstrate their scholarship by writing and publishing in their own fields. They have the moral right to claim such work as their own property (this is sometimes referred to loosely, rather than in the legal sense, as 'intellectual property'). Hence, the academic community requires that all academic authors attribute the ownership of ideas, text and other forms of work to the original writers.

There are two intertwined strands to avoiding plagiarism: the need to maintain your academic integrity (that is, your honesty) by giving correct attribution to sources; and the need to demonstrate your critical thinking skills (Ch 16) – namely, your ability to analyse, synthesise and create new meaning from complex textual information.

Citation

In the academic environment, citation involves linking an idea within a new text to information or data derived from another source document and its author(s). This gives recognition to the original author by providing sufficient information from the publication details so that the reader can locate the original document, if they wish. Integration of the ideas of others can be done:

- by direct quotation – that is, writing down what they wrote word for word
- by paraphrasing the idea in words that are different from those of the original author
- by summarising the general ideas of the original author in less detail than in paraphrasing.

Whichever of these methods is adopted, the actual attribution in the text (the publishing details) will follow the citation and referencing style required for your writing.

Referencing

There are two usages in the context of academic writing: providing information in the text about authorship of the original source material; and providing the publication details in some kind of footnote, reference list or bibliography in accordance with the citation and referencing style being followed. The rationale for this is:

- to protect the 'intellectual property' of the original author by acknowledging their contribution
- to provide readers with specific bibliographical information.

By structuring and presenting your views with appropriate attention to the published evidence, you enhance the quality of your research and acknowledge the contribution of others to the literature. Thus, learning how to cite and reference is essential to successful academic writing and will help you to achieve the highest standards in your work.

> **Details of specific referencing styles**
>
> There are many referencing styles, each with very specific rules for layout and punctuation. Space precludes detailed descriptions here; instead the focus is on principles. The companion text *How to Cite, Reference and Avoid Plagiarism at University* by McMillan and Weyers (2013) focuses on five of the main styles – American Psychological Association (APA), Chicago, Harvard, Modern Language Association and Vancouver – and should be consulted for guidance.

AVOIDING PLAGIARISM

The concept of plagiarism as an ethical issue was introduced in **Chapter 18** and it is assumed that you will wish to safeguard yourself against the risks of this academic misdeed. This is not always a straightforward task. There is a very thin line between unintended and deliberate plagiarism. Some people think (wrongly) that plagiarism can be avoided by:

- creating a patchwork of quotations from original text
- substituting one or two words with synonyms
- rearranging the wording of the original text
- reordering the original sentences
- or mixing any of the above strategies.

These misconceptions can lead to unintended plagiarism, when the writer has not understood the conventions and practices of engaging with the work of others within their own work. Instead, the right way to avoid plagiarism is to:

- cite the work of others when this is due
- quote others' work where this is appropriate (within limits), with due citation
- paraphrase the ideas or text of others, with due citation.

As can be seen, the key is 'appropriate' citation. For example, a piece of text that incorporates too high a proportion of quotes from other sources might be considered to plagiarise just as much as one that fails to acknowledge its sources via citation. There can be no exceptions to the norm of citation etiquette, and you must preserve your academic integrity by following these academic conventions.

> **? When is quotation plagiarism?**
>
> In many disciplines, if more than 10 per cent of a piece of work, article or book chapter is devoted to quotation, this is regarded as a form of plagiarism. The heavy reliance on the literature as a source of words shows limited original thinking without real analysis or discussion of the issues, and may even imply lack of understanding. However, it should be noted that in some disciplines – for example, English literature – more extensive quotation may be expected and thus does not constitute plagiarism, unless it has not been correctly attributed to its author.

METHODS AND STYLES OF CITATION

There are two fundamental ways of citing authors within the text, which are used according to your purpose.

Information-prominent citation

Here the text provides the idea or result first, and then provides the citation. This approach tends to be used when the statement being made is regarded as generally accepted in the field of study. For example:

> Providing enough copies of essential texts is a problem for university librarians and this can be a factor in students using the internet as their first research choice (Monaghan, 2012).

Alternatively, the statement may relate to literature that is less recent and that provides the foundation of a thread of research or reasoning. For example:

> Books have developed from handwritten texts illuminated by scribes to mass-produced paperbacks that bring the printed word to all (Francis, 1971).

Note that these examples follow the Harvard style, in which the author's name and the date of publication are given in brackets.

Author-prominent citation

Author-prominent citation is used when the statement is more recent or contemporary, or when the stress is on the ownership of the finding or idea – as when comparing two schools of thought. For example:

> O'Donnell (2010) surmised that the implications of downloading lengthy texts from the internet may infringe the intellectual property rights of authors. Smith (2011), on the other hand...

This example, again, follows the Harvard style, where the author's name is included as part of the sentence (in these examples as the subject of the sentence); the date of publication is encased in round brackets and follows immediately after the name of the author.

> **Deciding how many citations to include** ✔
>
> A whole string of citations does not add to the merit of writing if these are not germane to the purpose of discussion in the text. It is better to build up a cogent analysis of the existing literature, identifying seminal works from which to build the framework of your analysis. From there you can then include additional citations that support your particular line of investigation, or which illuminate or characterise contrasting views or evidence with which you may or may not agree. If you look at a few articles in your own field, you will obtain a sense of the extent to which multiple references are the norm, or whether only the more recent publications are cited. If there is a single principle to apply, it is that the citations should be relevant to the purpose of the author making the citations.

Conveying attitude in citation

To help direct your reader along a particular line of thought and to help build your discussion, your choice of verb reporting the authorship of the source material is important. This verb choice will be dictated by the function you are trying to perform by using the source material as supporting evidence. Thus, for example, you may wish to introduce material performing the following functions, namely, to:

- provide factual information
- present evidence that is non-controversial and universally accepted
- express opinion
- support or refute ideas or research within your own discussion
- offer alternatives – viewpoints or approaches that are either positive or negative.

Table 24.1 itemises some potential reasons for citing the work of others. These are categorised according to whether they mark the beginning of a research theme (the accepted view in a particular field), whether they take a positive or negative view of existing literature, or whether they are outlining processes described in the literature.

Table 24.1 Reasons for citing the work of others. This table is derived from **www.garfield.library.upenn.edu/papers/vladivostok.html** [Accessed 6 November 2013].

Rationale for citation	Positive context	Negative context	Processes involved
Indicating key reading to establish the context of work	Validating claims in earlier literature	Critiquing published literature reporting earlier research	Identifying methodology, equipment, etc.
Acknowledging the work of early investigators in a particular field	Acknowledging previous well-received work in a field	Identifying work that is not well-written, or related to existing literature	Authenticating data and classes of fact
Identifying original publications in which an idea or concept was first introduced	Identifying seminal literature	Rejecting the work or ideas of others (negative claims)	Alerting researchers to forthcoming work
Identifying the original publication describing an eponymic concept or terms such as Parkinson's Disease, the Peter Principle, Asperger's Syndrome or Boyle's Law	Acknowledging priority	Disputing the 'priority claims' of others, that is, questioning claims of 'ownership' of the instigation of a research theme or aspect within it or of ground-breaking achievements	Challenging the validity or merit of the work of others in respect of procedural methods or data interpretation

Whatever your purpose in citing the work of others, in order to make the citation you will have to attribute the idea to the original author. However, how you report that work will reflect 'attitude' – that could be, how the content reflects the work of the original author as perceived in the academic world, or how you view the content. Within your discussion, it makes a considerable difference to interpretation if you report: 'Brown contended that...' (meaning 'disputed in face of controversy') as opposed to: 'Brown noted that...' (meaning 'made special mention of...'), and both take the reader much further in their understanding of the case that has been compiled in the text than simply 'Brown said that...' or Brown stated that...'. Table 24.2 provides some examples of positive- and negative-attitude verbs that are commonly used to report the work of others in academic texts.

Table 24.2 Attitude verbs used to report the work of others. This table derives from analysis of academic discourse across a range of disciplines. This is by no means comprehensive, but it reflects the diversity of expressions used in relation to citing the ideas and work of others. The shading groups the verbs by the function given in column 3. Part A of the table deals with positive connotations, while Part B covers negative connotations.

Attitude verb in past tense	Definition in present tense	Function(s)
A. Positive connotation examples		
concurred with the view	be in accord	agreeing
supported the view	concur	agreeing
alleged	assert without proof	affirming
asserted	state firmly	affirming/declaring
averred	declare positively	affirming
declared	state emphatically	affirming/alleging
decreed	decide authoritatively	affirming/dictating
professed	claim forcefully	affirming/declaring
contended	dispute in face of controversy	alleging/maintaining
claimed	state to be true when open to question	alleging/maintaining
explained	make understandable	clarifying/simplifying
proclaimed	announce officially and publicly	clarifying
expounded the view	simplify by giving detail	clarifying/elucidating
reflected	make a statement of opinion	commenting/observing
affirmed	maintain to be true	confirming/validating
established	make of truth based on evidence	confirming
conjectured	infer from inconclusive evidence	conjecturing/surmising
guessed	form an opinion with little evidence	conjecturing/surmising
hypothesised	believe tentatively without evidence	conjecturing/theorising
inferred	conclude from evidence or facts	conjecturing/theorising
supposed	consider as a suggestion	conjecturing/suggesting
surmised	infer without sufficient evidence	conjecturing/guessing
defined something as…	state precise meaning	describing
characterised	categorise	describing
believed	accept as true or real	judging

Continued overleaf

Attitude verb in past tense	Definition in present tense	Function(s)
judged	form an opinion through reasoning	judging/evaluating
commented	explain judgementally	judging/interpreting
held the view	have an opinion	judging/opining
insisted	express an opinion strongly	judging strongly
noted	make special mention of…	judging/commenting
observed	understand through known facts	judging
opined that…	express a view	judging/stating belief
posited the view	put forward an idea for consideration	judging/offering opinion
stated	express particulars in words	judging/formulating
suggested	present for consideration	proposing/suggesting
advanced the view	bring to notice	proposing
proposed	put forward for consideration	proposing/proffering
B. Negative connotation examples		
warned	recommend caution	advising against
diverged	take different routes	differing
disagreed	to have a different opinion	disagreeing with
disputed	question on basis of poor evidence	disagreeing with
doubted	consider unlikely	disagreeing with
opposed	be resistant to an idea	disagreeing with
criticised	judge on basis of good and bad points	disapproving
disdained	regard with scorn	disapproving/despise
questioned the view	express uncertainty	doubting/disputing

Your choice of 'reporting verb' might reflect your own attitude or that of the original author. You can use such choices to construct your own argument and subliminally lead your reader through the analysis or argument you are presenting. Table 24.2 also provides you with options in some groups so that you avoid repeatedly using the same wording.

Use of tense in reporting the work of others

Citation of the work of others has to be placed in a time-frame. However, there is some inconsistency in practice, in that some writers use the present tense to report the literature while others adopt a simple past tense. Those who favour the present tense might argue that the text is in front of the reader and therefore it is acceptable to use the present tense ('Brown contends that…'). However, other writers would state that:

- the research work has already been done
- a view has already been presented for consideration by the academic world.

Hence, they reason that the simple past tense should be used ('Brown observed that…').

The choice you make between these alternatives should reflect normal practice for your discipline, or perhaps your supervisor's preference. You should ensure that you are consistent in the tense that you use, but note that the present tense is used, regardless of time-frame, to describe habitual conditions – for example, 'Traditionalists argue that…'.

Secondary citation in reporting the work of others ('secondary referencing')

Secondary citation occurs when a writer wishes to refer to a source that they have not read themselves. This could be because the original is out of print, or unavailable to them for other reasons. Formerly, secondary citation/referencing was rare because it was discouraged or disallowed. This remains the policy in some of the more common referencing styles. However, with the diminution of library book stocks and concomitant rise in availability of online sources that may refer to less well-publicised literature, the incidence of secondary citation has become more prevalent.

Figure 24.1 shows how to cite a secondary reference in the text following the Harvard style. Note that the source that should be listed in the references is the text that you have read, not the reference for the unread text. It is advisable to check the guidance given in your subject, since attitudes to secondary citation can differ from one referencing style to another and also different regulations or conventions may apply in your discipline.

> **An information-prominent secondary citation would be presented as:**
>
> One of the most powerful criticisms is that reading on-screen is, for many people, a painful activity (Owen, 2007 cited in Peel, 2010).

> **An author-prominent secondary citation would be presented as:**
>
> Owen (2007 cited in Peel, 2010) considered that 'one of the most powerful criticisms of reading on-screen is that, for many people, this is a painful activity'.

Figure 24.1 Two examples of secondary referencing in the Harvard style. These examples use the form of words 'cited in' but it would be equally acceptable to use the form 'quoted in' where material had been quoted. Note that secondary referencing can be used in paraphrased citations as well as in direct quotations.

QUOTATION TECHNIQUES

Quoting text directly from source material has a place in academic writing in many disciplines, although in some it is rarely used. If permitted, quotation is best used sparingly. It would be very easy to drift inadvertently into plagiarism should too great a proportion of your writing rely on direct extracts from the work of others.

Before you decide to quote from the literature you have sourced, you should consider why you want to include the exact words used by the original author. Some questions to contemplate include:

- ❏ Will this quotation strengthen my discussion?
- ❏ Will the extract place special emphasis on the author's findings or viewpoint?
- ❏ Will the extract present a point that could be counter-argued?
- ❏ Will the words used make the author's point in a particularly powerful way that would be weakened if paraphrased?

Only if your response to any of these questions is 'yes' should you seriously consider including a quotation. To quote correctly, you will need to assemble the following:

- the exact words from the text (sometimes described as '*verbatim* text')
- page number(s) or, in the case of journals, volume and page number where the quote appeared
- the publication details (see below).

Since different citation styles require different information, you might need all or only some of the following publication details:

- author(s)
- date of publication
- edition
- editor(s)
- title (of book, chapter or article)
- journal title (if applicable)
- place of publication
- publisher.

Collecting these details is a routine part of note-making practice (**Ch 10**).

Characteristics of quotations

The layout of quotations can differ from one discipline to another, but some key guidelines can help you follow the general rules appropriately. Check the conventions in your particular discipline or subject area. In general, quotations may be laid out in one of the following formats:

- Long quotes consist of 30 or more words (some propose 40 words) of prose, or two lines of poetry or more, and should:
    - be indented by five character spaces from the left-hand margin
    - not include quotation marks at the beginning and end (quotation marks should only be included if used in the original text)
    - be printed in single-line spacing (although some styles require double-line spacing)
    - be followed by the author(s) surname, year of publication and page number separated by a full colon (:), or date of publication followed by page number printed as p. xx, depending on the preferred citation convention.
- Short quotes consist of fewer than 30 words and should:
    - be integrated within the sentence
    - include the author(s) name within the sentence, where it often performs the role of the subject of the sentence. In this case, the date of publication should be in round brackets (...) immediately after the author name
    - give the page reference in round brackets (...) at the end of the quotation in the form 'p. xx'.

These two methods are illustrated in Figure 24.2. Note that there are minor variations regarding punctuation across citation styles, so it is important to consult your handbook to check for any deviations from the 'official' style. In some student writing, quotations can be found 'dangling' under the title of a chapter or within the text – that is, without introduction or context – so that the reader has no indication of the significance or relevance of the words quoted. Expecting your readers to make the connections for themselves is not indicative of well-explained logic and discussion. Thus, through your own writing, you should ensure that any quotation used in the text has a purpose and clear connection to the context in which it is found, possibly in the form of some related discussion.

> An essential prerequisite for monitoring demographic trends is efficient garnering of population data which means that the population census is essential to this process. Thus, while early records were relatively primitive in nature, more recent records that have been derived from computerised census data identify the relationship between birth rate and death rate as factors in population growth. This is described as the demographic transition model and is explained by Kay and Campbell (2011) as comprising
>
> > ... four stages: high birth rate with fluctuating but high death rate; high birth rate with falling death rate; falling birth rate and falling death rate; and low birth rate with low death rate.
> >
> > (Kay and Campbell, 2011, p. 23)
>
> More recent studies have attempted to interrogate the demographic transition model in order to identify socio-economic and ethnicity patterns from the birth-rate:death-rate data.

(a) Long quotation. This 'indentation' method is used where the quote is 30+ words or three lines of text. Note the positioning of the citation.

> Simpson (1953) claimed that one factor affecting the demographic transition model involved 'the changing roles of women as key contributors to the economy since these roles impact on their traditional child-bearing roles' (p.63).

(b) Short quotation. This 'in text' method is used where the quote is less than 30 words or three lines of text. Note the positioning of the citation and that the quotation forms a part of the sentence, so the full stop is placed after the final quotation mark. This is different from the punctuation required in direct speech (the actual words said) in a novel or a newspaper report, for example.

Figure 24.2 Layouts for 'long' and 'short' quotations.

What forms of quotation marks should be used?

1. **Single or double quote marks.** Approaches to the use of quotation marks, which are sometimes called 'inverted commas', differ according to whether the text follows British English or American English.
   - British English: single quotation marks are used around the text to mark the exact words spoken or written. Any quote-within-the-quote is placed in double quotation marks.
   - American English: double quotation marks are used around the text to mark the exact words spoken or written. Any quote-within-the-quote is placed in single quotation marks.

   Note that these conventions apply in most cases, but there are some disciplines that do not follow them. If this appears to be the case, consult your handbook or supervisor.

2. **'Curly' ('round') quotes or 'straight' quotes.** Curly quotes are the inverted comma symbols that were used traditionally by typographers. In word processors, these are sometimes referred to as 'smart quotes'. The single ones look like 'this' and double ones look like "this". They resemble miniature digits 6 or 66 before the quotation words and digits 9 or 99 after the quotation. Straight quotes are the inverted comma symbols that are often used by typewriters and word processors. They are sometimes referred to as 'dumb quotes'. The single ones look like this: ' and double ones look like this: ". There is no difference in form between the straight quote marks before and after the quotation. Ideally, 'curly' and 'straight' styles of quotation marks should not be mixed within the same document.

SUMMARISING AND PARAPHRASING

While quotation must replicate exactly the words in the original work of an author, the central concept of both summarising and paraphrasing is that writers use their own words rather than those of the original author, except in the following situations:

- where, within the paraphrase or summary, a direct quotation from the source document is used
- where there is use of the same or similar wording to state aspects that are common knowledge – for example, dates, well-known facts or anything regarded as published in the public

domain in information/reference sources such as dictionaries or encyclopaedias
- where 'shared', subject-specific language has been reproduced from the original.

Figure 24.3 illustrates the difference between these two approaches, which can be explained as follows:

1 Summarising: while recognising that technical terms or 'shared language' can be retained, the aim is to use your own words in writing (but giving less detail than in a paraphrase) to:
   - put across the general idea
   - state the main points briefly
   - include only the views of the original author.

2 Paraphrasing: while recognising that technical terms or 'shared language' can be retained, the aim is to use your own words in writing (but giving more detail than in a summary) to:
   - explain the key idea(s)
   - clarify their meaning
   - include only the views of the original author.

A. Original text (51 words)

E-books are a function of the internet era and make access to otherwise unattainable material possible to wider audiences. The globalisation of literature means that individual authors can present their work to a wider audience without incurring abortive publication costs. This facility constitutes a considerable threat to publishers of traditional books.

Source: Watt, W. (2011) *The demise of the book*. Cambridge: The Printing Press (page 13)

B. Summarised text (19 words)

With the advent of e-books, individual authors are faced with new approaches to publication of their work (Watt, 2011).

C. Paraphrased text (40 words)

Watt (2011) notes that there is concern amongst publishers of hard-copy printed books that the advent of e-books marks the end of their monopoly of the literature market since authors can publish directly from the internet thus avoiding publishing costs.

Figure 24.3 **Examples of summarised and paraphrased text.** Examples B and C follow the Harvard Style; B follows information-prominent citation and C follows author-prominent citation.

As well as indicating variation in content, the examples shown in Figure 24.3 demonstrate visually the relative difference in length. Paraphrasing will reduce the original text but not as much as a summary, which will be significantly shorter than the original text or section. The choice may relate to whether you wish to introduce an idea in more general terms by summarising or elucidate a discussion in greater detail by paraphrasing.

The advantage of summarising and paraphrasing in these ways is that there is much less risk of plagiarism because you are using your own words and writing style to create the shorter version; you are also demonstrating your ability to engage with the material and reach conclusions that demonstrate your critical thinking skills (**Ch 16**). In addition, as you become more practised and at ease with the process, you will be able to summarise or paraphrase spontaneously.

AN OUTLINE OF REFERENCING STYLES

As a researcher, you will meet a range of referencing styles during your literature searching and reading. Being aware of the conventions associated with these styles is important as they may differ from those with which you are familiar.

Figure 24.4 shows typical components of a Reference List or Bibliography (sometimes called 'Works Cited'). The layout and punctuation differ from one style to another. In practice, authors and universities tend to adhere to styles that are the norm for their disciplines or the departments within their institutions, or the publishers of academic journals in their subject area.

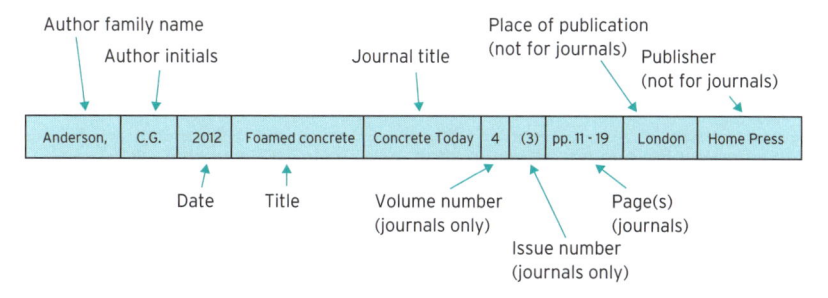

| Anderson, | C.G. | 2012 | Foamed concrete | Concrete Today | 4 | (3) | pp. 11 - 19 | London | Home Press |

Labels: Author family name, Author initials, Date, Title, Journal title, Volume number (journals only), Issue number (journals only), Page(s) (journals), Place of publication (not for journals), Publisher (not for journals)

Figure 24.4 The main components of a reference, as listed in a Reference section (or Bibliography or 'Works Cited' section). The precise details of order and punctuation will depend on the referencing style used.

Referencing systems can be classified as follows (note that there are many permutations of each these approaches).

- Author name/date (sometimes called parenthetical) systems are used in the social sciences and humanities, as well as the natural sciences (for example, 'Campbell and Hutton (2012) suggested that...'). However, there are significant differences in layout and language related to these and you should consult the guidelines you have been given for your recommended style.
- Numeric/footnote plus reference/bibliography list systems are used in scientific styles to give information in a numbered footnote about authorship on the same page as the citation first appears (for example, 'In the view of Campbell and Hutton[15]...'). Numbering may be full-size or superscript.
- Author name/page number systems are used in some disciplines within the humanities and include the Modern Language Association (MLA) style (for example, 'In the view of Campbell and Hutton (133)...').
- Numeric systems (sometimes called numbered or scientific systems) are used most commonly in the sciences (for example, 'In the view of Campbell and Hutton (15)...' or 'In the view of Campbell and Hutton[15]...'). The number relates to the number of the reference in the reference list. It would be inadvisable to use this type of system unless you have been told specifically to do so.

Five commonly used referencing systems are illustrated in Table 24.3. This takes as an example a citation and reference to a journal article, but there are specific formats for other forms of publication – each differing according to the style adopted. Examples include: books, chapters in books, newspaper articles, e-journals, e-books and websites – extending recently to blogs and wikis.

Table 24.3 Five commonly used referencing styles. With each is shown the format of a citation and reference that would be used when referring to material from an article in a journal. For formats used with other types of source, see McMillan and Weyers (2013).

1 American Psychological Association (APA) style This is used in both sciences and social sciences. It follows a name/date style. Note that APA spacing for the Reference List should be double-line.

In publishing, for example, several notorious cases of plagiarism exist where the text and plot of a best seller have close similarities to the text and plot of another book by another author (Scribner, 2006).

Scribner, A. (2006). Authorship by proxy: the case of the non-original best-seller. *Journal of Professional Ethics* 2(3), 51–59.

2 Chicago Style This style is used in the scientific community and social sciences where a scientific approach has been followed. It follows a numeric/footnote style. Note that there are two options for laying out the Footnotes and the Reference List:

1. Footnotes are at the bottom of the page beneath a line across the page or as a list of endnotes at the end of the text with a full bibliography of all works cited at the end of the text.

2. Full citations in the footnotes or endnotes for the first mention and thereafter as concise notes; there is no bibliography.

> In publishing, for example, there are several notorious cases where a best seller has been shown to be closely similar to another book by another author.[2]
>
> Footnote or Endnote
> 2. A. Scribner, "Authorship by Proxy: the Case of the Non-original Best-seller," *Journal of Professional Ethics*, 2, no.3 (2006): 59.
>
> Bibliography
> Scribner, A. "Authorship by Proxy: the Case of the Non-original Best-seller." *Journal of Professional Ethics* 2, no.3 (2006): 59.

3 Harvard Style which was not named after the US Harvard University but after John Harvard, an American clergyman, who bequeathed his library of books to Cambridge College, Massachusetts in 1637. This is one of the most commonly used styles and is accepted in disciplines across social and life sciences as well as in engineering. It follows the author/date style.

> In publishing, for example, there are several notorious cases where a best seller has been shown to be closely similar to another book by another author (Scribner, 2006).
>
> Scribner, A., 2006. Authorship by proxy: the case of the non-original best-seller. *Journal of Professional Ethics* 2(3), 51–59.

4 Modern Language Association (MLA) Style as its name suggests is designed to suit disciplines in the humanities. It follows the author/page number style. Note URLs are no longer used but the medium is included at the end of the 'Works cited' (MLA term for Reference List). Also, double line-spacing is required for the reference list in this style.

> In publishing, for example, there are several notorious cases where a best seller has been shown to be closely similar to another book by another author (Scribner 35).
>
> Scribner, A. "Authorship by Proxy: the Case of the Non-original Best-seller."
>
> *Journal of Professional Ethics* 2(3) (2006): 51–59. Print.

5 Vancouver Style is most commonly used in the medicine and related fields. It follows the numeric (scientific) style.

> In publishing, for example, there are several notorious cases where a best seller has been shown to be closely similar to another book by another author. (1)
>
> 1. Scribner A. Authorship by proxy: the case of the non-original best-seller. *J Prof Ethics* 2006 Mar 3; 2(3): 51–59.

ACTION POINTS

24.1 Look carefully at all five citation and referencing methods to make yourself aware of some of the permutations. You may find that you need to access, read or cite material that is presented in ways other than the referencing system that you have to follow in your manuscript. Understanding other layouts and ways in which bibliographical information is presented will help you deconstruct this and allow you to present details as required by the regulations of your university. The specific details of the major referencing styles can be found in the companion text by McMillan and Weyers (2013) or in the 'instructions to authors' sections of relevant journals.

24.2 Find out about the citation and referencing style expected for your written submission. Your supervisor should be able to guide you, or talk through the options, and the format may be specified in departmental or university rules. Once you know this, you can ensure that you format any citations and references you use in draft text in the correct way, saving a lot of time and effort later on. At this stage you should consider whether to use a referencing software package, such as EndNote or Zotero (**Ch 11**).

24.3 Examine your use of language when citing references. Use an earlier piece of your own academic writing or your project proposal. Do you use the same forms of wording repeatedly? Examine the options mentioned in this chapter (especially in Table 24.2) to judge whether you can expand your repertoire and provide more variety and accuracy in your writing.

25 REVIEWING, EDITING AND PROOFREADING

How to enhance the quality of your write-up

Looking critically at your own writing is essential if you want to produce work of the highest quality. Developing editing skills will allow you to improve the sense, grammar and syntax of your project write-up.

KEY TOPICS
- The value of reviewing, editing and proofreading
- The reviewing, editing and proofreading process

Writing is a process. It begins with a plan and it finishes with reviewing, editing and proofreading. This means that you should re-read your text critically and edit it before submitting it for assessment. The effort you invest in this final stage will contribute greatly to the quality of your project submission. Ideally, you should leave a gap of time between completing the writing and beginning the reviewing process, as this allows you to distance yourself from the work and helps you look at it as a new reader would.

THE VALUE OF REVIEWING, EDITING AND PROOFREADING

Many students do not appreciate the potential complexity of the review process, and fail to pay enough emphasis, either in effort or time, to this crucial aspect of the writing. Text that is not revised in this way will be unlikely to receive as favourable a reading – and possibly as high a mark – as one that has been fully reviewed, edited and proofread. It is the mix of style, content, structure and presentation that will influence your grading. Thus, anything you can do to improve the perception of your work by going through these final stages will be to your advantage. In the longer term, learning how to edit your work properly will help you to develop a skill of critical analysis that will stand you in good stead throughout your career.

> **Definitions: reviewing, editing and proofreading**
>
> **Reviewing** – appraising critically; that is, examining a task or project to ensure that it meets the requirements and objectives of the task and that the overall sense is conveyed as well.
>
> **Editing** – revising and correcting later drafts of a piece of writing to arrive at a final version; usually, this involves the smaller but no less important details, such as correct punctuation, spelling, grammar and layout.
>
> **Proofreading** – checking a printed copy for errors of any sort.

THE REVIEWING, EDITING AND PROOFREADING PROCESS

At this stage you are performing the role of editor. This means that you are looking critically at your text for content, relevance and sense, as well as for flaws in layout, grammar, punctuation and spelling. You should also check for consistency in all aspects – for example, in the use of terminology, in spelling and in presentational features such as font and point size, layout of paragraphs and labelling of tables and diagrams.

Clearly, there are a lot of aspects to cover, and some degree of overlap in different aspects of the process. Some people prefer to go through their text in one sweep, amending any flaws as they go; others, in particular professional writers, take a staged approach – reading through their text several times and looking at a different aspect each time. Here are five aspects to consider in the reviewing process:

1 content and relevance
2 clarity, style and coherence
3 grammatical correctness
4 spelling and punctuation
5 presentation.

Table 25.1 provides a quick checklist of key aspects to consider under each of these themes. Table 25.2 gives some strategies you can adopt

Table 25.1 **Proofreading and editing checklists.** Each heading represents a 'sweep' of your text, checking for the aspects shown.

Content and relevance
❏ The structure is appropriate
❏ The text shows objectivity
❏ The examples are relevant
❏ All sources are correctly cited
❏ The facts presented are accurate
Clarity, style and coherence
❏ The aims and objectives are clear
❏ What you wrote is what you meant to write
❏ The text is fluent, with appropriate use of signpost words
❏ The style is academic and appropriate for the genre
❏ The content and style of each section is consistent
❏ The tense used in each section is suited to the time-frame of your text and is consistent
❏ The lengths of the text sections are balanced appropriately
Grammatical correctness
❏ All sentences are complete and make sense
❏ Paragraphs have been correctly used
❏ Suggestions made by the grammar checker have been accepted/rejected
❏ The text has been checked against your own checklist of recurrent grammatical errors
❏ The text is consistent in adopting either British English or American English conventions, as appropriate
Spelling and punctuation
❏ Any obvious 'typos' have been corrected by reading for meaning
❏ The text has been spell-checked and looked at for your 'own' most-often misspelt words
❏ A check has been made for spelling of subject-specific words and words from other languages
❏ Punctuation has been checked, if possible by the 'reading aloud' method
❏ Proper names are correctly capitalised
❏ Overlong sentences have been divided
Presentation
❏ The text length is neither too short nor too long and meets the word-count target, if any
❏ The presentational aspects are as required by your department
❏ The Bibliography/Reference List is correctly formatted in accordance with regulations, if applicable
❏ Page numbers have been included (in position stipulated, if given)
❏ The figures and tables are in appropriate format

Table 25.2 Editing strategies. The reviewing/editing/proofreading process can be done in a single 'sweep'. As you become more experienced, you will become adept at doing this. However, initially, it might help you to focus on each of these three broad aspects in a separate 'sweep' of the text. Note that the first two sections combine pairs of aspects considered in Table 25.1.

Content and relevance; clarity, style and coherence
• Read text aloud – your ears will help you to identify errors that your eyes miss. • Revisit the task or question. Check your interpretation against the task as set. • Work on a hard copy using editing symbols to correct errors. • Check that the aims you set out in your introduction have been met. • Read objectively and assess whether the text makes sense. Look for inconsistencies in argument. • Confirm that all your facts are correct. • Insert additional or overlooked evidence that strengthens the whole. • Remove anything that is not relevant or alter the text so that it is clear and unambiguous. Reducing text by 10–25 per cent can improve quality considerably. • Honestly and critically assess your material to ensure that you have attributed ideas to the sources, that is, check that you have not committed plagiarism. • Remodel any expressions that are too informal for academic contexts. • Eliminate gendered or discriminatory language. • Consider whether the different parts link together well – if not, introduce signpost words to guide the reader through the text.
Grammatical correctness, spelling and punctuation
• Check for fluency in sentence and paragraph structure – remodel as required. • Check sentence length – remodel to shorter or longer sentences. Sometimes shorter sentences are more effective than longer ones. • Ensure that you have been consistent in spelling conventions, for example, either following British English or American English spelling. • Spelling errors – use the spellchecker but be prepared to double-check in a standard dictionary if you are in doubt. • Check for cumbersome constructions – divide or restructure sentence(s); consider whether active or passive is more suitable. Consider using vocabulary that might convey your point more eloquently. • Check use of 'absolute' terms to maintain objectivity.
Presentation
• Check that titles and subtitles are appropriate to the style of the work and stand out by using bold or underlining (not both). • Check that you have made good use of white space, that is, not crammed the text into too tight a space, and that your text is neat and legible. • If word-processed, check that you have followed standard typing conventions. Follow any 'house style' rules stipulated by your department. • Check that your reference list consistently follows a recognised method. • Check that all citations in the text are matched by an entry in the reference list and *vice versa*. • Ensure that all pages are numbered and are stapled, clipped or bound as appropriate. Ensure that the cover page is included. • Check that your name, matriculation number and course number are included. You may wish to add this information as a footnote that appears on each page. • Check that numbering of diagrams, charts and other visual material is in sequence and consistently presented. • Ensure that supporting material is added in sequence as appendices, footnotes, endnotes or as a glossary as applicable.

when going through the editing process. Professional proofreaders have developed a system of symbols to speed up the editing and proofreading process. You may wish to adopt some of these yourself, and you are certainly likely to see some of them, and other 'informal' marks, on work returned by your supervisor. Table 25.3 illustrates some of the more commonly used symbols.

The word processor has the potential to make the reviewing and editing task much easier. Here are some tips for using this software effectively:

- Use the word-count facility to check on length
- Check page breaks and general layout using the 'View' facility
- Change words or phrases throughout a document using the 'Find & Replace' facility
- Don't rely entirely on the spell- and grammar-checker (**Ch 23**).

> **Proofread from a hard copy**
>
> Reading through your work laid out on paper, which is the format in which your marker/examiner will probably see it, will help you identify errors and inconsistencies more readily than might be possible on-screen. A printout also allows you to see the whole work in overview, and focus on the way the text 'flows'. If necessary, spread the pages out on the desk in front of you. A paper version is also easier to annotate.

If you are struggling with the sense of a particular piece of text, one useful approach is to map your work to obtain an overview. 'Label' each paragraph with a topic heading, and list these in a linear way on a separate paper. This will provide you with a 'snapshot' of your text and will allow you to appraise the order, check against any original plan and adjust the position of parts as you feel necessary. As noted, reading your text aloud is another tried-and-tested technique to ensure that what you have written actually makes sense. Your ears will hear the errors that your eyes might miss on a silent reading of the text. This will help you correct grammatical and spelling inconsistencies, as well as punctuation omissions.

Maintaining consistency is a key element of proofreading. This is relevant at two levels:

1 The way you have spaced out the text, punctuated and spelt words needs to be the same throughout your report or paper. **Chapter 27** deals with other aspects of this type, but it is valuable to keep them in mind at this stage.

Table 25.3 Common proofreading symbols. Your supervisor may use a variety of symbols on your writing to indicate errors, corrections or suggestions. Apart from issues relating to content, these can also apply to punctuation, spelling, presentation or grammar. The symbols provide a kind of 'shorthand' that acts as a code to help you see how you might be able to amend your text so that it reads correctly and fluently. You can use these marks yourself when editing and proofreading your work. In this table, some of the more commonly used correction marks are shown alongside their meanings. The sample text shows how these symbols may be used, either in the text or the margin, to indicate where a change is recommended.

Correction mark	Meaning
⌐ (np)	(new) paragraph
≢	change CAPITALS to small letters (lower case)
～～～	change into **bold** type
≡	change into CAPITALS
⌒	close up (delete space)
/ or ⁊ or ⊢⊣	delete
⋏	insert a word or letter
⋎	insert space
.... or (STET)	leave unchanged
Insert punctuation symbol in a circle (P)	punctuation
plag.	plagiarism
⟶	run on (no new paragraph)
Sp.	spelling
⊔⊓	transpose text
?	what do you mean?
??	text does not seem to make sense
✓	good point/correct
✗	error

Text   *margin*

The correction marks that t⌒utors use in students' texts are generally made to help identify where there have been errors of sp⋏lin⋏or punctuation. They can ~~often~~ indicate where there is lack of paragraphing or grammatical accuracy. If you find that work is returned to you with such |marks|correction|, then it is worthwhile spending some time analysing the common errors as well as the comments, because this will help you to improve the quality of presentation and content of your work⋏this reviewing can have a positive effect on your assessed mark.

In the margin, the error symbols are separated by a slash (/).

288   The writing process

2 The elements of your text must be coherent. For example, your Introduction and Conclusion should complement and not contradict each other.

You may need to stick to a word limit for your submission. Remember that too few words can be just as bad as too many. The key point is that your writing must be clear to your reader. Sometimes this means giving a longer explanation; sometimes it means simplifying what you have written. However, if at this review stage your writing is over the word-count limit, you may need to carry out a specific sweep of the text to cut down on redundant material. This can often be beneficial as it 'tightens' the text, making the underlying logic clearer.

How much time should I leave for proofreading?

Effective proofreading is an important determinant of the final quality of your writing and should therefore not be rushed. The answer to this question depends on your text's length and your reading speed when editing. However, there is another factor to consider, which is that it can be valuable to 'distance' yourself in time from your draft writing so you can view it more critically. A suitable 'resting period' for the draft should be built into your timetable.

ACTION POINTS

25.1 Make time for checking. When planning the writing phase (**Ch 21**), ensure that you have allowed adequate time for reviewing and proofreading. You will not want to spoil all your hard work by skimping on this final stage. Try to leave a break between finishing the final draft and returning to check the whole text, as then you will return to your work with a fresh and possibly more critical eye.

25.2 Learn the main proofreading symbols (Table 25.3). This is a valuable skill that will speed up the editing process for you at all stages and will also help you interpret feedback from your supervisor.

25.3 Create your own 'style sheet'. At an early stage, decide on the way in which you wish to present your work (**Ch 27**). You might note, for example, font sizes and line spacing for different headings and details of figure and table arrangements. The list can also include points such as preferred terminology, the spelling of difficult words and recurrent grammatical errors.

26

ACTING ON FEEDBACK

How to interpret and learn from what your supervisor writes on your drafts

Your supervisor may provide written feedback on drafts of your work. It is essential that you understand and act upon these comments if you want to improve your text.

KEY TOPICS
→ Types of feedback
→ Examples of feedback comments and what they mean

Your final manuscript, whether in report or alternative format, represents an extensive writing process and your supervisor may wish to monitor progress by reading through your draft work at various stages.

TYPES OF FEEDBACK

Written feedback may be provided on your scripts and other work. This may take the form of handwritten comments over your draft text, and a summary commenting on your work or explaining what changes are needed. Alternatively, your supervisor may use a tool such as the 'Track Changes' facility in Microsoft Word. This allows amendments to your work. In addition, your supervisor may use the 'Comments' facility in Word, to add explanations or ideas. The 'Help' menu explains how to accept or delete amendments and comments.

The annotations and comments on your manuscript may relate to presentational aspects, such as spelling, grammar and punctuation, as well as to content. The presentational factors outlined in **Chapter 25** should not be discounted nor regarded as minor details, for if the errors in these areas are many, then this may divert your supervisor's attention away from the equally important content. Similarly, if the structure of the work is weak, this too will impede their appreciation of your content. This may mean that the feedback you get is less about content and more about any shortcomings in your writing and structure. You can avoid this by paying particular attention to the simple things, such as intensive checking of grammar, spelling and punctuation, which you should be able to correct fairly easily and so leave your supervisor with a clear path to understanding the logic of your work and the content that it contains. This means paying due attention to the reviewing, editing and proofreading stage (**Ch 25**).

> **Be mentally prepared to learn from the views of your supervisor**
>
> You may initially feel that feedback is unfair, harsh or that it misunderstands the approach you were trying to take to the topic. A natural reaction might be to dismiss many of the comments. However, you should recognise that your supervisor probably has a much deeper understanding of the topic than you, and concede that if you want to do well in a subject then you need to gain a better understanding of what makes a good dissertation or project from the academic's point of view.

Some feedback may be verbal and informal – for example, a comment given as you work in the lab, or an observation during a tutorial or seminar. If you have the opportunity to have scheduled meetings with your supervisor, then you can bring up feedback issues then. However, it will help both of you if you attend these meetings well-prepared with a list of topics or queries that you wish to discuss. These may relate to a clarification of comments on draft material or to matters that arise out of these comments. Being prepared with your own 'agenda' will save time in the meeting and also give you a framework for discussion that will help you to develop your work in the direction that your supervisor has recommended.

✓ Always read the feedback and make sure you understand it

Your supervisor's feedback should give you constructive direction for developing the structure and style of your work, as well as encouraging you to develop a deeper understanding of the topic. A student who ignores advice from a supervisor would be unwise.

- Spend some time reviewing comments and considering how you intend to act on them.
- Always make sure you understand the feedback. Check with fellow students or your supervisor if you cannot read the comment or do not understand why it has been made.
- Make a note of common or repeated errors, even in peripheral topics, so that you can avoid them in later drafts.

EXAMPLES OF FEEDBACK COMMENTS AND WHAT THEY MEAN

Different supervisors use different terms to express similar meanings, and because they work quickly, their handwritten comments are sometimes untidy and may be difficult to interpret. This means that you may need help in deciphering their meaning. Table 26.1 illustrates feedback comments that are frequently made and explains how you should react in response in future drafts. This should be viewed alongside Table 25.3, which explains some proofreading symbols that may also be used. If a particular comment or mark does not make sense to you after reading these tables, then you should ask your supervisor for clarification.

? How often can I expect my supervisor to read my draft versions?

This can be a problematic issue. Some supervisors may choose to look at a number of versions, but others may not; up to a point, that is their choice. Remember that supervisors are busy people; they may have (many) other duties and be supervising many students, some on programmes other than yours (**Ch 6**). Moreover, the department may lay down a ruling that limits supervisors to surveying only one draft before submission.

Table 26.1 Common types of feedback annotation and how to act in response. Comments in the margin may be accompanied by underlining of word(s) or circling of phrases, sentences or paragraphs.

Types of comment and typical examples	Meaning and potential remedial action
REGARDING CONTENT	
Relevance Relevance? Importance? Value of example? So?	An example or quotation may not be apt, or you may not have explained its relevance. Think about the logic of your narrative or argument and whether there is a mismatch as implied, or whether you could add further explanation; choose a more appropriate example or quote.
Detail Give more information Example? Too much detail/waffle/padding	You are expected to flesh out your text with more detail or an example to illustrate your point; or, conversely, you may have provided too much information. It may be that your work lacks substance and you appear to have compensated by putting in too much description rather than analysis, for example.
Specific factual comment or comment on your approach You could have included ... What about ...? Why didn't you ...?	Depends on context, but it should be obvious what is required to accommodate the comment.
Expressions of approval Good! Excellent! ✓ (may be repeated)	You got this right or chose a good example. Keep up the good work!
Expressions of disapproval Poor Weak No! ✗ (may be repeated)	Sometimes obvious, but may not be clear. The implication is that your examples or logic could be improved. If you are unsure of what is wrong, then you should speak with your lecturer or supervisor.
REGARDING STRUCTURE	
Fault in logic or argument Logic! Non sequitur (does not follow)	Your argument or line of logic is faulty. This may require quite radical changes to your approach to the topic.
Failure to introduce topic clearly Where are you going with this? Unclear	What is your understanding of the topic? What parameters will confine your discussion? How do you intend to develop this aspect?

Continued overleaf

Types of comment and typical examples	Meaning and potential remedial action
REGARDING STRUCTURE (Continued)	
Failure to construct a logical discussion Imbalanced discussion Weak on pros and cons	When you have to compare and contrast in any way, then it is important that you give each element in your discussion equal coverage.
Failure to conclude dissertation or report clearly So what? Conclusion?	You have to leave a 'take-home message' that sums up the most salient features of your writing and you should not include new material in this section. This is to demonstrate your ability to think critically and define the key aspects.
Heavy dependency on quotations Watch out for over-quotation Too many quotations	There is a real danger of plagiarism if you include too many direct quotations from text (Ch 24). You have to demonstrate that you can synthesise the information from sources as evidence of your understanding. However, in a subject like English literature or law, quotation may be a key characteristic of writing. In this case, quotation is permitted, provided that it is supported by critical comment.
Move text Loops and arrows	Suggestion for changing order of text, usually to enhance the flow or logic.
REGARDING PRESENTATION	
Minor proofing errors sp. (usually in margin – spelling) ⋏ (insert material here) ⌐ (break paragraph here) ⁊ (delete this material) P (punctuation error)	A (minor) correction is required. Table 25.3 provides more detail of likely proofreading symbols.
Citations Reference (required) Refl Reference (or bibliography) list omitted	You have not provided supporting evidence, argument or quotation with a reference to the original source. This is important in academic work and if you fail to do it, you may be considered guilty of plagiarism. If you omit a reference list, this will invalidate your work and imply that you have done no specialist reading.
Tidiness Untidy Can't read	Your document may be difficult to follow because of poor layout, inconsistent numbering of sections, and typos.

Types of comment and typical examples	Meaning and potential remedial action
REGARDING PRESENTATION (Continued)	
Failure to follow recommended format *Please follow departmental template for reports* *Order!*	If the department or school provides a template for the submission of dissertations and reports, then you must follow it. There are good reasons, such as the need to follow professional conventions, especially in sciences; you must conform. If you don't, then your grade may be reduced.

If you are disappointed about the extent of feedback you are given, consider first that there may be good reasons for this. For example, a research project is an opportunity for students to show their abilities as independent thinkers. If they receive a great deal of staff attention and time as they go through the research and writing process, then this compromises the integrity of the work as exclusively that of the student. Therefore, if there is a restriction on feedback in your department, then you should be sure to optimise the opportunity by submitting a draft version that is almost complete, is as free as you can make it of basic presentational errors and is well-organised. This means that when you submit this to your supervisor you can do so with confidence.

ACTION POINTS

26.1 Check out your department's assessment criteria for dissertations and project reports. As explained above, these may help you interpret feedback and understand how to reach the standard you want to achieve.

26.2 Decide what to do about feedback comments you frequently receive. For instance, does your supervisor always comment about your spelling or grammar, or suggest you should use more examples, or ask for more citations to be included? If so, look at relevant chapters in this book to see if you can adjust appropriately, or seek assistance from the Academic Support Service in your institution.

26.3 Learn to criticise drafts of your own work. This is equivalent to giving feedback to yourself and is an essential academic skill. Annotate drafts of your own work – this is an important way to refine it and improve its quality. Stages you can adopt when reviewing your written work are discussed in **Chapter 23**.

27 PRESENTING YOUR PROJECT FOR ASSESSMENT

How to submit your work appropriately

Your final manuscript must be presented according to the appropriate academic conventions and specific university rules. You will need to create a well-prepared submission that follows the established standards of academic writing in your discipline.

KEY TOPICS

→ Following institutional guidance for the presentation of research projects
→ Laying out your text
→ Incorporating figures and tables
→ Formatting, printing and binding

The quality of your submission will be determined by a combination of factors, but principally:

- activities that take place before you write, such as researching your sources, conducting experiments or analysing the literature
- the way you express your ideas in writing.

Your examiners will be expected to verify that your manuscript has been submitted according to the local rules. Its presentation will also make a statement about the overall care you have taken in conducting your analysis and preparing the content, and might therefore influence your examiners. This chapter provides reminders of what may seem to be the 'cosmetic' details of layout and visual elements, but which, in fact, reflect the standards you should attach to all aspects of your work.

Good presentation involves accuracy, consistency and attention to detail. For this reason it is often associated with editing and proofreading (**Ch 25**). You will need to allocate time to get these aspects right, so when you plan the writing-up process, you should allow for adding this final 'polish' to your work.

> **Why does good presentation matter?**
> - it may form an element of the assessment
> - it helps the marker or examiner understand what you have written
> - it shows you can adopt professional standards in your work
> - if you have taken care with meticulous presentation, then this suggests that the work it reports will have been done with equal attention to detail
> - it demonstrates you have acquired important skills that will transfer to other subjects and, later, to employment.

FOLLOWING INSTITUTIONAL GUIDANCE FOR THE PRESENTATION OF RESEARCH PROJECTS

Acceptable reporting structures depend on the discipline and subject, as discussed in **Chapter 22**. You should research this carefully before you start to write up, by consulting the course handbook or other regulations. Institutions also provide information about structural formats and presentation. Sometimes this is very prescriptive and relates to the appearance and layout; however, sometimes only minimal direction is provided.

You may have to search for the information on your university's website, through the university library, the Registry, the Media or Printing Services Department or your own school or faculty. If you have difficulty in locating these guidelines, then a good starting point would be your departmental office, your supervisor or the course tutor. The specifications will include aspects such as:

- details on submission process, binding formats and, possibly, the number of copies to be provided

- inclusion and possibly layout of certain introductory elements – namely, title page (title, author, year of presentation), abstract, declaration as to originality of the document (both student and supervisor), acknowledgements and table of contents (**Ch 22**)

- expected length of the research project submission (either in pages or words)

- page and margin sizes; page numbering; justification and indentation
- font, point size and line spacing (usually 1.5 or double line)
- numbering of chapters, headings and sub-headings
- layout of diagrams, illustrations and other visuals, including photographs
- inclusion of glossaries, footnotes, endnotes and reference list or bibliography (referencing style may be prescribed by the department, which, in turn, may follow relevant professional standards).

LAYING OUT YOUR TEXT

There are a number of conventions regarding the presentation of academic writing of different types, including scientific reports, case studies and theoretical papers. These are discussed below and some important aspects are summarised in checklist form in Table 27.1.

Table 27.1 Checklist for conventions in the presentation of academic writing.

Abbreviations
❏ In some disciplines the abbreviations i.e. and e.g. are acceptable in academic text; in others these are not used; etc. should never be used in academic text
❏ &, the ampersand, is not commonly used in text, although it is used routinely in certain referencing styles
❏ Where abbreviations are used to express units, for example, SI units, then this is acceptable
❏ Subject-specific dictionaries will provide most common abbreviations used in a particular field
Acronyms
❏ Do not use acronyms in the title of a paper or thesis
❏ Provide an alphabetical list of abbreviations and acronyms at the beginning of technical reports and manuals
❏ Define acronyms the first time that they appear in the text
❏ Only capitalise definitions of acronyms if they are proper nouns
❏ Form plurals of acronyms only by adding -s, as in QUANGOs – do not add an apostrophe
❏ Some acronyms become 'words' in their own right: NATO (North Atlantic Treaty Organisation)
Fonts and point size
❏ The norms are either Times New Roman or Arial
❏ The point size is usually 12 point
❏ Larger point size is usually selected for chapter headings and sub-headings

- ❏ The same font and selected point sizes should be used consistently throughout the work
- ❏ Latin words such as *et al.* (and others) and *in vitro,* should be printed in italics
- ❏ If emphasis is required – usually rarely in academic writing – then use only one feature: either bold or italics or underlining, but not any combination of these

Headings and sub-headings

Conventions and preferences differ. Check with your department or supervisor about presentation 'rules' that will apply to your thesis. In the absence of any other instruction, the following approach may be followed:

- ❏ Use a capital only at the first letter of a title and at proper nouns within the title
- ❏ Full stops are not necessary in titles
- ❏ If a strap line, introduced by a colon, is used after the title, place the words following in lower case unless they are proper names (initial capital) or acronyms
- ❏ Sub-headings, if used/permitted, need to be laid out consistently using the same font and point size throughout

Lists

- ❏ Each point on bulleted lists should begin with a capital letter provided that there is no preceding 'sentence stem' introducing the list (usually ending with a colon)

Punctuation

- ❏ If in doubt, add punctuation where you would normally pause, if you were to read your work aloud
- ❏ For bullet points, the academic conventions vary. (a) One commonly used convention in some disciplines requires no full stops at the end of each bullet (particularly if the bullet consists of only a few words). Where the bullet extends into more than one sentence, then the last sentence and any intervening ones are finished by full stops. (b) In other areas, the convention adopted is to use a full stop at the end if the bullet point is a complete sentence and a semi-colon if the bullet is incomplete. (c) Another option commonly used is one in which a phrase or sentence 'stem' (followed by a full colon) introduces the bulleted list. The bullets that follow each 'complete' the introductory stem as a sentence. Thus, the list of bullets creates an extended sentence in which each bullet is an element. In such cases a semi-colon is used at the end of each bullet point and a full-stop after the last bullet.
- ❏ Whichever citation system you use (Ch 24), ensure that the punctuation format is followed consistently

Spelling

- ❏ In some disciplines, for example, chemistry, the internationally recognised convention is to use American spelling for words such as, sulfur, analyze, organization
- ❏ Spell-checking is not a guarantee of error-free spelling; ensure that you check your work by reading it through to avoid errors such as: from/form – both are perfectly good words but if you mean one and not the other, the spell-checker would not identify the error

Printing

The project research document should always be printed on only one side of the paper – this makes it easier to read, and if you make a significant error you may only have to reprint a single sheet.

Font

There are two main choices: serif types, with extra strokes at the end of the main strokes of each letter, and sans serif types, without these strokes (see Figure 27.1). The type to use is usually left to personal preference (although this may be that of your supervisor rather than you), but a serif font is said to be easier to read. More likely to be specified is the point size (pt) of the font, which will probably be 11 or 12 point for ease of reading. You should avoid using elaborate font types as generally they may not help the reader to assimilate what you have written. For the same reason, you should not use too many forms of emphasis. Choose italics or bold and stick with one only. Symbols are often used in academic work, and in Microsoft Word these can be added using the 'Insert>Symbol' menu.

> **Serif font**
> Times roman 11 pt
> Times roman 12 pt
> Times roman 14 pt
>
> **Sans serif font**
> Arial 11 pt
> Arial 12 pt
> Arial 14 pt

Figure 27.1 Examples of the main types of font at different point sizes.

Line spacing and margins

Text that is spaced at least at 1.5–2 lines apart is easier to read. The exception is where you wish to use long quotations; these should be indented and typed in single-line spacing (**Ch 24**). A typical custom is for left-hand margins to be 4 cm and the right-hand margins 2.5 cm. These conventions allow space for any marker's comments and ensure that the text can be read if a left-hand binding is used.

Paragraphs

The key thing to remember about layout is to make good use of the 'white space'. This means that you should lay out your paragraphs clearly and consistently. Some people prefer the indentation method, where the paragraph begins on the fourth character space from the left-hand margin (Figure 27.2a). Others prefer the blocked paragraph style – that is, where all paragraphs begin on the left-hand margin, but are separated by a double-line space (Figure 27.2b). The space between paragraphs should be roughly equivalent to a missing line.

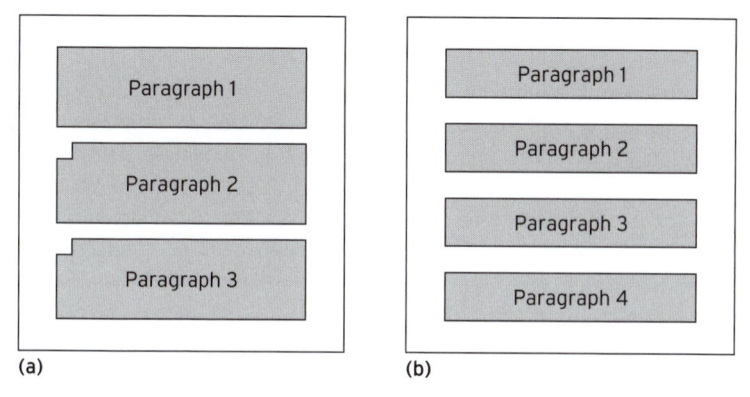

Figure 27.2 Types of paragraph layout: (a) indented and (b) blocked. Note that in the indented model, by convention the first paragraph in any section is not indented.

In Microsoft Word these aspects can be controlled using the 'Format>Paragraph' menu.

Sub-headings

In some disciplines, use of sub-headings is acceptable or even favoured, though in others these 'signpost' strategies are discouraged. It is best to consult your supervisor about this if you are uncertain. Sub-headings are usually in bold.

Punctuation

Standard punctuation applies to all types of academic writing. One decision you may wish to make is about spaces between sentences – whether to use one or two. This is generally a matter of personal preference. Take special care to ensure the punctuation of the reference list follows the appropriate convention and is consistent (**Ch 24**).

Word count

You may be asked not to exceed a specific word count and this can be checked using the word count feature of your word processor. If you greatly exceed this limit this will almost certainly impact on your presentation, as you will confront the reader with too much information and will probably not be writing in the expected concise fashion.

> ✓ **Working to a word count**
>
> When working to a word count, you should consider the balance of the sections in your manuscript because excessively cutting from one section might adversely affect the final result. For example, drawing to an abrupt end in your Conclusion section because of word-count problems is not a good idea as this section is often given significant weighting in assessment.

Citations and references

Providing citations and a reference list is standard practice, as discussed in **Chapter 24**. You must be consistent in the referencing style you adopt, and some disciplines impose strict subject-specific conventions. If in doubt, consult your course handbook, institutional regulations or library guidelines.

Quotations, numbers and formulae

Quotations can be integrated into the text when short, but are usually presented as a 'special' type of paragraph when long. In either case, the source and date of publication are provided after the quotation. **Chapter 24** provides detailed guidance on the presentation of quotations. Some disciplines – for example, English Literature and Law – have very specific rules for the way in which quotations are laid out and referenced. In such cases, consult your course handbook or ask for guidance from a tutor.

Chapter 20 includes information on the presentation of numbers in text. Short formulae or equations can be included in the text, but they are probably better presented on a separate line and indented, thus:

$$\alpha + 4\beta/\eta^2\pi = 0 \qquad \text{(Eqn. 27.1)}$$

Where a large number of formulae are included, they can be numbered for ease of cross-reference, as shown above.

INCORPORATING FIGURES AND TABLES

In many disciplines, you will be expected to support your discussion with visual material or data, and it is important that you do so in a fashion that best helps the reader to assimilate the information. You must also follow any specific presentational rules that apply in your subject area.

> **Inserting figures in text**
>
> Integrated suites of office-type software allow you to insert the graphs you produced using the spreadsheet program into text produced with the word-processing program. The two programs can even be linked so that changes on the spreadsheet data automatically appear in the graph within the word-processed file. Consult the manual or 'Help' facility to find out how to do this. In Microsoft Word, digital photographs can be inserted using the 'Insert>Picture>From File' command.

Figures

The academic convention is to include a wide range of visual material under the term 'Figure' (in some disciplines, 'Fig.' for short). This includes graphs, diagrams, charts, sketches, pictures and photographs, although in some disciplines and contexts the latter may be referred to as 'plates'.

The following set of guidelines should be adopted when including figures.

- All figures should be referred to in the text. There are 'standard' formulations for doing this, such as 'Figure 4 shows that...', or '... results for one treatment were higher than for the other (see Figure 2)'. Find out what is appropriate from the literature or texts in your subject area.

- Figures should be numbered in the order they are referred to in the text. If you are including the figures within the main body of text (usually more convenient for the reader) then they should appear at the next suitable position in the text after the first time of mention. At the very least this will be after the paragraph that includes the first citation, but more normally will be at the top of the following page.

- Figures should be positioned at the top or bottom of a page, rather than sandwiched between blocks of text. This looks neater and makes the text easier to read.

- Each figure must have a legend, which will include the figure number, a title and some text (often a key to the symbols and line styles used). The convention is for figure legends to appear below each figure. Your aim should be to make each figure self-contained. That is, a reader who knows the general subject area should be able to work out what your figure shows, without reference to other material.

Choosing the right type of figure to display information is an art in itself (Chs 9 and 20). Although there are technical reasons why some forms of data should be presented in particular ways (for example, frequency distributions in a histogram rather than a bar chart), your main focus should always be on selecting a method that will help the reader assimilate the information presented most effectively.

> ✓ **Don't automatically accept the graphical output from spreadsheets and other programs**
>
> These are not always in the accepted style for academic work. For example, the default output for many charts produced by the Microsoft Office Excel spreadsheet includes a grey background and horizontal gridlines, neither of which is generally used in academic contexts (Ch 20).

When presenting individual figures, clarity should be your main aim – ensuring, for example, that the different slices of a pie chart or the lines and symbols in a graph are clearly distinguishable from one another. Consistency is also important, so you should use the same line or shading for the same entity in all your figures (for example, hollow symbols for 'controls'). The widespread availability of colour printers should help with this, but some departments may insist on the use of black and white, since this was the convention when colour printing was prohibitively expensive. If you are using colour, keep it 'tasteful' and remember that certain colour combinations are not easily differentiated by some readers.

If you have doubts about the precise style or arrangement of figures and tables, follow the model shown in texts or journal articles from your subject area.

Tables

The rules for presenting tables are essentially similar to those for figures, with the important exception that a table legend should appear above the table. It is quite common to provide additional information as a footnote to a table (Ch 20).

FORMATTING, PRINTING AND BINDING

There will come a time when you consider your document is ready for the final stages of presentation; this involves several tasks where attention to detail is essential.

- Final inspection for consistency – this will depend on the nature of the research, but could involve spelling checks, consistency in punctuation, explanation of abbreviations at first use, fonts for headings and so on.
- Formatting – you will need to check each page carefully and in sequence to see that spacing conventions have been obeyed and that there are no untidy 'widows' and 'orphans' – paragraphs where splits between pages result in one or few lines on either side. Any tables or figures should be in the correct position and orientation.
- Numbering – you will need to ensure that all pages are numbered correctly and in true sequence, as well as the figures, tables and other numbered elements, such as case studies.
- Contents page – you can only complete this once the final page numbering is known. You will also then be able to complete the lists of figures and tables with page numbering.
- References – you need to run a final check to ensure (a) that all citations in the text have a corresponding entry in the reference list and (b) that all entries in the reference list are actually cited. Checking the formatting of references is a very tedious task, but essential.

Take pride and pleasure from your work

By the time that you reach this final stage you will have spent many, many hours on producing the final version. What you are handling now will be the product of those hours and the culmination of study and thinking about a complex research issue. Even though your energy reserves may be low, keep your standards up to ensure that your submission is of the best possible quality. At this time, you should take huge pride in what you have done – the breadth of the research, the triumph over problems and the sense that you have done the job and done it well.

When these checks are complete, you will be ready for printing. This should be carried out using a good-quality (laser) printer and good-quality paper. You will need several copies – one for yourself and one or more for handing in, depending on the departmental rule. Although there is an expense attached, this printing is probably best carried out by a specialist photocopying or printing service. They can also advise on binding options.

> **ACTION POINTS**
>
> **27.1 Look at a recently submitted project report or paper to gauge the overall standard of presentation expected.** Ask a past student (perhaps someone in your supervisor's research group) whether you can look at their successful submission, or ask your supervisor whether he or she can show you a past example that was rated highly. Examine this carefully for aspects of presentation mentioned in this chapter.
>
> **27.2 Prepare well for printing out your final version.** Many students opt to print out their final copies using their own word processor and printer. Should you choose to do this rather than use the services of a professional printing company, be sure that, before you begin, you have sufficient paper and ink to allow you to complete the necessary processes. Finding that your supplies run out part way through the process could involve you in significant delays and even make you miss the submission deadline.
>
> **27.3 Make good use of the 'dead time' after submission.** By all means take a well-deserved break, but take advantage of the 'free' time you now have to prepare for a *viva* if you have one, or for other forms of assessment, if these apply.

LIST OF REFERENCES

Anderson, L. and Krathwohl, D. A., 2001. *Taxonomy for Learning, Teaching and Assessing: A Revision of Bloom's Taxonomy of Educational Objectives.* New York: Longman.

Bloom, B. S., Englehart, M. D., Furst, E. J., Holl, W. H. and Krathwohl, D. R., 1956. *Taxonomy of Educational Objectives: Cognitive Domain.* New York: McKay.

CILIP, 2012. Chartered Institute of Library and Information Professionals: Information literacy: definition. Available at: ***http://www.cilip.org.uk/get-involved/advocacy/information-literacy/Pages/definition.aspx*** [Accessed 6 November 2013].

Cohen L., Manion, L. and Morrison, K., 2007. *Research Methods in Education,* 6th ed. London: Routledge-Falmer.

Denzin, N. and Lincoln Y., eds., 2005. *The Sage Handbook of Qualitative Research,* 3rd ed. London: Sage.

Lakin, S., 2010a. *How to Improve Your Maths Skills.* Harlow: Pearson Education.

Lakin, S., 2010b. *How to Use Statistics.* Harlow: Pearson Education.

McMillan, K. M. and Weyers, J. D. B., 2013. *How to Cite, Reference and Avoid Plagiarism at University.* Harlow: Pearson Education.

McMillan, K. M and Weyers, J. D. B., 2014. *How to Write for University: Academic Writing for Success.* Harlow: Pearson Education.

Robson, C., 2011. *Real World Research,* 3rd ed. New York: John Wiley.

Sana, L., 2000. *Textbook of Research Ethics: Theory and Practise.* New York: Kluwer Academic.

SCONUL, 2011. Society of College, National and University Libraries: The Seven Pillars of Information Literacy model. Available at: ***http://www.sconul.ac.uk/sites/default/files/documents/coremodel.pdf*** [Accessed 6 November 2013].

Shamoo, A. E. and Resnik, D. B., 2009. *Responsible Conduct of Research,* 2nd ed. Oxford: Oxford University Press.

Strauss, A. and Corbin, J., 2007. *Basics of Qualitative Research: Techniques and Procedures for Developing Grounded Theory,* 3rd ed. London: Sage.

URLS FOR WEBSITES QUOTED IN THE TEXT

Chapter 5

http://www.smartdraw.com [Accessed 6 November 2013].

http://www.rememberthemilk.com/services/ [Accessed 9 April 2014]

http://www.wunderlist.com [Accessed 9 April 2014]

Chapter 7

http://www.bl.uk [Accessed 6 November 2013]

http://ec.europa.eu/europedirect/visit_us/edc/index_en.htm [Accessed 6 November 2013].

http://www.parliament.uk/ [Accessed 6 November 2013].

http://www.statistics.gov.uk/hub/index.html [Accessed 6 November 2013].

Chapter 8

http://wokinfo.com/ [Accessed 6 November 2013].

Chapter 10

http://www.vark-learn.com/english/index.asp [Accessed 6 November 2013].

Chapter 11

http://www.ipo.gov.uk/ [Accessed 6 November 2013].

Chapter 22

http://www.somis.dundee.ac.uk/calendar/senate/hdtheses.htm [Accessed 6 November 2013].

Chapter 24

http://www.garfield.library.upenn.edu/papers/vladivostok.html [Accessed 6 November 2013].

HOW TO COMPLETE A SUCCESSFUL RESEARCH PROJECT

KATHLEEN McMILLAN & JONATHAN WEYERS

A practical, step-by-step guide to planning, researching and writing a research project for undergraduate students approaching a research project for the first time.

Undertaking a large-scale, original research project can be extremely daunting and challenging to any student. This book delivers timely, practical, hands-on guidance based on real-life experience from students and lecturers alike. It will be an invaluable tutorial and reference for any student approaching an undergraduate or masters research project for the first time.

HOW TO COMPLETE A SUCCESSFUL RESEARCH PROJECT guides the student through all of the key areas that they will need to deliver a successful research project, providing practical guidance, examples, hints and tips for success on areas such as:

- Choosing a theme and topic for your research
- Writing the proposal
- Analysing and evaluating data
- Successful academic writing styles and conventions
- Correct citing, referencing and avoiding plagiarism
- Ethics in research
- Researching and compiling the literature survey

An essential guide to academic success!

£17.99
STUDY SKILLS

ISBN 978-0-273-77392-4

eBOOK also available

Visit our website at
www.pearson-books.com